T0307498

基本法

The Basic Law

©2023 City University of Hong Kong

All rights reserved. No part of this publication may be reproduced, stored in a retrieval system, or transmitted, in any form or by any means, electronic, mechanical, photocopying, recording, Internet or otherwise, without the prior written permission of the City University of Hong Kong Press.

ISBN: 978-962-937-674-1

Published by
City University of Hong Kong Press
Tat Chee Avenue
Kowloon, Hong Kong
Website: www.cityu.edu.hk/upress
E-mail: upress@cityu.edu.hk

Printed in Hong Kong

中華人民共和國
香港特別行政區基本法
及相關憲制性法律文件

The Basic Law
of the Hong Kong Special Administrative Region
of the People's Republic of China
and Related Constitutional Instruments

2023

香港城市大學出版社
City University of Hong Kong Press

目錄

Table of Contents

Order of the State Council of the People's Republic of China No. 221 *163*

**全國人民代表大會和全國人民代表大會常務委員會決定
（按公布時間排列）**

**Decisions of the National People's Congress and
the Standing Committee of the National People's Congress**
(By Chronological Order)

**全國人民代表大會常務委員會關於《中華人民共和國
香港特別行政區基本法》附件三的決定**

Decisions of the Standing Committee of the National People's Congress on Annex III to the Basic Law of the Hong Kong Special Administrative Region of the People's Republic of China

全國人民代表大會常務委員會關於《中華人民共和國國籍法》和《中華人民共和國香港特別行政區基本法》的解釋

**Interpretations by the Standing Committee
of the National People's Congress on the Nationality Law
of the People's Republic of China and on the Basic Law
of the Hong Kong Special Administrative Region
of the People's Republic of China**

前言

在網絡發達的今天,《基本法》全部條文均可在網上瀏覽,透過流動裝置也可隨時隨地找到相關條文。但要仔細學習研讀,一本紙本的《基本法》仍然極有功用,不可或缺。

我很高興見到香港城市大學香港基本法實施研究計劃編輯出版這本輕便裝《基本法》。這本首先因應學術需要而構思製作的《基本法》,不但精緻輕巧,便於攜帶,適合大專院校師生學習使用;其內文附相關條文旁註以利檢索的編排方式,尤其適合法律及相關專業人士和公務人員隨身攜帶,方便隨時查閱使用。中英文雙語並列也是充分考慮到香港社會大眾的實際需要。

《基本法》作為憲制性法律文件,條文自然有份量,但這本輕便版《基本法》卻是舉重若輕,攜帶起來沒有一點負擔,顯然製作和設計上花了一番心思。我相信它定能滿足有興趣研習及了解《基本法》人士的期待。

Foreword

In today's technologically advanced society, all articles of the Basic Law of the Hong Kong Special Administrative Region (Basic Law) can be found on the Internet. They can also be searched for through any mobile device, anytime and anywhere. However, if one wants to study the Basic Law thoroughly, a printed edition is indispensable.

I was delighted to learn that the Implementation of the Hong Kong Basic Law Research Project of City University of Hong Kong is publishing a new edition of the Basic Law, designed specially in response to academic needs. It is not only light and handy, but is suitable for the study of tertiary education scholars and students. Related articles and instruments are cross-referenced, making it a simple-to-use reference for legal professionals and civil servants on the move. Its bilingual layout has taken into consideration practical needs.

As a constitutional instrument, the Basic Law undoubtedly carries a lot of weight. Yet, its importance has not laid any burden on this lightweight edition. The production and design of this new version of the Basic Law evidently took some ingenuity. I believe it can satisfy the expectations of those who are interested in learning and understanding the Basic Law.

　　因應香港城市大學香港基本法實施研究計劃首席研究員 (Principal Investigator)、法律學院教授朱國斌博士之盛情邀請,特為之序。

梁愛詩,GBM,JP
全國人民代表大會常務委員會
香港基本法委員會前副主任
香港特別行政區政府首任律政司司長 (1997–2005)
二零一七年陽春三月,香港

I have to thank Dr. ZHU Guobin, the principal investigator of the Implementation of the Hong Kong Basic Law Research Project and Professor of the Law School of City University of Hong Kong for his sincere invitation to add this foreword.

Elsie Leung Oi-Sie, GBM, JP
Former Vice Chairman of the Basic Law Committee
under the Standing Committee of the National People's Congress
First Secretary for Justice (1997–2005)
of the Hong Kong Special Administrative Region
Spring, March 2017, Hong Kong

2023年版序言

《中華人民共和國香港特別行政區基本法及相關憲制性法律文件》（"袖珍版基本法"）自2017年出版以來，獲得了學術界、法律專業界、公務人員和社會大眾的歡迎和認同。編輯出版本法律文本之初衷是"為《基本法》教學與研究需要，為推廣及普及《基本法》知識，為方便查閱法律文本"（參見"編輯出版說明"）。應該說，出版的目的實現了。編者與出版人為之欣慰。

過去的六年是不平凡的六年。六年過去了，香港社會與政治生態發生了重大變化，憲制性法律隨之得以發展。就《基本法》及其實施而言，全國人民代表大會及其常務委員會因應時勢需求，制定通過了若干件關涉香港政治生活與法律發展的重要法律文件，這包括《全國人民代表大會關於建立健全香港特別行政區維護國家安全的法律制度和執行機制的決定》（2020）、全國人民代表大會常務委員會通過的《中華人民共和國香港特別行政區維護國家安全法》（2020），以及《全國人民代表大會關於完善香港特別行政區選舉制度的決定》（2021）等。

作為2017年版編者，經與出版社商議，我們決定出版《袖珍版基本法》第二版即2023年版，既能方便學術界和

Preface to 2023 Edition

The Basic Law of the Hong Kong Special Administrative Region of the People's Republic of China and Related Constitutional Instruments (hereafter referred to as the *"Pocket Edition of the Basic Law"*) has been welcomed and recognized by the academic community, legal professionals, public servants, and the general public since it was published in 2017. The original intention of editing this sourcebook was to facilitate access to the legal texts for the needs of teaching and research on the Basic Law, and to promote and popularize knowledge of the Basic Law (see "Editor's Notes"). It should be said that the purpose of publication has been achieved, and both the editor and publisher are pleased.

The past six years have been extraordinary. Six years on, Hong Kong's social and political ecology has undergone major changes, and constitutional laws have developed accordingly. As far as the Basic Law and its implementation are concerned, the National People's Congress and its Standing Committee have formulated and adopted a number of important legal documents related to Hong Kong's political life and legal development in response to the needs of the times, including *Decision of the National People's Congress on Establishing and Improving the Legal System and Enforcement Mechanisms for the Hong Kong Special Administrative Region to Safeguard National Security* (2020), *Law of the People's Republic of China on Safeguarding National Security in the Hong Kong Special Administrative Region* adopted by the Standing Committee of the National People's Congress (2020), *Decision of the National People's Congress on Improving the Electoral System of the Hong Kong Special Administrative Region* (2021), and so on.

As the editor of the 2017 edition, after consultation with the publisher, we have decided to publish the second edition of the *Pocket Edition of the Basic Law*, the 2023 edition. It can not only

法律專業人士的日常參閱使用，滿足社會大眾了解學習研究《基本法》的需求，又能紀錄香港憲制性法律的發展歷程。2023年版《袖珍版基本法》不僅保留了第一版收錄的全部法律，還增補了上一次未收錄的全國人民代表大會常務委員會的兩件決定，以及加入了2017年7月之後由全國人民代表大會及其常務委員會通過的全部相關法律。鑒於《香港特別行政區維護國家安全法》在香港憲制秩序建構完善過程中和法律體系中的重要性以及社會對它的關注度，2023年版《袖珍版基本法》還以"附錄"形式收入了《香港特別行政區維護國家安全法》和全國人民代表大會常務委員會對該法的第一次解釋 (2021)。

2023年版《袖珍版基本法》仍然保留原來的結構安排，並承繼第一版之編輯特徵，如雙語對照、分類編排、條文互檢、攜帶方便 (參見"編輯出版説明")。編者和出版人希望，《袖珍版基本法》繼續作為法律研究者、法律實踐者、公務人員乃至有興趣社會人士之案頭書、口袋書，服務讀者與用戶。

是為序。

朱國斌
香港城市大學法律學院教授
香港城市大學香港基本法實施研究計劃首席研究員
二零二三年六月，獅子山下

facilitate the daily reference and use by academia and legal professionals, but also meet the needs of the public to understand and study the Basic Law, and record the development of Hong Kong's constitutional law. The 2023 *Pocket Edition of the Basic Law* retains all the laws included in the first edition, incorporates two decisions of the Standing Committee of the National People's Congress that were not included in the previous edition, and adds in it all relevant constitutional instruments adopted after its publication in 2017 by the National People's Congress and its Standing Committee. In view of the importance of the Law on Safeguarding National Security in the Hong Kong Special Administrative Region in the process of constructing and improving the constitutional order and legal system in Hong Kong, as well as the attention paid to it by the Hong Kong and international communities, the 2023 *Pocket Edition of the Basic Law* also includes as appendixes this Law and the first Interpretation of it by the Standing Committee of the National People's Congress (2021).

The 2023 *Pocket Edition of the Basic Law* retains the original structural arrangement and inherits the editorial features of the first edition, such as bilingual referencing, classification by category, cross referencing, and ease of carrying (see "Editor's Notes"). The editor and the publisher hope that this *Pocket Edition of the Basic Law* will continue to serve, as a desk book and pocket book, for legal researchers, legal practitioners, public servants and even interested members of the public.

Zhu Guobin, PhD
Professor, School of Law
Principal Investigator of the Implementation
of the Hong Kong Basic Law Research Project,
City University of Hong Kong
June 2023, Hong Kong

編輯出版說明

　　為《基本法》教學與研究需要，為推廣及普及《基本法》知識，為方便查閱法律文本，香港城市大學「香港基本法實施研究計劃」決定編輯出版一本輕便裝本《基本法》（包含其他相關憲制性法律文件），希望為法律與相關專業人士、公職人員，及大眾提供一本精緻輕巧、方便攜帶、易於查檢的《基本法》匯編本。它收錄《基本法》正文（共9章160條條文以及三份附件），和與《基本法》有直接關聯的現行憲制性法律文件，包括全國人民代表大會及其常務委員會分別就《基本法》實施作出的相關決定和法律解釋。

　　這本便攜式法律匯編具有如下特點：

雙語對照

香港特別行政區實行雙語法律制度，所有法例均有中文及英文兩種版本。這個輕便裝本，中英雙語並列，目的為便於讀者對照閱讀，不用翻頁就能在兩文之間互相檢索。

分類編排

過去出版的《基本法》及相關憲制性文件匯編，一般只直接按頒布時序排列，未有從內容及其性質上進行分類。除《基本法》正文單列外，本匯編特別將共20份重要憲制性決定及釋法文件，分為一般性「決定」（11份）、「關於附件三的決定」（3份）及「法律解釋」（6份）三部分，每部分再按時序排列。

Editor's Notes

For teaching and research purposes and to promote the Basic Law, the Implementation of the Hong Kong Basic Law Research Project of City University of Hong Kong has decided to publish a pocket-sized edition of the Basic Law, which includes the Basic Law full text (a total of 9 chapters consisting of 160 articles, plus 3 annexes) and all directly related constitutional instruments, including the decisions and legal interpretations of the Basic Law by the National People's Congress and its standing committee. It is hoped that this lightweight edition can provide an easy and convenient reference for legal professionals, civil servants and the public alike.

The pocket-sized edition of the Basic Law has the following features:

Bilingual Reference

As the Hong Kong Special Administrative Region employs a bilingual legal system where all legislation, including the Basic Law, are enacted in both Chinese and English, this pocket-sized edition provides a parallel, bilingual display which allows readers easy cross-referencing without having to turn pages.

Classification by Category

In previous editions of the Basic Law and constitution-related documents, most instruments have been arranged solely in chronological order. In addition to the full text of the Basic Law, this new edition includes 20 important constitutional decisions and legal interpretations of the Basic Law, which are first divided into 3 categories: Decisions (11 instruments), Decisions regarding Annex III (3 instruments) and Legal Interpretations (6 instruments). Each category is further arranged chronologically, allowing readers to easily search for specific content.

條文互檢

本匯編根據每項條文內容所提及或指涉的另一或幾個條
文或文件,於旁邊附註,便利讀者迅速檢閱相關條文或文
件。此外,編輯附註在文中以符號(如"*")標示,附註內
容見同一頁底部。

攜帶方便

它精緻小巧,尤其適合大專院校師生、法律和相關專業人
士,以及公職人員隨身攜帶,並隨時查閱。

香港基本法實施研究計劃

香港城市大學

二零一七年三月

二零二三年六月更新

Clear Cross References
In this edition, whenever an article refers to other articles, page numbers to the relevant articles are provided, allowing readers easy access to further information. In addition, editorial notes are clearly indicated by symbols such as "*", and footnotes can be found at the bottom of the pages.

Easy to Carry
This lightweight and handy edition is especially suitable for tertiary education scholars and students, legal professionals and civil servants for quick and easy referencing.

The Implementation
of the Hong Kong Basic Law Research Project
City University of Hong Kong
March 2017
Updated June 2023

中華人民共和國
香港特別行政區基本法

The Basic Law
of the Hong Kong Special Administrative Region
of the People's Republic of China

中華人民共和國主席令

第二十六號

Anx I (p 124),
Anx II (p 142),
Anx III (p 156)

《中華人民共和國香港特別行政區基本法》，包括附件一：《香港特別行政區行政長官的產生辦法》，附件二：《香港特別行政區立法會的產生辦法和表決程序》，附件三：《在香港特別行政區實施的全國性法律》，以及香港特別行政區區旗、區徽圖案，已由中華人民共和國第七屆全國人民代表大會第三次會議於1990年4月4日通過，現予公布，自1997年7月1日起實施。

中華人民共和國主席　楊尚昆

1990年4月4日

Decree of the President of the People's Republic of China

No. 26

I hereby promulgate the Basic Law of the Hong Kong Special Administrative Region of the People's Republic of China, including Annex I, Method for the Selection of the Chief Executive of the Hong Kong Special Administrative Region, Annex II, Method for the Formation of the Legislative Council of the Hong Kong Special Administrative Region and Its Voting Procedures, Annex III, National Laws to be Applied in the Hong Kong Special Administrative Region, and designs of the regional flag and regional emblem of the Hong Kong Special Administrative Region, which was adopted at the Third Session of the Seventh National People's Congress of the People's Republic of China on 4 April 1990 and shall be put into effect as of 1 July 1997.

Anx I (p 125), Anx II (p 143), Anx III (p 157)

(Signed)
Yang Shangkun
President of the People's Republic of China
4 April 1990

中華人民共和國
香港特別行政區基本法

(1990年4月4日第七屆全國人民代表大會第三次會議通過
1990年4月4日中華人民共和國主席令第二十六號公布
自1997年7月1日起施行)

The Basic Law
of the Hong Kong Special Administrative Region
of the People's Republic of China

(Adopted at the Third Session
of the Seventh National People's Congress on 4 April 1990

Promulgated by Order No. 26 of the President
of the People's Republic of China on 4 April 1990

Effective as of 1 July 1997)

序言

香港自古以來就是中國的領土,一八四〇年鴉片戰爭以後被英國佔領。一九八四年十二月十九日,中英兩國政府簽署了關於香港問題的聯合聲明,確認中華人民共和國政府於一九九七年七月一日恢復對香港行使主權,從而實現了長期以來中國人民收回香港的共同願望。

為了維護國家的統一和領土完整,保持香港的繁榮和穩定,並考慮到香港的歷史和現實情況,國家決定,在對香港恢復行使主權時,根據中華人民共和國憲法第三十一條的規定,設立香港特別行政區,並按照"一個國家,兩種制度"的方針,不在香港實行社會主義的制度和政策。國家對香港的基本方針政策,已由中國政府在中英聯合聲明中予以闡明。

根據中華人民共和國憲法,全國人民代表大會特制定中華人民共和國香港特別行政區基本法,規定香港特別行政區實行的制度,以保障國家對香港的基本方針政策的實施。

Preamble

Hong Kong has been part of the territory of China since ancient times; it was occupied by Britain after the Opium War in 1840. On 19 December 1984, the Chinese and British Governments signed the Joint Declaration on the Question of Hong Kong, affirming that the Government of the People's Republic of China will resume the exercise of sovereignty over Hong Kong with effect from 1 July 1997, thus fulfilling the long-cherished common aspiration of the Chinese people for the recovery of Hong Kong.

Upholding national unity and territorial integrity, maintaining the prosperity and stability of Hong Kong, and taking account of its history and realities, the People's Republic of China has decided that upon China's resumption of the exercise of sovereignty over Hong Kong, a Hong Kong Special Administrative Region will be established in accordance with the provisions of Article 31 of the Constitution of the People's Republic of China, and that under the principle of "one country, two systems", the socialist system and policies will not be practised in Hong Kong. The basic policies of the People's Republic of China regarding Hong Kong have been elaborated by the Chinese Government in the Sino-British Joint Declaration.

In accordance with the Constitution of the People's Republic of China, the National People's Congress hereby enacts the Basic Law of the Hong Kong Special Administrative Region of the People's Republic of China, prescribing the systems to be practised in the Hong Kong Special Administrative Region, in order to ensure the implementation of the basic policies of the People's Republic of China regarding Hong Kong.

第一章　總則

第一條

Art 12

香港特別行政區是中華人民共和國不可分離的部分。

第二條

Art 43, 59, 66, 80

全國人民代表大會授權香港特別行政區依照本法的規定實行高度自治，享有行政管理權、立法權、獨立的司法權和終審權。

第三條

Art 24

香港特別行政區的行政機關和立法機關由香港永久性居民依照本法有關規定組成。

第四條

Art 25–40

香港特別行政區依法保障香港特別行政區居民和其他人的權利和自由。

第五條

香港特別行政區不實行社會主義制度和政策，保持原有的資本主義制度和生活方式，五十年不變。

Chapter I: General Principles

Article 1
The Hong Kong Special Administrative Region is an inalienable part of the People's Republic of China.

Art 12

Article 2
The National People's Congress authorizes the Hong Kong Special Administrative Region to exercise a high degree of autonomy and enjoy executive, legislative and independent judicial power, including that of final adjudication, in accordance with the provisions of this Law.

Art 43, 59, 66, 80

Article 3
The executive authorities and legislature of the Hong Kong Special Administrative Region shall be composed of permanent residents of Hong Kong in accordance with the relevant provisions of this Law.

Art 24

Article 4
The Hong Kong Special Administrative Region shall safeguard the rights and freedoms of the residents of the Hong Kong Special Administrative Region and of other persons in the Region in accordance with law.

Art 25–40

Article 5
The socialist system and policies shall not be practised in the Hong Kong Special Administrative Region, and the previous capitalist system and way of life shall remain unchanged for 50 years.

第六條

Art 29, 105

香港特別行政區依法保護私有財產權。

第七條

Art 120–123

香港特別行政區境內的土地和自然資源屬於國家所有,由香港特別行政區政府負責管理、使用、開發、出租或批給個人、法人或團體使用或開發,其收入全歸香港特別行政區政府支配。

第八條

Art 11, 73, 160

香港原有法律,即普通法、衡平法、條例、附屬立法和習慣法,除同本法相抵觸或經香港特別行政區的立法機關作出修改者外,予以保留。

第九條

香港特別行政區的行政機關、立法機關和司法機關,除使用中文外,還可使用英文,英文也是正式語文。

第十條

Anx III (p 156)

香港特別行政區除懸掛中華人民共和國國旗和國徽外,還可使用香港特別行政區區旗和區徽。

Anx III (p 160)

　　香港特別行政區的區旗是五星花蕊的紫荊花紅旗。

Article 6

The Hong Kong Special Administrative Region shall protect the right of private ownership of property in accordance with law.

Art 29, 105

Article 7

The land and natural resources within the Hong Kong Special Administrative Region shall be State property. The Government of the Hong Kong Special Administrative Region shall be responsible for their management, use and development and for their lease or grant to individuals, legal persons or organizations for use or development. The revenues derived therefrom shall be exclusively at the disposal of the government of the Region.

Art 120–123

Article 8

The laws previously in force in Hong Kong, that is, the common law, rules of equity, ordinances, subordinate legislation and customary law shall be maintained, except for any that contravene this Law, and subject to any amendment by the legislature of the Hong Kong Special Administrative Region.

Art 11, 73, 160

Article 9

In addition to the Chinese language, English may also be used as an official language by the executive authorities, legislature and judiciary of the Hong Kong Special Administrative Region.

Article 10

Apart from displaying the national flag and national emblem of the People's Republic of China, the Hong Kong Special Administrative Region may also use a regional flag and regional emblem.

Anx III (p 157)

The regional flag of the Hong Kong Special Administrative Region is a red flag with a bauhinia highlighted by five star-tipped stamens.

Anx III (p 161)

Anx III (p 160)

　　香港特別行政區的區徽，中間是五星花蕊的紫荊花，周圍寫有"中華人民共和國香港特別行政區"和英文"香港"。

第十一條

序言

根據中華人民共和國憲法第三十一條，香港特別行政區的制度和政策，包括社會、經濟制度，有關保障居民的基本權利和自由的制度，行政管理、立法和司法方面的制度，以及有關政策，均以本法的規定為依據。

Art 8, 68, 73

　　香港特別行政區立法機關制定的任何法律，均不得同本法相抵觸。

The regional emblem of the Hong Kong Special Administrative
Region is a bauhinia in the centre highlighted by five star-tipped
stamens and encircled by the words "Hong Kong Special
Administrative Region of the People's Republic of China" in
Chinese and "HONG KONG" in English.

Anx III (p 161)

Article 11

In accordance with Article 31 of the Constitution of the People's
Republic of China, the systems and policies practised in the
Hong Kong Special Administrative Region, including the social
and economic systems, the system for safeguarding the
fundamental rights and freedoms of its residents, the executive,
legislative and judicial systems, and the relevant policies, shall be
based on the provisions of this Law.

Preamble

No law enacted by the legislature of the Hong Kong Special
Administrative Region shall contravene this Law.

Art 8, 68, 73

第二章　中央和香港特別行政區的關係

第十二條

Art 1

香港特別行政區是中華人民共和國的一個享有高度自治權的地方行政區域，直轄於中央人民政府。

第十三條

Inst 28 (p 354)

中央人民政府負責管理與香港特別行政區有關的外交事務。

中華人民共和國外交部在香港設立機構處理外交事務。

Art 126,
150–157

中央人民政府授權香港特別行政區依照本法自行處理有關的對外事務。

第十四條

Inst 19 (p 312)

中央人民政府負責管理香港特別行政區的防務。

香港特別行政區政府負責維持香港特別行政區的社會治安。

Chapter II: Relationship between the Central Authorities and the Hong Kong Special Administrative Region

Article 12

The Hong Kong Special Administrative Region shall be a local administrative region of the People's Republic of China, which shall enjoy a high degree of autonomy and come directly under the Central People's Government.

Art 1

Article 13

The Central People's Government shall be responsible for the foreign affairs relating to the Hong Kong Special Administrative Region.

Inst 28 (p 355)

The Ministry of Foreign Affairs of the People's Republic of China shall establish an office in Hong Kong to deal with foreign affairs.

The Central People's Government authorizes the Hong Kong Special Administrative Region to conduct relevant external affairs on its own in accordance with this Law.

Art 126, 150–157

Article 14

The Central People's Government shall be responsible for the defence of the Hong Kong Special Administrative Region.

Inst 19 (p 312)

The Government of the Hong Kong Special Administrative Region shall be responsible for the maintenance of public order in the Region.

　　中央人民政府派駐香港特別行政區負責防務的軍隊不干預香港特別行政區的地方事務。香港特別行政區政府在必要時，可向中央人民政府請求駐軍協助維持社會治安和救助災害。

　　駐軍人員除須遵守全國性的法律外，還須遵守香港特別行政區的法律。

　　駐軍費用由中央人民政府負擔。

第十五條

Art 43-45, 48 (5)–(7), 61

中央人民政府依照本法第四章的規定任命香港特別行政區行政長官和行政機關的主要官員。

第十六條

Art 62

香港特別行政區享有行政管理權，依照本法的有關規定自行處理香港特別行政區的行政事務。

第十七條

Art 21, 66, 73 (1)

香港特別行政區享有立法權。

　　香港特別行政區的立法機關制定的法律須報全國人民代表大會常務委員會備案。備案不影響該法律的生效。

Military forces stationed by the Central People's Government in the Hong Kong Special Administrative Region for defence shall not interfere in the local affairs of the Region. The Government of the Hong Kong Special Administrative Region may, when necessary, ask the Central People's Government for assistance from the garrison in the maintenance of public order and in disaster relief.

In addition to abiding by national laws, members of the garrison shall abide by the laws of the Hong Kong Special Administrative Region.

Expenditure for the garrison shall be borne by the Central People's Government.

Article 15

The Central People's Government shall appoint the Chief Executive and the principal officials of the executive authorities of the Hong Kong Special Administrative Region in accordance with the provisions of Chapter IV of this Law.

Art 43-45, 48 (5)–(7), 61

Article 16

The Hong Kong Special Administrative Region shall be vested with executive power. It shall, on its own, conduct the administrative affairs of the Region in accordance with the relevant provisions of this Law.

Art 62

Article 17

The Hong Kong Special Administrative Region shall be vested with legislative power.

Art 21, 66, 73 (1)

Laws enacted by the legislature of the Hong Kong Special Administrative Region must be reported to the Standing Committee of the National People's Congress for the record. The reporting for record shall not affect the entry into force of such laws.

Inst 4 (p 192)

　　全國人民代表大會常務委員會在徵詢其所屬的香港特別行政區基本法委員會後，如認為香港特別行政區立法機關制定的任何法律不符合本法關於中央管理的事務及中央和香港特別行政區的關係的條款，可將有關法律發回，但不作修改。經全國人民代表大會常務委員會發回的法律立即失效。該法律的失效，除香港特別行政區的法律另有規定外，無溯及力。

第十八條

Art 8

在香港特別行政區實行的法律為本法以及本法第八條規定的香港原有法律和香港特別行政區立法機關制定的法律。

Anx III (p 156),
Inst 19 (p 312),
Inst 20 (p 316),
Inst 21 (p 318),
Inst 22 (p 320),
Inst 23 (p 322)

　　全國性法律除列於本法附件三者外，不在香港特別行政區實施。凡列於本法附件三之法律，由香港特別行政區在當地公布或立法實施。

Anx III (p 156),
Inst 4 (p 192),
Inst 19 (p 312),
Inst 20 (p 316),
Inst 21 (p 318),
Inst 22 (p 320),
Inst 23 (p 322),

　　全國人民代表大會常務委員會在徵詢其所屬的香港特別行政區基本法委員會和香港特別行政區政府的意見後，可對列於本法附件三的法律作出增減，任何列入附件三的法律，限於有關國防、外交和其他按本法規定不屬於香港特別行政區自治範圍的法律。

If the Standing Committee of the National People's Congress, after consulting the Committee for the Basic Law of the Hong Kong Special Administrative Region under it, considers that any law enacted by the legislature of the Region is not in conformity with the provisions of this Law regarding affairs within the responsibility of the Central Authorities or regarding the relationship between the Central Authorities and the Region, the Standing Committee may return the law in question but shall not amend it. Any law returned by the Standing Committee of the National People's Congress shall immediately be invalidated. This invalidation shall not have retroactive effect, unless otherwise provided for in the laws of the Region.

Inst 4 (p 193)

Article 18

The laws in force in the Hong Kong Special Administrative Region shall be this Law, the laws previously in force in Hong Kong as provided for in Article 8 of this Law, and the laws enacted by the legislature of the Region.

Art 8

National laws shall not be applied in the Hong Kong Special Administrative Region except for those listed in Annex III to this Law. The laws listed therein shall be applied locally by way of promulgation or legislation by the Region.

Anx III (p 157),
Inst 19 (p 313),
Inst 20 (p 317),
Inst 21 (p 319),
Inst 22 (p 321),
Inst 23 (p 323),

The Standing Committee of the National People's Congress may add to or delete from the list of laws in Annex III after consulting its Committee for the Basic Law of the Hong Kong Special Administrative Region and the government of the Region. Laws listed in Annex III to this Law shall be confined to those relating to defence and foreign affairs as well as other matters outside the limits of the autonomy of the Region as specified by this Law.

Anx III (p 157),
Inst 4 (p 193),
Inst 19 (p 313),
Inst 20 (p 317),
Inst 21 (p 319),
Inst 22 (p 321),
Inst 23 (p 323),

　　全國人民代表大會常務委員會決定宣布戰爭狀態或因香港特別行政區內發生香港特別行政區政府不能控制的危及國家統一或安全的動亂而決定香港特別行政區進入緊急狀態，中央人民政府可發布命令將有關全國性法律在香港特別行政區實施。

第十九條

Art 2

香港特別行政區享有獨立的司法權和終審權。

Art 80, 81

　　香港特別行政區法院除繼續保持香港原有法律制度和原則對法院審判權所作的限制外，對香港特別行政區所有的案件均有審判權。

Inst 28 (p 354)

　　香港特別行政區法院對國防、外交等國家行為無管轄權。香港特別行政區法院在審理案件中遇有涉及國防、外交等國家行為的事實問題，應取得行政長官就該等問題發出的證明文件，上述文件對法院有約束力。行政長官在發出證明文件前，須取得中央人民政府的證明書。

第二十條

香港特別行政區可享有全國人民代表大會和全國人民代表大會常務委員會及中央人民政府授予的其他權力。

In the event that the Standing Committee of the National People's Congress decides to declare a state of war or, by reason of turmoil within the Hong Kong Special Administrative Region which endangers national unity or security and is beyond the control of the government of the Region, decides that the Region is in a state of emergency, the Central People's Government may issue an order applying the relevant national laws in the Region.

Article 19

The Hong Kong Special Administrative Region shall be vested with independent judicial power, including that of final adjudication.

Art 2

The courts of the Hong Kong Special Administrative Region shall have jurisdiction over all cases in the Region, except that the restrictions on their jurisdiction imposed by the legal system and principles previously in force in Hong Kong shall be maintained.

Art 80, 81

The courts of the Hong Kong Special Administrative Region shall have no jurisdiction over acts of state such as defence and foreign affairs. The courts of the Region shall obtain a certificate from the Chief Executive on questions of fact concerning acts of state such as defence and foreign affairs whenever such questions arise in the adjudication of cases. This certificate shall be binding on the courts. Before issuing such a certificate, the Chief Executive shall obtain a certifying document from the Central People's Government.

Inst 28 (p 355)

Article 20

The Hong Kong Special Administrative Region may enjoy other powers granted to it by the National People's Congress, the Standing Committee of the National People's Congress or the Central People's Government.

第二十一條

Inst 24 (p 326)

香港特別行政區居民中的中國公民依法參與國家事務的管理。

　　根據全國人民代表大會確定的名額和代表產生辦法，由香港特別行政區居民中的中國公民在香港選出香港特別行政區的全國人民代表大會代表，參加最高國家權力機關的工作。

第二十二條

中央人民政府所屬各部門、各省、自治區、直轄市均不得干預香港特別行政區根據本法自行管理的事務。

　　中央各部門、各省、自治區、直轄市如需在香港特別行政區設立機構，須徵得香港特別行政區政府同意並經中央人民政府批准。

　　中央各部門、各省、自治區、直轄市在香港特別行政區設立的一切機構及其人員均須遵守香港特別行政區的法律。

Article 21

Chinese citizens who are residents of the Hong Kong Special Administrative Region shall be entitled to participate in the management of state affairs according to law.

Inst 24 (p 327)

In accordance with the assigned number of seats and the selection method specified by the National People's Congress, the Chinese citizens among the residents of the Hong Kong Special Administrative Region shall locally elect deputies of the Region to the National People's Congress to participate in the work of the highest organ of state power.

Article 22

No department of the Central People's Government and no province, autonomous region, or municipality directly under the Central Government may interfere in the affairs which the Hong Kong Special Administrative Region administers on its own in accordance with this Law.

If there is a need for departments of the Central Government, or for provinces, autonomous regions, or municipalities directly under the Central Government to set up offices in the Hong Kong Special Administrative Region, they must obtain the consent of the government of the Region and the approval of the Central People's Government.

All offices set up in the Hong Kong Special Administrative Region by departments of the Central Government, or by provinces, autonomous regions, or municipalities directly under the Central Government, and the personnel of these offices shall abide by the laws of the Region.

Inst 25 (p 332)

　　中國其他地區的人進入香港特別行政區須辦理批准手續，其中進入香港特別行政區定居的人數由中央人民政府主管部門徵求香港特別行政區政府的意見後確定。

　　香港特別行政區可在北京設立辦事機構。

第二十三條

Inst 15 (p 286),
Inst 23 (p 322)
App 1 (p 378),
App 2 (p 446)

香港特別行政區應自行立法禁止任何叛國、分裂國家、煽動叛亂、顛覆中央人民政府及竊取國家機密的行為，禁止外國的政治性組織或團體在香港特別行政區進行政治活動，禁止香港特別行政區的政治性組織或團體與外國的政治性組織或團體建立聯繫。

For entry into the Hong Kong Special Administrative Region, people from other parts of China must apply for approval. Among them, the number of persons who enter the Region for the purpose of settlement shall be determined by the competent authorities of the Central People's Government after consulting the government of the Region.

Inst 25 (p 333)

The Hong Kong Special Administrative Region may establish an office in Beijing.

Article 23

The Hong Kong Special Administrative Region shall enact laws on its own to prohibit any act of treason, secession, sedition, subversion against the Central People's Government, or theft of state secrets, to prohibit foreign political organizations or bodies from conducting political activities in the Region, and to prohibit political organizations or bodies of the Region from establishing ties with foreign political organizations or bodies.

Inst 15 (p 287),
Inst 23 (p 323)
App 1 (p 379),
App 2 (p 447)

第三章　居民的基本權利和義務

第二十四條

香港特別行政區居民，簡稱香港居民，包括永久性居民和非永久性居民。

Inst 25 (p 332)

香港特別行政區永久性居民為：

(一)　在香港特別行政區成立以前或以後在香港出生的中國公民；

(二)　在香港特別行政區成立以前或以後在香港通常居住連續七年以上的中國公民；

Inst 25 (p 336)

(三)　第(一)、(二)兩項所列居民在香港以外所生的中國籍子女；

(四)　在香港特別行政區成立以前或以後持有效旅行證件進入香港、在香港通常居住連續七年以上並以香港為永久居住地的非中國籍的人；

Chapter III: Fundamental Rights and Duties of the Residents

Article 24

Residents of the Hong Kong Special Administrative Region ("Hong Kong residents") shall include permanent residents and non-permanent residents.

Inst 25 (p 333)

The permanent residents of the Hong Kong Special Administrative Region shall be:

(1)   Chinese citizens born in Hong Kong before or after the establishment of the Hong Kong Special Administrative Region;

(2)   Chinese citizens who have ordinarily resided in Hong Kong for a continuous period of not less than seven years before or after the establishment of the Hong Kong Special Administrative Region;

(3)   Persons of Chinese nationality born outside Hong Kong of those residents listed in categories (1) and (2);

Inst 25 (p 327)

(4)   Persons not of Chinese nationality who have entered Hong Kong with valid travel documents, have ordinarily resided in Hong Kong for a continuous period of not less than seven years and have taken Hong Kong as their place of permanent residence before or after the establishment of the Hong Kong Special Administrative Region;

（五）　　在香港特別行政區成立以前或以後第（四）項所列居民在香港所生的未滿二十一周歲的子女；

（六）　　第（一）至（五）項所列居民以外在香港特別行政區成立以前只在香港有居留權的人。

以上居民在香港特別行政區享有居留權和有資格依照香港特別行政區法律取得載明其居留權的永久性居民身份證。

香港特別行政區非永久性居民為：有資格依照香港特別行政區法律取得香港居民身份證，但沒有居留權的人。

第二十五條

Art 24 (1)–(6), 42

香港居民在法律面前一律平等。

第二十六條

Art 24 (1)–(4)

香港特別行政區永久性居民依法享有選舉權和被選舉權。

第二十七條

香港居民享有言論、新聞、出版的自由，結社、集會、遊行、示威的自由，組織和參加工會、罷工的權利和自由。

(5) Persons under 21 years of age born in Hong Kong of those residents listed in category (4) before or after the establishment of the Hong Kong Special Administrative Region; and

(6) Persons other than those residents listed in categories (1) to (5), who, before the establishment of the Hong Kong Special Administrative Region, had the right of abode in Hong Kong only.

The above-mentioned residents shall have the right of abode in the Hong Kong Special Administrative Region and shall be qualified to obtain, in accordance with the laws of the Region, permanent identity cards which state their right of abode.

The non-permanent residents of the Hong Kong Special Administrative Region shall be persons who are qualified to obtain Hong Kong identity cards in accordance with the laws of the Region but have no right of abode.

Article 25
All Hong Kong residents shall be equal before the law.

Art 24 (1)–(6), 42

Article 26
Permanent residents of the Hong Kong Special Administrative Region shall have the right to vote and the right to stand for election in accordance with law.

Art 24 (1)–(4)

Article 27
Hong Kong residents shall have freedom of speech, of the press and of publication; freedom of association, of assembly, of procession and of demonstration; and the right and freedom to form and join trade unions, and to strike.

第二十八條

香港居民的人身自由不受侵犯。

香港居民不受任意或非法逮捕、拘留、監禁。禁止任意或非法搜查居民的身體、剝奪或限制居民的人身自由。禁止對居民施行酷刑、任意或非法剝奪居民的生命。

第二十九條

Art 6

香港居民的住宅和其他房屋不受侵犯。禁止任意或非法搜查、侵入居民的住宅和其他房屋。

第三十條

香港居民的通訊自由和通訊秘密受法律的保護。除因公共安全和追查刑事犯罪的需要，由有關機關依照法律程序對通訊進行檢查外，任何部門或個人不得以任何理由侵犯居民的通訊自由和通訊秘密。

第三十一條

Inst 24 (p 326)

香港居民有在香港特別行政區境內遷徙的自由，有移居其他國家和地區的自由。香港居民有旅行和出入境的自由。有效旅行證件的持有人，除非受到法律制止，可自由離開香港特別行政區，無需特別批准。

Article 28

The freedom of the person of Hong Kong residents shall be inviolable.

No Hong Kong resident shall be subjected to arbitrary or unlawful arrest, detention or imprisonment. Arbitrary or unlawful search of the body of any resident or deprivation or restriction of the freedom of the person shall be prohibited. Torture of any resident or arbitrary or unlawful deprivation of the life of any resident shall be prohibited.

Article 29

The homes and other premises of Hong Kong residents shall be inviolable. Arbitrary or unlawful search of, or intrusion into, a resident's home or other premises shall be prohibited.

Art 6

Article 30

The freedom and privacy of communication of Hong Kong residents shall be protected by law. No department or individual may, on any grounds, infringe upon the freedom and privacy of communication of residents except that the relevant authorities may inspect communication in accordance with legal procedures to meet the needs of public security or of investigation into criminal offences.

Article 31

Hong Kong residents shall have freedom of movement within the Hong Kong Special Administrative Region and freedom of emigration to other countries and regions. They shall have freedom to travel and to enter or leave the Region. Unless restrained by law, holders of valid travel documents shall be free to leave the Region without special authorization.

Inst 24 (p 327)

第三十二條

香港居民有信仰的自由。

Art 137, 141   香港居民有宗教信仰的自由,有公開傳教和舉行、參加宗教活動的自由。

第三十三條

香港居民有選擇職業的自由。

第三十四條

Ar 137, 140 香港居民有進行學術研究、文學藝術創作和其他文化活動的自由。

第三十五條

香港居民有權得到秘密法律諮詢、向法院提起訴訟、選擇律師及時保護自己的合法權益或在法庭上為其代理和獲得司法補救。

    香港居民有權對行政部門和行政人員的行為向法院提起訴訟。

第三十六條

Art 145 香港居民有依法享受社會福利的權利。勞工的福利待遇和退休保障受法律保護。

第三十七條

香港居民的婚姻自由和自願生育的權利受法律保護。

Article 32
Hong Kong residents shall have freedom of conscience.

Hong Kong residents shall have freedom of religious belief and freedom to preach and to conduct and participate in religious activities in public.

Art 137, 141

Article 33
Hong Kong residents shall have freedom of choice of occupation.

Article 34
Hong Kong residents shall have freedom to engage in academic research, literary and artistic creation, and other cultural activities.

Art 137, 140

Article 35
Hong Kong residents shall have the right to confidential legal advice, access to the courts, choice of lawyers for timely protection of their lawful rights and interests or for representation in the courts, and to judicial remedies.

Hong Kong residents shall have the right to institute legal proceedings in the courts against the acts of the executive authorities and their personnel.

Article 36
Hong Kong residents shall have the right to social welfare in accordance with law. The welfare benefits and retirement security of the labour force shall be protected by law.

Art 145

Article 37
The freedom of marriage of Hong Kong residents and their right to raise a family freely shall be protected by law.

第三十八條

香港居民享有香港特別行政區法律保障的其他權利和自由。

第三十九條

Art 27

《公民權利和政治權利國際公約》、《經濟、社會與文化權利的國際公約》和國際勞工公約適用於香港的有關規定繼續有效,通過香港特別行政區的法律予以實施。

香港居民享有的權利和自由,除依法規定外不得限制,此種限制不得與本條第一款規定抵觸。

第四十條

Art 122

"新界"原居民的合法傳統權益受香港特別行政區的保護。

第四十一條

Art 24

在香港特別行政區境內的香港居民以外的其他人,依法享有本章規定的香港居民的權利和自由。

第四十二條

香港居民和在香港的其他人有遵守香港特別行政區實行的法律的義務。

Article 38

Hong Kong residents shall enjoy the other rights and freedoms safeguarded by the laws of the Hong Kong Special Administrative Region.

Article 39

The provisions of the International Covenant on Civil and Political Rights, the International Covenant on Economic, Social and Cultural Rights, and international labour conventions as applied to Hong Kong shall remain in force and shall be implemented through the laws of the Hong Kong Special Administrative Region.

Art 27

The rights and freedoms enjoyed by Hong Kong residents shall not be restricted unless as prescribed by law. Such restrictions shall not contravene the provisions of the preceding paragraph of this Article.

Article 40

The lawful traditional rights and interests of the indigenous inhabitants of the "New Territories" shall be protected by the Hong Kong Special Administrative Region.

Art 122

Article 41

Persons in the Hong Kong Special Administrative Region other than Hong Kong residents shall, in accordance with law, enjoy the rights and freedoms of Hong Kong residents prescribed in this Chapter.

Art 24

Article 42

Hong Kong residents and other persons in Hong Kong shall have the obligation to abide by the laws in force in the Hong Kong Special Administrative Region.

第四章 政治體制

第一節 行政長官

第四十三條

香港特別行政區行政長官是香港特別行政區的首長,代表香港特別行政區。

Art 15

香港特別行政區行政長官依照本法的規定對中央人民政府和香港特別行政區負責。

第四十四條

Art 15,
24 (1)–(4)

香港特別行政區行政長官由年滿四十周歲,在香港通常居住連續滿二十年並在外國無居留權的香港特別行政區永久性居民中的中國公民擔任。

第四十五條

Art 15

香港特別行政區行政長官在當地通過選舉或協商產生,由中央人民政府任命。

Anx I (p 124),
Inst 8 (p 222),
Inst 10 (p 236),
Inst 11 (p 246),
Inst 13 (p 260),
Inst 18 (p 302)

行政長官的產生辦法根據香港特別行政區的實際情況和循序漸進的原則而規定,最終達至由一個有廣泛代表性的提名委員會按民主程序提名後普選產生的目標。

Chapter IV: Political Structure

Section 1: The Chief Executive

Article 43

The Chief Executive of the Hong Kong Special Administrative Region shall be the head of the Hong Kong Special Administrative Region and shall represent the Region.

Art 15

The Chief Executive of the Hong Kong Special Administrative Region shall be accountable to the Central People's Government and the Hong Kong Special Administrative Region in accordance with the provisions of this Law.

Article 44

The Chief Executive of the Hong Kong Special Administrative Region shall be a Chinese citizen of not less than 40 years of age who is a permanent resident of the Region with no right of abode in any foreign country and has ordinarily resided in Hong Kong for a continuous period of not less than 20 years.

Art 15,
24 (1)–(4)

Article 45

The Chief Executive of the Hong Kong Special Administrative Region shall be selected by election or through consultations held locally and be appointed by the Central People's Government.

Art 15

The method for selecting the Chief Executive shall be specified in the light of the actual situation in the Hong Kong Special Administrative Region and in accordance with the principle of gradual and orderly progress. The ultimate aim is the selection of the Chief Executive by universal suffrage upon nomination by a broadly representative nominating committee in accordance with democratic procedures.

Anx I (p 125),
Inst 8 (p 223),
Inst 10 (p 237),
Inst 11 (p 247),
Inst 13 (p 261),
Inst 18 (p 303)

Anx I (p 124)　　　　行政長官產生的具體辦法由附件一《香港特別行政區行政長官的產生辦法》規定。

第四十六條

香港特別行政區行政長官任期五年,可連任一次。

第四十七條

香港特別行政區行政長官必須廉潔奉公、盡忠職守。

　　　行政長官就任時應向香港特別行政區終審法院首席法官申報財產,記錄在案。

第四十八條

Art 60香港特別行政區行政長官行使下列職權:

(一)　　領導香港特別行政區政府;

(二)　　負責執行本法和依照本法適用於香港特別行政區的其他法律;

Art 76(三)　　簽署立法會通過的法案,公布法律;

　　　　簽署立法會通過的財政預算案,將財政預算、決算報中央人民政府備案;

(四)　　決定政府政策和發布行政命令;

The specific method for selecting the Chief Executive is *Anx I (p 125)* prescribed in Annex I "Method for the Selection of the Chief Executive of the Hong Kong Special Administrative Region".

Article 46

The term of office of the Chief Executive of the Hong Kong Special Administrative Region shall be five years. He or she may serve for not more than two consecutive terms.

Article 47

The Chief Executive of the Hong Kong Special Administrative Region must be a person of integrity, dedicated to his or her duties.

The Chief Executive, on assuming office, shall declare his or her assets to the Chief Justice of the Court of Final Appeal of the Hong Kong Special Administrative Region. This declaration shall be put on record.

Article 48

The Chief Executive of the Hong Kong Special Administrative *Art 60* Region shall exercise the following powers and functions:

(1) To lead the government of the Region;

(2) To be responsible for the implementation of this Law and other laws which, in accordance with this Law, apply in the Hong Kong Special Administrative Region;

(3) To sign bills passed by the Legislative Council and to *Art 76* promulgate laws;

To sign budgets passed by the Legislative Council and report the budgets and final accounts to the Central People's Government for the record;

(4) To decide on government policies and to issue executive orders;

Art 15, 61,
99, 101

(五) 提名並報請中央人民政府任命下列主要官員：各司司長、副司長，各局局長，廉政專員，審計署署長，警務處處長，入境事務處處長，海關關長；建議中央人民政府免除上述官員職務；

Art 88

(六) 依照法定程序任免各級法院法官；

(七) 依照法定程序任免公職人員；

(八) 執行中央人民政府就本法規定的有關事務發出的指令；

Art 150–152

(九) 代表香港特別行政區政府處理中央授權的對外事務和其他事務；

Art 73 (2)–(3)

(十) 批准向立法會提出有關財政收入或支出的動議；

Art 73 (10)

(十一) 根據安全和重大公共利益的考慮，決定政府官員或其他負責政府公務的人員是否向立法會或其屬下的委員會作證和提供證據；

(十二) 赦免或減輕刑事罪犯的刑罰；

(十三) 處理請願、申訴事項。

(5) To nominate and to report to the Central People's Government for appointment the following principal officials: Secretaries and Deputy Secretaries of Departments, Directors of Bureaux, Commissioner Against Corruption, Director of Audit, Commissioner of Police, Director of Immigration and Commissioner of Customs and Excise; and to recommend to the Central People's Government the removal of the above-mentioned officials;

Art 15, 61, 99, 101

(6) To appoint or remove judges of the courts at all levels in accordance with legal procedures;

Art 88

(7) To appoint or remove holders of public office in accordance with legal procedures;

(8) To implement the directives issued by the Central People's Government in respect of the relevant matters provided for in this Law;

(9) To conduct, on behalf of the Government of the Hong Kong Special Administrative Region, external affairs and other affairs as authorized by the Central Authorities;

Art 150–152

(10) To approve the introduction of motions regarding revenues or expenditure to the Legislative Council;

Art 73 (2)–(3)

(11) To decide, in the light of security and vital public interests, whether government officials or other personnel in charge of government affairs should testify or give evidence before the Legislative Council or its committees;

Art 73 (10)

(12) To pardon persons convicted of criminal offences or commute their penalties; and

(13) To handle petitions and complaints.

第四十九條

香港特別行政區行政長官如認為立法會通過的法案不符合香港特別行政區的整體利益，可在三個月內將法案發回立法會重議，立法會如以不少於全體議員三分之二多數再次通過原案，行政長官必須在一個月內簽署公布或按本法第五十條的規定處理。

第五十條

香港特別行政區行政長官如拒絕簽署立法會再次通過的法案或立法會拒絕通過政府提出的財政預算案或其他重要法案，經協商仍不能取得一致意見，行政長官可解散立法會。

Art 70

行政長官在解散立法會前，須徵詢行政會議的意見。行政長官在其一任任期內只能解散立法會一次。

第五十一條

香港特別行政區立法會如拒絕批准政府提出的財政預算案，行政長官可向立法會申請臨時撥款。如果由於立法會已被解散而不能批准撥款，行政長官可在選出新的立法會前的一段時期內，按上一財政年度的開支標準，批准臨時短期撥款。

Art 73

Article 49

If the Chief Executive of the Hong Kong Special Administrative Region considers that a bill passed by the Legislative Council is not compatible with the overall interests of the Region, he or she may return it to the Legislative Council within three months for reconsideration. If the Legislative Council passes the original bill again by not less than a two-thirds majority of all the members, the Chief Executive must sign and promulgate it within one month, or act in accordance with the provisions of Article 50 of this Law.

Article 50

If the Chief Executive of the Hong Kong Special Administrative Region refuses to sign a bill passed the second time by the Legislative Council, or the Legislative Council refuses to pass a budget or any other important bill introduced by the government, and if consensus still cannot be reached after consultations, the Chief Executive may dissolve the Legislative Council.

Art 70

The Chief Executive must consult the Executive Council before dissolving the Legislative Council. The Chief Executive may dissolve the Legislative Council only once in each term of his or her office.

Article 51

If the Legislative Council of the Hong Kong Special Administrative Region refuses to pass the budget introduced by the government, the Chief Executive may apply to the Legislative Council for provisional appropriations. If appropriation of public funds cannot be approved because the Legislative Council has already been dissolved, the Chief Executive may, prior to the election of the new Legislative Council, approve provisional short-term appropriations according to the level of expenditure of the previous fiscal year.

Art 73

第五十二條

香港特別行政區行政長官如有下列情況之一者必須辭職：

(一)　　因嚴重疾病或其他原因無力履行職務；

Art 50

(二)　　因兩次拒絕簽署立法會通過的法案而解散立法會，重選的立法會仍以全體議員三分之二多數通過所爭議的原案，而行政長官仍拒絕簽署；

(三)　　因立法會拒絕通過財政預算案或其他重要法案而解散立法會，重選的立法會繼續拒絕通過所爭議的原案。

第五十三條

Art 43, 48

香港特別行政區行政長官短期不能履行職務時，由政務司長、財政司長、律政司長依次臨時代理其職務。

Inst 27 (p 348)

行政長官缺位時，應在六個月內依本法第四十五條的規定產生新的行政長官。行政長官缺位期間的職務代理，依照上款規定辦理。

Article 52

The Chief Executive of the Hong Kong Special Administrative Region must resign under any of the following circumstances:

(1) When he or she loses the ability to discharge his or her duties as a result of serious illness or other reasons;

(2) When, after the Legislative Council is dissolved because he or she twice refuses to sign a bill passed by it, the new Legislative Council again passes by a two-thirds majority of all the members the original bill in dispute, but he or she still refuses to sign it; and

Art 50

(3) When, after the Legislative Council is dissolved because it refuses to pass a budget or any other important bill, the new Legislative Council still refuses to pass the original bill in dispute.

Article 53

If the Chief Executive of the Hong Kong Special Administrative Region is not able to discharge his or her duties for a short period, such duties shall temporarily be assumed by the Administrative Secretary, Financial Secretary or Secretary of Justice in this order of precedence.

Art 43

In the event that the office of Chief Executive becomes vacant, a new Chief Executive shall be selected within six months in accordance with the provisions of Article 45 of this Law. During the period of vacancy, his or her duties shall be assumed according to the provisions of the preceding paragraph.

Inst 27 (p 349)

第五十四條

香港特別行政區行政會議是協助行政長官決策的機構。

第五十五條

Art 46, 104

香港特別行政區行政會議的成員由行政長官從行政機關的主要官員、立法會議員和社會人士中委任，其任免由行政長官決定。行政會議成員的任期應不超過委任他的行政長官的任期。

Art 24 (1)–(4)

香港特別行政區行政會議成員由在外國無居留權的香港特別行政區永久性居民中的中國公民擔任。

行政長官認為必要時可邀請有關人士列席會議。

第五十六條

Art 43, 48

香港特別行政區行政會議由行政長官主持。

行政長官在作出重要決策、向立法會提交法案、制定附屬法規和解散立法會前，須徵詢行政會議的意見，但人事任免、紀律制裁和緊急情況下採取的措施除外。

行政長官如不採納行政會議多數成員的意見，應將具體理由記錄在案。

Article 54

The Executive Council of the Hong Kong Special Administrative Region shall be an organ for assisting the Chief Executive in policy-making.

Article 55

Members of the Executive Council of the Hong Kong Special Administrative Region shall be appointed by the Chief Executive from among the principal officials of the executive authorities, members of the Legislative Council and public figures. Their appointment or removal shall be decided by the Chief Executive. The term of office of members of the Executive Council shall not extend beyond the expiry of the term of office of the Chief Executive who appoints them.

Art 46, 104

Members of the Executive Council of the Hong Kong Special Administrative Region shall be Chinese citizens who are permanent residents of the Region with no right of abode in any foreign country.

Art 24 (1)–(4)

The Chief Executive may, as he or she deems necessary, invite other persons concerned to sit in on meetings of the Council.

Article 56

The Executive Council of the Hong Kong Special Administrative Region shall be presided over by the Chief Executive.

Art 43, 48

Except for the appointment, removal and disciplining of officials and the adoption of measures in emergencies, the Chief Executive shall consult the Executive Council before making important policy decisions, introducing bills to the Legislative Council, making subordinate legislation, or dissolving the Legislative Council.

If the Chief Executive does not accept a majority opinion of the Executive Council, he or she shall put the specific reasons on record.

第五十七條

Art 48 (5)

香港特別行政區設立廉政公署,獨立工作,對行政長官負責。

第五十八條

Art 48 (5)

香港特別行政區設立審計署,獨立工作,對行政長官負責。

第二節　行政機關

第五十九條

Art 2

香港特別行政區政府是香港特別行政區行政機關。

第六十條

Art 43

香港特別行政區政府的首長是香港特別行政區行政長官。

香港特別行政區政府設政務司、財政司、律政司和各局、處、署。

第六十一條

Art 15, 24 (1)–(4), 48 (5)

香港特別行政區的主要官員由在香港通常居住連續滿十五年並在外國無居留權的香港特別行政區永久性居民中的中國公民擔任。

Article 57

A Commission Against Corruption shall be established in the Hong Kong Special Administrative Region. It shall function independently and be accountable to the Chief Executive.

Art 48 (5)

Article 58

A Commission of Audit shall be established in the Hong Kong Special Administrative Region. It shall function independently and be accountable to the Chief Executive.

Art 48 (5)

Section 2: The Executive Authorities

Article 59

The Government of the Hong Kong Special Administrative Region shall be the executive authorities of the Region.

Art 2

Article 60

The head of the Government of the Hong Kong Special Administrative Region shall be the Chief Executive of the Region.

Art 43

A Department of Administration, a Department of Finance, a Department of Justice, and various bureaux, divisions and commissions shall be established in the Government of the Hong Kong Special Administrative Region.

Article 61

The principal officials of the Hong Kong Special Administrative Region shall be Chinese citizens who are permanent residents of the Region with no right of abode in any foreign country and have ordinarily resided in Hong Kong for a continuous period of not less than 15 years.

*Art 15,
24 (1)–(4),
48 (5)*

第六十二條

Art 16

香港特別行政區政府行使下列職權:

(一)　制定並執行政策;

(二)　管理各項行政事務;

Art 150–152
Inst 19 (p 286)

(三)　辦理本法規定的中央人民政府授權的對外事務;

(四)　編制並提出財政預算、決算;

(五)　擬定並提出法案、議案、附屬法規;

(六)　委派官員列席立法會並代表政府發言。

第六十三條

Art 60

香港特別行政區律政司主管刑事檢察工作,不受任何干涉。

第六十四條

Art 73
(2)–(5)

香港特別行政區政府必須遵守法律,對香港特別行政區立法會負責:執行立法會通過並已生效的法律;定期向立法會作施政報告;答覆立法會議員的質詢;徵稅和公共開支須經立法會批准。

第六十五條

原由行政機關設立諮詢組織的制度繼續保留。

Article 62

The Government of the Hong Kong Special Administrative Region shall exercise the following powers and functions:

(1) To formulate and implement policies;

(2) To conduct administrative affairs;

(3) To conduct external affairs as authorized by the Central People's Government under this Law;

(4) To draw up and introduce budgets and final accounts;

(5) To draft and introduce bills, motions and subordinate legislation; and

(6) To designate officials to sit in on the meetings of the Legislative Council and to speak on behalf of the government.

Art 16

Art 150–152
Inst 19 (p 286)

Article 63

The Department of Justice of the Hong Kong Special Administrative Region shall control criminal prosecutions, free from any interference.

Art 60

Article 64

The Government of the Hong Kong Special Administrative Region must abide by the law and be accountable to the Legislative Council of the Region: it shall implement laws passed by the Council and already in force; it shall present regular policy addresses to the Council; it shall answer questions raised by members of the Council; and it shall obtain approval from the Council for taxation and public expenditure.

Art 73
(2)–(5)

Article 65

The previous system of establishing advisory bodies by the executive authorities shall be maintained.

第三節　立法機關

第六十六條

Art 2, 17

香港特別行政區立法會是香港特別行政區的立法機關。

第六十七條

Art 24, 26

香港特別行政區立法會由在外國無居留權的香港特別行政區永久性居民中的中國公民組成。但非中國籍的香港特別行政區永久性居民和在外國有居留權的香港特別行政區永久性居民也可以當選為香港特別行政區立法會議員，其所佔比例不得超過立法會全體議員的百分之二十。

第六十八條

Inst 8 (p222),
Inst 10 (p236),
Inst 12 (p254),
Inst 13 (p 260),
Inst 16 (p292),
Inst 17 (p296),
Inst 18 (p302)

Anx II (p 142)

香港特別行政區立法會由選舉產生。

立法會的產生辦法根據香港特別行政區的實際情況和循序漸進的原則而規定，最終達至全部議員由普選產生的目標。

立法會產生的具體辦法和法案、議案的表決程序由附件二《香港特別行政區立法會的產生辦法和表決程序》規定。

Section 3: The Legislature

Article 66

The Legislative Council of the Hong Kong Special Administrative Region shall be the legislature of the Region.

Art 2, 17

Article 67

The Legislative Council of the Hong Kong Special Administrative Region shall be composed of Chinese citizens who are permanent residents of the Region with no right of abode in any foreign country. However, permanent residents of the Region who are not of Chinese nationality or who have the right of abode in foreign countries may also be elected members of the Legislative Council of the Region, provided that the proportion of such members does not exceed 20 percent of the total membership of the Council.

Art 24, 26

Article 68

The Legislative Council of the Hong Kong Special Administrative Region shall be constituted by election.

The method for forming the Legislative Council shall be specified in the light of the actual situation in the Hong Kong Special Administrative Region and in accordance with the principle of gradual and orderly progress. The ultimate aim is the election of all the members of the Legislative Council by universal suffrage.

The specific method for forming the Legislative Council and its procedures for voting on bills and motions are prescribed in Annex II: "Method for the Formation of the Legislative Council of the Hong Kong Special Administrative Region and Its Voting Procedures".

Inst 8 (p223),
Inst 10 (p237),
Inst 12 (p255),
Inst 13 (p 261),
Inst 16 (p293),
Inst 17 (p297),
Inst 18 (p303),

Anx II (p 143)

第六十九條

Inst 16 (p292)

香港特別行政區立法會除第一屆任期為兩年外，每屆任期四年。

第七十條

Art 50, 68

香港特別行政區立法會如經行政長官依本法規定解散，須於三個月內依本法第六十八條的規定，重行選舉產生。

第七十一條

香港特別行政區立法會主席由立法會議員互選產生。

Art 24

香港特別行政區立法會主席由年滿四十周歲，在香港通常居住連續滿二十年並在外國無居留權的香港特別行政區永久性居民中的中國公民擔任。

Article 69

The term of office of the Legislative Council of the Hong Kong Special Administrative Region shall be four years, except the first term which shall be two years.

Inst 16 (p293)

Article 70

If the Legislative Council of the Hong Kong Special Administrative Region is dissolved by the Chief Executive in accordance with the provisions of this Law, it must, within three months, be reconstituted by election in accordance with Article 68 of this Law.

Art 50, 68

Article 71

The President of the Legislative Council of the Hong Kong Special Administrative Region shall be elected by and from among the members of the Legislative Council.

The President of the Legislative Council of the Hong Kong Special Administrative Region shall be a Chinese citizen of not less than 40 years of age, who is a permanent resident of the Region with no right of abode in any foreign country and has ordinarily resided in Hong Kong for a continuous period of not less than 20 years.

Art 24

第七十二條

香港特別行政區立法會主席行使下列職權:

(一)　主持會議;

(二)　決定議程,政府提出的議案須優先列入議程;

(三)　決定開會時間;

(四)　在休會期間可召開特別會議;

(五)　應行政長官的要求召開緊急會議;

(六)　立法會議事規則所規定的其他職權。

第七十三條

香港特別行政區立法會行使下列職權:

Art 11, 17, 48 (一)　根據本法規定並依照法定程序制定、修改和廢除法律;

Art 49 (二)　根據政府的提案,審核、通過財政預算;

(三)　批准稅收和公共開支;

(四)　聽取行政長官的施政報告並進行辯論;

Art 64 (五)　對政府的工作提出質詢;

(六)　就任何有關公共利益問題進行辯論;

Art 90 (七)　同意終審法院法官和高等法院首席法官的任免;

Article 72

The President of the Legislative Council of the Hong Kong Special Administrative Region shall exercise the following powers and functions:

(1) To preside over meetings;

(2) To decide on the agenda, giving priority to government bills for inclusion in the agenda;

(3) To decide on the time of meetings;

(4) To call special sessions during the recess;

(5) To call emergency sessions on the request of the Chief Executive; and

(6) To exercise other powers and functions as prescribed in the rules of procedure of the Legislative Council.

Article 73

The Legislative Council of the Hong Kong Special Administrative Region shall exercise the following powers and functions:

Art 11, 17, 48

(1) To enact, amend or repeal laws in accordance with the provisions of this Law and legal procedures;

(2) To examine and approve budgets introduced by the government;

Art 49

(3) To approve taxation and public expenditure;

(4) To receive and debate the policy addresses of the Chief Executive;

(5) To raise questions on the work of the government;

Art 64

(6) To debate any issue concerning public interests;

(7) To endorse the appointment and removal of the judges of the Court of Final Appeal and the Chief Judge of the High Court;

Art 90

(八)　接受香港居民申訴並作出處理;

Art 52　(九)　如立法會全體議員的四分之一聯合動議,指控行政長官有嚴重違法或瀆職行為而不辭職,經立法會通過進行調查,立法會可委託終審法院首席法官負責組成獨立的調查委員會,並擔任主席。調查委員會負責進行調查,並向立法會提出報告。如該調查委員會認為有足夠證據構成上述指控,立法會以全體議員三分之二多數通過,可提出彈劾案,報請中央人民政府決定;

Art 48 (II)　(十)　在行使上述各項職權時,如有需要,可傳召有關人士出席作證和提供證據。

第七十四條

Anx II (p 142)　香港特別行政區立法會議員根據本法規定並依照法定程序提出法律草案,凡不涉及公共開支或政治體制或政府運作者,可由立法會議員個別或聯名提出。凡涉及政府政策者,在提出前必須得到行政長官的書面同意。

(8) To receive and handle complaints from Hong Kong residents;

(9) If a motion initiated jointly by one-fourth of all the members of the Legislative Council charges the Chief Executive with serious breach of law or dereliction of duty and if he or she refuses to resign, the Council may, after passing a motion for investigation, give a mandate to the Chief Justice of the Court of Final Appeal to form and chair an independent investigation committee. The committee shall be responsible for carrying out the investigation and reporting its findings to the Council. If the committee considers the evidence sufficient to substantiate such charges, the Council may pass a motion of impeachment by a two-thirds majority of all its members and report it to the Central People's Government for decision; and *Art 52*

(10) To summon, as required when exercising the above-mentioned powers and functions, persons concerned to testify or give evidence. *Art 48 (11)*

Article 74

Members of the Legislative Council of the Hong Kong Special Administrative Region may introduce bills in accordance with the provisions of this Law and legal procedures. Bills which do not relate to public expenditure or political structure or the operation of the government may be introduced individually or jointly by members of the Council. The written consent of the Chief Executive shall be required before bills relating to government policies are introduced. *Anx II (p 143)*

第七十五條

香港特別行政區立法會舉行會議的法定人數為不少於全體議員的二分之一。

Art 11

　　立法會議事規則由立法會自行制定,但不得與本法相抵觸。

第七十六條

Art 48 (3)

香港特別行政區立法會通過的法案,須經行政長官簽署、公布,方能生效。

第七十七條

香港特別行政區立法會議員在立法會的會議上發言,不受法律追究。

第七十八條

香港特別行政區立法會議員在出席會議時和赴會途中不受逮捕。

Article 75

The quorum for the meeting of the Legislative Council of the Hong Kong Special Administrative Region shall be not less than one half of all its members.

The rules of procedure of the Legislative Council shall be made by the Council on its own, provided that they do not contravene this Law.

Art 11

Article 76

A bill passed by the Legislative Council of the Hong Kong Special Administrative Region may take effect only after it is signed and promulgated by the Chief Executive.

Art 48 (3)

Article 77

Members of the Legislative Council of the Hong Kong Special Administrative Region shall be immune from legal action in respect of their statements at meetings of the Council.

Article 78

Members of the Legislative Council of the Hong Kong Special Administrative Region shall not be subjected to arrest when attending or on their way to a meeting of the Council.

第七十九條

Inst 17 (p296)

香港特別行政區立法會議員如有下列情況之一,由立法會主席宣告其喪失立法會議員的資格:

(一)　因嚴重疾病或其他情況無力履行職務;

(二)　未得到立法會主席的同意,連續三個月不出席會議而無合理解釋者;

(三)　喪失或放棄香港特別行政區永久性居民的身份;

(四)　接受政府的委任而出任公務人員;

(五)　破產或經法庭裁定償還債務而不履行;

(六)　在香港特別行政區區內或區外被判犯有刑事罪行,判處監禁一個月以上,並經立法會出席會議的議員三分之二通過解除其職務;

Art 104,
Inst 29 (p368)

(七)　行為不檢或違反誓言而經立法會出席會議的議員三分之二通過譴責。

Article 79

The President of the Legislative Council of the Hong Kong Special Administrative Region shall declare that a member of the Council is no longer qualified for the office under any of the following circumstances: Inst 17 (p297)

(1) When he or she loses the ability to discharge his or her duties as a result of serious illness or other reasons;

(2) When he or she, with no valid reason, is absent from meetings for three consecutive months without the consent of the President of the Legislative Council;

(3) When he or she loses or renounces his or her status as a permanent resident of the Region;

(4) When he or she accepts a government appointment and becomes a public servant;

(5) When he or she is bankrupt or fails to comply with a court order to repay debts;

(6) When he or she is convicted and sentenced to imprisonment for one month or more for a criminal offence committed within or outside the Region and is relieved of his or her duties by a motion passed by two-thirds of the members of the Legislative Council present; and

(7) When he or she is censured for misbehaviour or breach of oath by a vote of two-thirds of the members of the Legislative Council present. Art 104, Inst 29 (p369)

第四節　司法機關

第八十條

Art 2, 19

香港特別行政區各級法院是香港特別行政區的司法機關，行使香港特別行政區的審判權。

第八十一條

香港特別行政區設立終審法院、高等法院、區域法院、裁判署法庭和其他專門法庭。高等法院設上訴法庭和原訟法庭。

Art 19, 91

　　原在香港實行的司法體制，除因設立香港特別行政區終審法院而產生變化外，予以保留。

第八十二條

香港特別行政區的終審權屬於香港特別行政區終審法院。終審法院可根據需要邀請其他普通法適用地區的法官參加審判。

第八十三條

香港特別行政區各級法院的組織和職權由法律規定。

Section 4: The Judiciary

Article 80

The courts of the Hong Kong Special Administrative Region at all levels shall be the judiciary of the Region, exercising the judicial power of the Region.

Art 2, 19

Article 81

The Court of Final Appeal, the High Court, district courts, magistrates' courts and other special courts shall be established in the Hong Kong Special Administrative Region. The High Court shall comprise the Court of Appeal and the Court of First Instance.

The judicial system previously practised in Hong Kong shall be maintained except for those changes consequent upon the establishment of the Court of Final Appeal of the Hong Kong Special Administrative Region.

Art 19, 91

Article 82

The power of final adjudication of the Hong Kong Special Administrative Region shall be vested in the Court of Final Appeal of the Region, which may as required invite judges from other common law jurisdictions to sit on the Court of Final Appeal.

Article 83

The structure, powers and functions of the courts of the Hong Kong Special Administrative Region at all levels shall be prescribed by law.

第八十四條

Art 18

香港特別行政區法院依照本法第十八條所規定的適用於香港特別行政區的法律審判案件，其他普通法適用地區的司法判例可作參考。

第八十五條

香港特別行政區法院獨立進行審判，不受任何干涉，司法人員履行審判職責的行為不受法律追究。

第八十六條

原在香港實行的陪審制度的原則予以保留。

第八十七條

香港特別行政區的刑事訴訟和民事訴訟中保留原在香港適用的原則和當事人享有的權利。

Art 28

　　任何人在被合法拘捕後，享有盡早接受司法機關公正審判的權利，未經司法機關判罪之前均假定無罪。

第八十八條

Art 48 (6)

香港特別行政區法院的法官，根據當地法官和法律界及其他方面知名人士組成的獨立委員會推薦，由行政長官任命。

Article 84

The courts of the Hong Kong Special Administrative Region shall adjudicate cases in accordance with the laws applicable in the Region as prescribed in Article 18 of this Law and may refer to precedents of other common law jurisdictions.

Art 18

Article 85

The courts of the Hong Kong Special Administrative Region shall exercise judicial power independently, free from any interference. Members of the judiciary shall be immune from legal action in the performance of their judicial functions.

Article 86

The principle of trial by jury previously practised in Hong Kong shall be maintained.

Article 87

In criminal or civil proceedings in the Hong Kong Special Administrative Region, the principles previously applied in Hong Kong and the rights previously enjoyed by parties to proceedings shall be maintained.

Anyone who is lawfully arrested shall have the right to a fair trial by the judicial organs without delay and shall be presumed innocent until convicted by the judicial organs.

Art 28

Article 88

Judges of the courts of the Hong Kong Special Administrative Region shall be appointed by the Chief Executive on the recommendation of an independent commission composed of local judges, persons from the legal profession and eminent persons from other sectors.

Art 48 (6)

第八十九條

香港特別行政區法院的法官只有在無力履行職責或行為
不檢的情況下,行政長官才可根據終審法院首席法官任
命的不少於三名當地法官組成的審議庭的建議,予以免
職。

香港特別行政區終審法院的首席法官只有在無力履
行職責或行為不檢的情況下,行政長官才可任命不少於五
名當地法官組成的審議庭進行審議,並可根據其建議,依
照本法規定的程序,予以免職。

第九十條

香港特別行政區終審法院和高等法院的首席法官,應由在
外國無居留權的香港特別行政區永久性居民中的中國公民
擔任。

除本法第八十八條和第八十九條規定的程序外,香
港特別行政區終審法院的法官和高等法院首席法官的任
命或免職,還須由行政長官徵得立法會同意,並報全國人
民代表大會常務委員會備案。

第九十一條

香港特別行政區法官以外的其他司法人員原有的任免制
度繼續保持。

（左側邊註）
Art 48 (6)

Art 24 (1)–(4),
88

Art 48 (6),
73 (7)

Art 81

Article 89

A judge of a court of the Hong Kong Special Administrative Region may only be removed for inability to discharge his or her duties, or for misbehaviour, by the Chief Executive on the recommendation of a tribunal appointed by the Chief Justice of the Court of Final Appeal and consisting of not fewer than three local judges.

Art 48 (6)

The Chief Justice of the Court of Final Appeal of the Hong Kong Special Administrative Region may be investigated only for inability to discharge his or her duties, or for misbehaviour, by a tribunal appointed by the Chief Executive and consisting of not fewer than five local judges and may be removed by the Chief Executive on the recommendation of the tribunal and in accordance with the procedures prescribed in this Law.

Article 90

The Chief Justice of the Court of Final Appeal and the Chief Judge of the High Court of the Hong Kong Special Administrative Region shall be Chinese citizens who are permanent residents of the Region with no right of abode in any foreign country.

Art 24 (1)–(4), 88

In the case of the appointment or removal of judges of the Court of Final Appeal and the Chief Judge of the High Court of the Hong Kong Special Administrative Region, the Chief Executive shall, in addition to following the procedures prescribed in Articles 88 and 89 of this Law, obtain the endorsement of the Legislative Council and report such appointment or removal to the Standing Committee of the National People's Congress for the record.

Art 48 (6), 73 (7)

Article 91

The Hong Kong Special Administrative Region shall maintain the previous system of appointment and removal of members of the judiciary other than judges.

Art 81

第九十二條

Art 82

香港特別行政區的法官和其他司法人員,應根據其本人的司法和專業才能選用,並可從其他普通法適用地區聘用。

第九十三條

香港特別行政區成立前在香港任職的法官和其他司法人員均可留用,其年資予以保留,薪金、津貼、福利待遇和服務條件不低於原來的標準。

對退休或符合規定離職的法官和其他司法人員,包括香港特別行政區成立前已退休或離職者,不論其所屬國籍或居住地點,香港特別行政區政府按不低於原來的標準,向他們或其家屬支付應得的退休金、酬金、津貼和福利費。

第九十四條

香港特別行政區政府可參照原在香港實行的辦法,作出有關當地和外來的律師在香港特別行政區工作和執業的規定。

第九十五條

香港特別行政區可與全國其他地區的司法機關通過協商依法進行司法方面的聯繫和相互提供協助。

Article 92

Judges and other members of the judiciary of the Hong Kong Special Administrative Region shall be chosen on the basis of their judicial and professional qualities and may be recruited from other common law jurisdictions.

Art 82

Article 93

Judges and other members of the judiciary serving in Hong Kong before the establishment of the Hong Kong Special Administrative Region may all remain in employment and retain their seniority with pay, allowances, benefits and conditions of service no less favourable than before.

The Government of the Hong Kong Special Administrative Region shall pay to judges and other members of the judiciary who retire or leave the service in compliance with regulations, including those who have retired or left the service before the establishment of the Hong Kong Special Administrative Region, or to their dependants, all pensions, gratuities, allowances and benefits due to them on terms no less favourable than before, irrespective of their nationality or place of residence.

Article 94

On the basis of the system previously operating in Hong Kong, the Government of the Hong Kong Special Administrative Region may make provisions for local lawyers and lawyers from outside Hong Kong to work and practise in the Region.

Article 95

The Hong Kong Special Administrative Region may, through consultations and in accordance with law, maintain juridical relations with the judicial organs of other parts of the country, and they may render assistance to each other.

第九十六條

在中央人民政府協助或授權下，香港特別行政區政府可與外國就司法互助關係作出適當安排。

第五節 區域組織

第九十七條

香港特別行政區可設立非政權性的區域組織，接受香港特別行政區政府就有關地區管理和其他事務的諮詢，或負責提供文化、康樂、環境衛生等服務。

第九十八條

區域組織的職權和組成方法由法律規定。

Article 96
With the assistance or authorization of the Central People's Government, the Government of the Hong Kong Special Administrative Region may make appropriate arrangements with foreign states for reciprocal juridical assistance.

Section 5: District Organizations

Article 97
District organizations which are not organs of political power may be established in the Hong Kong Special Administrative Region, to be consulted by the government of the Region on district administration and other affairs, or to be responsible for providing services in such fields as culture, recreation and environmental sanitation.

Article 98
The powers and functions of the district organizations and the method for their formation shall be prescribed by law.

第六節　公務人員

第九十九條

在香港特別行政區政府各部門任職的公務人員必須是香港特別行政區永久性居民。本法第一百零一條對外籍公務人員另有規定者或法律規定某一職級以下者不在此限。

　　公務人員必須盡忠職守，對香港特別行政區政府負責。

Art 24 (1)–(6), 101

第一百條

香港特別行政區成立前在香港政府各部門，包括警察部門任職的公務人員均可留用，其年資予以保留，薪金、津貼、福利待遇和服務條件不低於原來的標準。

第一百零一條

香港特別行政區政府可任用原香港公務人員中的或持有香港特別行政區永久性居民身份證的英籍和其他外籍人士擔任政府部門的各級公務人員，但下列各職級的官員必須由在外國無居留權的香港特別行政區永久性居民中的中國公民擔任：各司司長、副司長，各局局長，廉政專員，審計署署長，警務處處長，入境事務處處長，海關關長。

Art 24 (1)–(4), 48 (5), 99

Section 6: Public Servants

Article 99
Public servants serving in all government departments of the Hong Kong Special Administrative Region must be permanent residents of the Region, except where otherwise provided for in Article 101 of this Law regarding public servants of foreign nationalities and except for those below a certain rank as prescribed by law.

Public servants must be dedicated to their duties and be responsible to the Government of the Hong Kong Special Administrative Region.

Art 24 (1)–(6), 101

Article 100
Public servants serving in all Hong Kong government departments, including the police department, before the establishment of the Hong Kong Special Administrative Region, may all remain in employment and retain their seniority with pay, allowances, benefits and conditions of service no less favourable than before.

Article 101
The Government of the Hong Kong Special Administrative Region may employ British and other foreign nationals previously serving in the public service in Hong Kong, or those holding permanent identity cards of the Region, to serve as public servants in government departments at all levels, but only Chinese citizens among permanent residents of the Region with no right of abode in any foreign country may fill the following posts: the Secretaries and Deputy Secretaries of Departments, Directors of Bureaux, Commissioner Against Corruption, Director of Audit, Commissioner of Police, Director of Immigration and Commissioner of Customs and Excise.

Art 24 (1)–(4), 48 (5), 99

　　香港特別行政區政府還可聘請英籍和其他外籍人士擔任政府部門的顧問，必要時並可從香港特別行政區以外聘請合格人員擔任政府部門的專門和技術職務。上述外籍人士只能以個人身份受聘，對香港特別行政區政府負責。

第一百零二條

對退休或符合規定離職的公務人員，包括香港特別行政區成立前退休或符合規定離職的公務人員，不論其所屬國籍或居住地點，香港特別行政區政府按不低於原來的標準向他們或其家屬支付應得的退休金、酬金、津貼和福利費。

第一百零三條

公務人員應根據其本人的資格、經驗和才能予以任用和提升，香港原有關於公務人員的招聘、僱用、考核、紀律、培訓和管理的制度，包括負責公務人員的任用、薪金、服務條件的專門機構，除有關給予外籍人員特權待遇的規定外，予以保留。

The Government of the Hong Kong Special Administrative Region may also employ British and other foreign nationals as advisers to government departments and, when required, may recruit qualified candidates from outside the Region to fill professional and technical posts in government departments. These foreign nationals shall be employed only in their individual capacities and shall be responsible to the government of the Region.

Article 102

The Government of the Hong Kong Special Administrative Region shall pay to public servants who retire or who leave the service in compliance with regulations, including those who have retired or who have left the service in compliance with regulations before the establishment of the Hong Kong Special Administrative Region, or to their dependants, all pensions, gratuities, allowances and benefits due to them on terms no less favourable than before, irrespective of their nationality or place of residence.

Article 103

The appointment and promotion of public servants shall be on the basis of their qualifications, experience and ability. Hong Kong's previous system of recruitment, employment, assessment, discipline, training and management for the public service, including special bodies for their appointment, pay and conditions of service, shall be maintained, except for any provisions for privileged treatment of foreign nationals.

第一百零四條

Inst 29 (p 368)

香港特別行政區行政長官、主要官員、行政會議成員、立法會議員、各級法院法官和其他司法人員在就職時必須依法宣誓擁護中華人民共和國香港特別行政區基本法,效忠中華人民共和國香港特別行政區。

Article 104

When assuming office, the Chief Executive, principal officials, members of the Executive Council and of the Legislative Council, judges of the courts at all levels and other members of the judiciary in the Hong Kong Special Administrative Region must, in accordance with law, swear to uphold the Basic Law of the Hong Kong Special Administrative Region of the People's Republic of China and swear allegiance to the Hong Kong Special Administrative Region of the People's Republic of China.

Inst 29 (p 369)

第五章 經 濟

第一節 財政、金融、貿易和工商業

第一百零五條

Art 6

香港特別行政區依法保護私人和法人財產的取得、使用、處置和繼承的權利,以及依法徵用私人和法人財產時被徵用財產的所有人得到補償的權利。

徵用財產的補償應相當於該財產當時的實際價值,可自由兌換,不得無故遲延支付。

企業所有權和外來投資均受法律保護。

第一百零六條

香港特別行政區保持財政獨立。

香港特別行政區的財政收入全部用於自身需要,不上繳中央人民政府。

中央人民政府不在香港特別行政區徵稅。

第一百零七條

香港特別行政區的財政預算以量入為出為原則,力求收支平衡,避免赤字,並與本地生產總值的增長率相適應。

Chapter V: Economy

Section 1: Public Finance, Monetary Affairs, Trade, Industry and Commerce

Article 105

The Hong Kong Special Administrative Region shall, in accordance with law, protect the right of individuals and legal persons to the acquisition, use, disposal and inheritance of property and their right to compensation for lawful deprivation of their property.

Art 6

Such compensation shall correspond to the real value of the property concerned at the time and shall be freely convertible and paid without undue delay.

The ownership of enterprises and the investments from outside the Region shall be protected by law.

Article 106

The Hong Kong Special Administrative Region shall have independent finances.

The Hong Kong Special Administrative Region shall use its financial revenues exclusively for its own purposes, and they shall not be handed over to the Central People's Government.

The Central People's Government shall not levy taxes in the Hong Kong Special Administrative Region.

Article 107

The Hong Kong Special Administrative Region shall follow the principle of keeping expenditure within the limits of revenues in drawing up its budget, and strive to achieve a fiscal balance, avoid deficits and keep the budget commensurate with the growth rate of its gross domestic product.

第一百零八條

香港特別行政區實行獨立的稅收制度。

香港特別行政區參照原在香港實行的低稅政策,自行立法規定稅種、稅率、稅收寬免和其他稅務事項。

第一百零九條

香港特別行政區政府提供適當的經濟和法律環境,以保持香港的國際金融中心地位。

第一百一十條

香港特別行政區的貨幣金融制度由法律規定。

香港特別行政區政府自行制定貨幣金融政策,保障金融企業和金融市場的經營自由,並依法進行管理和監督。

第一百一十一條

港元為香港特別行政區法定貨幣,繼續流通。

港幣的發行權屬於香港特別行政區政府。港幣的發行須有百分之百的準備金。港幣的發行制度和準備金制度,由法律規定。

Article 108

The Hong Kong Special Administrative Region shall practise an independent taxation system.

The Hong Kong Special Administrative Region shall, taking the low tax policy previously pursued in Hong Kong as reference, enact laws on its own concerning types of taxes, tax rates, tax reductions, allowances and exemptions, and other matters of taxation.

Article 109

The Government of the Hong Kong Special Administrative Region shall provide an appropriate economic and legal environment for the maintenance of the status of Hong Kong as an international financial centre.

Article 110

The monetary and financial systems of the Hong Kong Special Administrative Region shall be prescribed by law.

The Government of the Hong Kong Special Administrative Region shall, on its own, formulate monetary and financial policies, safeguard the free operation of financial business and financial markets, and regulate and supervise them in accordance with law.

Article 111

The Hong Kong dollar, as the legal tender in the Hong Kong Special Administrative Region, shall continue to circulate.

The authority to issue Hong Kong currency shall be vested in the Government of the Hong Kong Special Administrative Region. The issue of Hong Kong currency must be backed by a 100 percent reserve fund. The system regarding the issue of Hong Kong currency and the reserve fund system shall be prescribed by law.

　　香港特別行政區政府，在確知港幣的發行基礎健全和發行安排符合保持港幣穩定的目的的條件下，可授權指定銀行根據法定權限發行或繼續發行港幣。

第一百一十二條

香港特別行政區不實行外匯管制政策。港幣自由兌換。繼續開放外匯、黃金、證券、期貨等市場。

　　香港特別行政區政府保障資金的流動和進出自由。

第一百一十三條

香港特別行政區的外匯基金，由香港特別行政區政府管理和支配，主要用於調節港元匯價。

第一百一十四條

Art 116

香港特別行政區保持自由港地位，除法律另有規定外，不徵收關稅。

第一百一十五條

Art 112

香港特別行政區實行自由貿易政策，保障貨物、無形財產和資本的流動自由。

The Government of the Hong Kong Special Administrative Region may authorize designated banks to issue or continue to issue Hong Kong currency under statutory authority, after satisfying itself that any issue of currency will be soundly based and that the arrangements for such issue are consistent with the object of maintaining the stability of the currency.

Article 112
No foreign exchange control policies shall be applied in the Hong Kong Special Administrative Region. The Hong Kong dollar shall be freely convertible. Markets for foreign exchange, gold, securities, futures and the like shall continue.

The Government of the Hong Kong Special Administrative Region shall safeguard the free flow of capital within, into and out of the Region.

Article 113
The Exchange Fund of the Hong Kong Special Administrative Region shall be managed and controlled by the government of the Region, primarily for regulating the exchange value of the Hong Kong dollar.

Article 114
The Hong Kong Special Administrative Region shall maintain the status of a free port and shall not impose any tariff unless otherwise prescribed by law.

Art 116

Article 115
The Hong Kong Special Administrative Region shall pursue the policy of free trade and safeguard the free movement of goods, intangible assets and capital.

Art 112

第一百一十六條

Art 114, 115
香港特別行政區為單獨的關稅地區。

香港特別行政區可以"中國香港"的名義參加《關稅和貿易總協定》、關於國際紡織品貿易安排等有關國際組織和國際貿易協定，包括優惠貿易安排。

香港特別行政區所取得的和以前取得仍繼續有效的出口配額、關稅優惠和達成的其他類似安排，全由香港特別行政區享有。

第一百一十七條

Art 112
香港特別行政區根據當時的產地規則，可對產品簽發產地來源證。

第一百一十八條

香港特別行政區政府提供經濟和法律環境，鼓勵各項投資、技術進步並開發新興產業。

第一百一十九條

香港特別行政區政府制定適當政策，促進和協調製造業、商業、旅遊業、房地產業、運輸業、公用事業、服務性行業、漁農業等各行業的發展，並注意環境保護。

Article 116
The Hong Kong Special Administrative Region shall be a separate *Art 114, 115* customs territory.

The Hong Kong Special Administrative Region may, using the name "Hong Kong, China", participate in relevant international organizations and international trade agreements (including preferential trade arrangements), such as the General Agreement on Tariffs and Trade and arrangements regarding international trade in textiles.

Export quotas, tariff preferences and other similar arrangements, which are obtained or made by the Hong Kong Special Administrative Region or which were obtained or made and remain valid, shall be enjoyed exclusively by the Region.

Article 117
The Hong Kong Special Administrative Region may issue its own *Art 112* certificates of origin for products in accordance with prevailing rules of origin.

Article 118
The Government of the Hong Kong Special Administrative Region shall provide an economic and legal environment for encouraging investments, technological progress and the development of new industries.

Article 119
The Government of the Hong Kong Special Administrative Region shall formulate appropriate policies to promote and co-ordinate the development of various trades such as manufacturing, commerce, tourism, real estate, transport, public utilities, services, agriculture and fisheries, and pay regard to the protection of the environment.

第二節 土地契約

第一百二十條

Art 160

香港特別行政區成立以前已批出、決定、或續期的超越一九九七年六月三十日年期的所有土地契約和與土地契約有關的一切權利，均按香港特別行政區的法律繼續予以承認和保護。

第一百二十一條

Art 160

從一九八五年五月二十七日至一九九七年六月三十日期間批出的，或原沒有續期權利而獲得續期的，超出一九九七年六月三十日年期而不超過二〇四七年六月三十日的一切土地契約，承租人從一九九七年七月一日起不補地價，但需每年繳納相當於當日該土地應課差餉租值百分之三的租金。此後，隨應課差餉租值的改變而調整租金。

第一百二十二條

Art 40, 160

原舊批約地段、鄉村屋地、丁屋地和類似的農村土地，如該土地在一九八四年六月三十日的承租人，或在該日以後批出的丁屋地承租人，其父系為一八九八年在香港的原有鄉村居民，只要該土地的承租人仍為該人或其合法父系繼承人，原定租金維持不變。

Section 2: Land Leases

Article 120

All leases of land granted, decided upon or renewed before the establishment of the Hong Kong Special Administrative Region which extend beyond 30 June 1997, and all rights in relation to such leases, shall continue to be recognized and protected under the law of the Region.

Art 160

Article 121

As regards all leases of land granted or renewed where the original leases contain no right of renewal, during the period from 27 May 1985 to 30 June 1997, which extend beyond 30 June 1997 and expire not later than 30 June 2047, the lessee is not required to pay an additional premium as from 1 July 1997, but an annual rent equivalent to 3 per cent of the rateable value of the property at that date, adjusted in step with any changes in the rateable value thereafter, shall be charged.

Art 160

Article 122

In the case of old schedule lots, village lots, small houses and similar rural holdings, where the property was on 30 June 1984 held by, or, in the case of small houses granted after that date, where the property is granted to, a lessee descended through the male line from a person who was in 1898 a resident of an established village in Hong Kong, the previous rent shall remain unchanged so long as the property is held by that lessee or by one of his lawful successors in the male line.

Art 40, 160

第一百二十三條

香港特別行政區成立以後滿期而沒有續期權利的土地契約，由香港特別行政區自行制定法律和政策處理。

第三節　航　運

第一百二十四條

香港特別行政區保持原在香港實行的航運經營和管理體制，包括有關海員的管理制度。

香港特別行政區政府自行規定在航運方面的具體職能和責任。

第一百二十五條

香港特別行政區經中央人民政府授權繼續進行船舶登記，並根據香港特別行政區的法律以"中國香港"的名義頒發有關證件。

第一百二十六條

Art 13 除外國軍用船隻進入香港特別行政區須經中央人民政府特別許可外，其他船舶可根據香港特別行政區法律進出其港口。

Article 123

Where leases of land without a right of renewal expire after the establishment of the Hong Kong Special Administrative Region, they shall be dealt with in accordance with laws and policies formulated by the Region on its own.

Section 3: Shipping

Article 124

The Hong Kong Special Administrative Region shall maintain Hong Kong's previous systems of shipping management and shipping regulation, including the system for regulating conditions of seamen.

The Government of the Hong Kong Special Administrative Region shall, on its own, define its specific functions and responsibilities in respect of shipping.

Article 125

The Hong Kong Special Administrative Region shall be authorized by the Central People's Government to continue to maintain a shipping register and issue related certificates under its legislation, using the name "Hong Kong, China".

Article 126

With the exception of foreign warships, access for which requires the special permission of the Central People's Government, ships shall enjoy access to the ports of the Hong Kong Special Administrative Region in accordance with the laws of the Region.

Art 13

第一百二十七條

香港特別行政區的私營航運及與航運有關的企業和私營
集裝箱碼頭，可繼續自由經營。

第四節　民用航空

第一百二十八條

香港特別行政區政府應提供條件和採取措施，以保持香
港的國際和區域航空中心的地位。

第一百二十九條

香港特別行政區繼續實行原在香港實行的民用航空管理
制度，並按中央人民政府關於飛機國籍標誌和登記標誌的
規定，設置自己的飛機登記冊。

Art 13

外國國家航空器進入香港特別行政區須經中央人民
政府特別許可。

Article 127

Private shipping businesses and shipping-related businesses and private container terminals in the Hong Kong Special Administrative Region may continue to operate freely.

Section 4: Civil Aviation

Article 128

The Government of the Hong Kong Special Administrative Region shall provide conditions and take measures for the maintenance of the status of Hong Kong as a centre of international and regional aviation.

Article 129

The Hong Kong Special Administrative Region shall continue the previous system of civil aviation management in Hong Kong and keep its own aircraft register in accordance with provisions laid down by the Central People's Government concerning nationality marks and registration marks of aircraft.

Access of foreign state aircraft to the Hong Kong Special Administrative Region shall require the special permission of the Central People's Government.

Art 13

第一百三十條

香港特別行政區自行負責民用航空的日常業務和技術管理,包括機場管理,在香港特別行政區飛行情報區內提供空中交通服務,和履行國際民航空組織的區域性航行規劃程序所規定的其他職責。

第一百三十一條

中央人民政府經同香港特別行政區政府磋商作出安排,為在香港特別行政區註冊並以香港為主要營業地的航空公司和中華人民共和國的其他航空公司,提供香港特別行政區和中華人民共和國其他地區之間的往返航班。

第一百三十二條

凡涉及中華人民共和國其他地區同其他國家和地區的往返並經停香港特別行政區的航班,和涉及香港特別行政區同其他國家和地區的往返並經停中華人民共和國其他地區航班的民用航空運輸協定,由中央人民政府簽訂。

中央人民政府在簽訂本條第一款所指民用航空運輸協定時,應考慮香港特別行政區的特殊情況和經濟利益,並同香港特別行政區政府磋商。

Article 130

The Hong Kong Special Administrative Region shall be responsible on its own for matters of routine business and technical management of civil aviation, including the management of airports, the provision of air traffic services within the flight information region of the Hong Kong Special Administrative Region, and the discharge of other responsibilities allocated to it under the regional air navigation procedures of the International Civil Aviation Organization.

Article 131

The Central People's Government shall, in consultation with the Government of the Hong Kong Special Administrative Region, make arrangements providing air services between the Region and other parts of the People's Republic of China for airlines incorporated in the Hong Kong Special Administrative Region and having their principal place of business in Hong Kong and other airlines of the People's Republic of China.

Article 132

All air service agreements providing air services between other parts of the People's Republic of China and other states and regions with stops at the Hong Kong Special Administrative Region and air services between the Hong Kong Special Administrative Region and other states and regions with stops at other parts of the People's Republic of China shall be concluded by the Central People's Government.

Art 13

In concluding the air service agreements referred to in the first paragraph of this Article, the Central People's Government shall take account of the special conditions and economic interests of the Hong Kong Special Administrative Region and consult the government of the Region.

　　中央人民政府在同外國政府商談有關本條第一款所指航班的安排時，香港特別行政區政府的代表可作為中華人民共和國政府代表團的成員參加。

第一百三十三條

香港特別行政區政府經中央人民政府具體授權可：

(一)　續簽或修改原有的民用航空運輸協定和協議；

(二)　談判簽訂新的民用航空運輸協定，為在香港特別行政區註冊並以香港為主要營業地的航空公司提供航線，以及過境和技術停降權利；

(三)　同沒有簽訂民用航空運輸協定的外國或地區談判簽訂臨時協議。

　　不涉及往返、經停中國內地而只往返、經停香港的定期航班，均由本條所指的民用航空運輸協定或臨時協議予以規定。

Representatives of the Government of the Hong Kong Special Administrative Region may, as members of the delegations of the Government of the People's Republic of China, participate in air service consultations conducted by the Central People's Government with foreign governments concerning arrangements for such services referred to in the first paragraph of this Article.

Article 133

Acting under specific authorizations from the Central People's Government, the Government of the Hong Kong Special Administrative Region may:

Art 134

(1) renew or amend air service agreements and arrangements previously in force;

(2) negotiate and conclude new air service agreements providing routes for airlines incorporated in the Hong Kong Special Administrative Region and having their principal place of business in Hong Kong and providing rights for over-flights and technical stops; and

(3) negotiate and conclude provisional arrangements with foreign states or regions with which no air service agreements have been concluded.

All scheduled air services to, from or through Hong Kong, which do not operate to, from or through the mainland of China shall be regulated by the air service agreements or provisional arrangements referred to in this Article.

第一百三十四條

中央人民政府授權香港特別行政區政府:

(一) 同其他當局商談並簽訂有關執行本法第一百三十三條所指民用航空運輸協定和臨時協議的各項安排;

(二) 對在香港特別行政區註冊並以香港為主要營業地的航空公司簽發執照;

(三) 依照本法第一百三十三條所指民用航空運輸協定和臨時協議指定航空公司;

(四) 對外國航空公司除往返、經停中國內地的航班以外的其他航班簽發許可證。

第一百三十五條

香港特別行政區成立前在香港註冊並以香港為主要營業地的航空公司和與民用航空有關的行業,可繼續經營。

Article 134

The Central People's Government shall give the Government of the Hong Kong Special Administrative Region the authority to:

Art 133

(1) negotiate and conclude with other authorities all arrangements concerning the implementation of the air service agreements and provisional arrangements referred to in Article 133 of this Law;

(2) issue licences to airlines incorporated in the Hong Kong Special Administrative Region and having their principal place of business in Hong Kong;

(3) designate such airlines under the air service agreements and provisional arrangements referred to in Article 133 of this Law; and

(4) issue permits to foreign airlines for services other than those to, from or through the mainland of China.

Article 135

Airlines incorporated and having their principal place of business in Hong Kong and businesses related to civil aviation functioning there prior to the establishment of the Hong Kong Special Administrative Region may continue to operate.

第六章　教育、科學、文化、體育、宗教、勞工和社會服務

第一百三十六條

香港特別行政區政府在原有教育制度的基礎上,自行制定有關教育的發展和改進的政策,包括教育體制和管理、教學語言、經費分配、考試制度、學位制度和承認學歷等政策。

社會團體和私人可依法在香港特別行政區興辦各種教育事業。

第一百三十七條

Art 32, 34

各類院校均可保留其自主性並享有學術自由,可繼續從香港特別行政區以外招聘教職員和選用教材。宗教組織所辦的學校可繼續提供宗教教育,包括開設宗教課程。

學生享有選擇院校和在香港特別行政區以外求學的自由。

第一百三十八條

香港特別行政區政府自行制定發展中西醫藥和促進醫療衛生服務的政策。社會團體和私人可依法提供各種醫療衛生服務。

Chapter VI: Education, Science, Culture, Sports, Religion, Labour and Social Services

Article 136
On the basis of the previous educational system, the Government of the Hong Kong Special Administrative Region shall, on its own, formulate policies on the development and improvement of education, including policies regarding the educational system and its administration, the language of instruction, the allocation of funds, the examination system, the system of academic awards and the recognition of educational qualifications.

Community organizations and individuals may, in accordance with law, run educational undertakings of various kinds in the Hong Kong Special Administrative Region.

Article 137
Educational institutions of all kinds may retain their autonomy and enjoy academic freedom. They may continue to recruit staff and use teaching materials from outside the Hong Kong Special Administrative Region. Schools run by religious organizations may continue to provide religious education, including courses in religion.

Art 32, 34

Students shall enjoy freedom of choice of educational institutions and freedom to pursue their education outside the Hong Kong Special Administrative Region.

Article 138
The Government of the Hong Kong Special Administrative Region shall, on its own, formulate policies to develop Western and traditional Chinese medicine and to improve medical and health services. Community organizations and individuals may provide various medical and health services in accordance with law.

第一百三十九條

香港特別行政區政府自行制定科學技術政策,以法律保護科學技術的研究成果、專利和發明創造。

香港特別行政區政府自行確定適用於香港的各類科學、技術標準和規格。

第一百四十條

Art 34

香港特別行政區政府自行制定文化政策,以法律保護作者在文學藝術創作中所獲得的成果和合法權益。

第一百四十一條

Art 32

香港特別行政區政府不限制宗教信仰自由,不干預宗教組織的內部事務,不限制與香港特別行政區法律沒有抵觸的宗教活動。

Art 6, 105

宗教組織依法享有財產的取得、使用、處置、繼承以及接受資助的權利。財產方面的原有權益仍予保持和保護。

Art 137

宗教組織可按原有辦法繼續興辦宗教院校、其他學校、醫院和福利機構以及提供其他社會服務。

香港特別行政區的宗教組織和教徒可與其他地方的宗教組織和教徒保持和發展關係。

Article 139

The Government of the Hong Kong Special Administrative Region shall, on its own, formulate policies on science and technology and protect by law achievements in scientific and technological research, patents, discoveries and inventions.

The Government of the Hong Kong Special Administrative Region shall, on its own, decide on the scientific and technological standards and specifications applicable in Hong Kong.

Article 140

The Government of the Hong Kong Special Administrative Region shall, on its own, formulate policies on culture and protect by law the achievements and the lawful rights and interests of authors in their literary and artistic creation.

Art 34

Article 141

The Government of the Hong Kong Special Administrative Region shall not restrict the freedom of religious belief, interfere in the internal affairs of religious organizations or restrict religious activities which do not contravene the laws of the Region.

Art 32

Religious organizations shall, in accordance with law, enjoy the rights to acquire, use, dispose of and inherit property and the right to receive financial assistance. Their previous property rights and interests shall be maintained and protected.

Art 6, 105

Religious organizations may, according to their previous practice, continue to run seminaries and other schools, hospitals and welfare institutions and to provide other social services.

Art 137

Religious organizations and believers in the Hong Kong Special Administrative Region may maintain and develop their relations with religious organizations and believers elsewhere.

第一百四十二條

香港特別行政區政府在保留原有的專業制度的基礎上，自行制定有關評審各種專業的執業資格的辦法。

在香港特別行政區成立前已取得專業和執業資格者，可依據有關規定和專業守則保留原有的資格。

香港特別行政區政府繼續承認在特別行政區成立前已承認的專業和專業團體，所承認的專業團體可自行審核和頒授專業資格。

香港特別行政區政府可根據社會發展需要並諮詢有關方面的意見，承認新的專業和專業團體。

第一百四十三條

香港特別行政區政府自行制定體育政策。民間體育團體可依法繼續存在和發展。

Article 142

The Government of the Hong Kong Special Administrative Region shall, on the basis of maintaining the previous systems concerning the professions, formulate provisions on its own for assessing the qualifications for practice in the various professions.

Persons with professional qualifications or qualifications for professional practice obtained prior to the establishment of the Hong Kong Special Administrative Region may retain their previous qualifications in accordance with the relevant regulations and codes of practice.

The Government of the Hong Kong Special Administrative Region shall continue to recognize the professions and the professional organizations recognized prior to the establishment of the Region, and these organizations may, on their own, assess and confer professional qualifications.

The Government of the Hong Kong Special Administrative Region may, as required by developments in society and in consultation with the parties concerned, recognize new professions and professional organizations.

Article 143

The Government of the Hong Kong Special Administrative Region shall, on its own, formulate policies on sports. Non-governmental sports organizations may continue to exist and develop in accordance with law.

第一百四十四條
香港特別行政區政府保持原在香港實行的對教育、醫療衛生、文化、藝術、康樂、體育、社會福利、社會工作等方面的民間團體機構的資助政策。原在香港各資助機構任職的人員均可根據原有制度繼續受聘。

第一百四十五條
Art 36

香港特別行政區政府在原有社會福利制度的基礎上，根據經濟條件和社會需要，自行制定其發展、改進的政策。

第一百四十六條
香港特別行政區從事社會服務的志願團體在不抵觸法律的情況下可自行決定其服務方式。

第一百四十七條
Art 36

香港特別行政區自行制定有關勞工的法律和政策。

第一百四十八條
Art 36, 141

香港特別行政區的教育、科學、技術、文化、藝術、體育、專業、醫療衛生、勞工、社會福利、社會工作等方面的民間團體和宗教組織同內地相應的團體和組織的關係，應以互不隸屬、互不干涉和互相尊重的原則為基礎。

Article 144

The Government of the Hong Kong Special Administrative Region shall maintain the policy previously practised in Hong Kong in respect of subventions for non-governmental organizations in fields such as education, medicine and health, culture, art, recreation, sports, social welfare and social work. Staff members previously serving in subvented organizations in Hong Kong may remain in their employment in accordance with the previous system.

Article 145

On the basis of the previous social welfare system, the Government of the Hong Kong Special Administrative Region shall, on its own, formulate policies on the development and improvement of this system in the light of the economic conditions and social needs.

Art 36

Article 146

Voluntary organizations providing social services in the Hong Kong Special Administrative Region may, on their own, decide their forms of service, provided that the law is not contravened.

Article 147

The Hong Kong Special Administrative Region shall on its own formulate laws and policies relating to labour.

Art 36

Article 148

The relationship between non-governmental organizations in fields such as education, science, technology, culture, art, sports, the professions, medicine and health, labour, social welfare and social work as well as religious organizations in the Hong Kong Special Administrative Region and their counterparts on the mainland shall be based on the principles of non-subordination, non-interference and mutual respect.

Art 36, 141

第一百四十九條

香港特別行政區的教育、科學、技術、文化、藝術、體育、專業、醫療衛生、勞工、社會福利、社會工作等方面的民間團體和宗教組織可同世界各國、各地區及國際的有關團體和組織保持和發展關係，各該團體和組織可根據需要冠用"中國香港"的名義，參與有關活動。

Art 141

Article 149

Non-governmental organizations in fields such as education, science, technology, culture, art, sports, the professions, medicine and health, labour, social welfare and social work as well as religious organizations in the Hong Kong Special Administrative Region may maintain and develop relations with their counterparts in foreign countries and regions and with relevant international organizations. They may, as required, use the name "Hong Kong, China" in the relevant activities.

Art 141

第七章 對外事務

第一百五十條

Art 13

香港特別行政區政府的代表,可作為中華人民共和國政府代表團的成員,參加由中央人民政府進行的同香港特別行政區直接有關的外交談判。

第一百五十一條

Art 116, 125,149

香港特別行政區可在經濟、貿易、金融、航運、通訊、旅遊、文化、體育等領域以"中國香港"的名義,單獨地同世界各國、各地區及有關國際組織保持和發展關係,簽訂和履行有關協議。

第一百五十二條

Art 13

對以國家為單位參加的、同香港特別行政區有關的、適當領域的國際組織和國際會議,香港特別行政區政府可派遣代表作為中華人民共和國代表團的成員或以中央人民政府和上述有關國際組織或國際會議允許的身份參加,並以"中國香港"的名義發表意見。

Art 116

香港特別行政區可以"中國香港"的名義參加不以國家為單位參加的國際組織和國際會議。

Chapter VII: External Affairs

Article 150

Representatives of the Government of the Hong Kong Special Administrative Region may, as members of delegations of the Government of the People's Republic of China, participate in negotiations at the diplomatic level directly affecting the Region conducted by the Central People's Government.

Art 13

Article 151

The Hong Kong Special Administrative Region may on its own, using the name "Hong Kong, China", maintain and develop relations and conclude and implement agreements with foreign states and regions and relevant international organizations in the appropriate fields, including the economic, trade, financial and monetary, shipping, communications, tourism, cultural and sports fields.

Art 116, 125, 149

Article 152

Representatives of the Government of the Hong Kong Special Administrative Region may, as members of delegations of the People's Republic of China, participate in international organizations or conferences in appropriate fields limited to states and affecting the Region, or may attend in such other capacity as may be permitted by the Central People's Government and the international organization or conference concerned, and may express their views, using the name "Hong Kong, China".

Art 13

The Hong Kong Special Administrative Region may, using the name "Hong Kong, China", participate in international organizations and conferences not limited to states.

Art 116

Art 116

　　對中華人民共和國已參加而香港也以某種形式參加了的國際組織，中央人民政府將採取必要措施使香港特別行政區以適當形式繼續保持在這些組織中的地位。

　　對中華人民共和國尚未參加而香港已以某種形式參加的國際組織，中央人民政府將根據需要使香港特別行政區以適當形式繼續參加這些組織。

第一百五十三條

中華人民共和國締結的國際協議，中央人民政府可根據香港特別行政區的情況和需要，在徵詢香港特別行政區政府的意見後，決定是否適用於香港特別行政區。

Art 39, 152

　　中華人民共和國尚未參加但已適用於香港的國際協議仍可繼續適用，中央人民政府根據需要授權或協助香港特別行政區政府作出適當安排，使其他有關國際協議適用於香港特別行政區。

The Central People's Government shall take the necessary steps to ensure that the Hong Kong Special Administrative Region shall continue to retain its status in an appropriate capacity in those international organizations of which the People's Republic of China is a member and in which Hong Kong participates in one capacity or another. *Art 116*

The Central People's Government shall, where necessary, facilitate the continued participation of the Hong Kong Special Administrative Region in an appropriate capacity in those international organizations in which Hong Kong is a participant in one capacity or another, but of which the People's Republic of China is not a member.

Article 153

The application to the Hong Kong Special Administrative Region of international agreements to which the People's Republic of China is or becomes a party shall be decided by the Central People's Government, in accordance with the circumstances and needs of the Region, and after seeking the views of the government of the Region.

International agreements to which the People's Republic of China is not a party but which are implemented in Hong Kong may continue to be implemented in the Hong Kong Special Administrative Region. The Central People's Government shall, as necessary, authorize or assist the government of the Region to make appropriate arrangements for the application to the Region of other relevant international agreements. *Art 39, 152*

第一百五十四條

Art 24,
Inst 24 (p 326)

中央人民政府授權香港特別行政區政府依照法律給持有香港特別行政區永久性居民身份證的中國公民簽發中華人民共和國香港特別行政區護照，給在香港特別行政區的其他合法居留者簽發中華人民共和國香港特別行政區的其他旅行證件。上述護照和證件，前往各國和各地區有效，並載明持有人有返回香港特別行政區的權利。

對世界各國或各地區的人入境、逗留和離境，香港特別行政區政府可實行出入境管制。

第一百五十五條

Art 13

中央人民政府協助或授權香港特別行政區政府與各國或各地區締結互免簽證協議。

第一百五十六條

Art 13

香港特別行政區可根據需要在外國設立官方或半官方的經濟和貿易機構，報中央人民政府備案。

Article 154

The Central People's Government shall authorize the Government of the Hong Kong Special Administrative Region to issue, in accordance with law, passports of the Hong Kong Special Administrative Region of the People's Republic of China to all Chinese citizens who hold permanent identity cards of the Region, and travel documents of the Hong Kong Special Administrative Region of the People's Republic of China to all other persons lawfully residing in the Region. The above passports and documents shall be valid for all states and regions and shall record the holder's right to return to the Region.

The Government of the Hong Kong Special Administrative Region may apply immigration controls on entry into, stay in and departure from the Region by persons from foreign states and regions.

Art 24, Inst 24 (p 327)

Article 155

The Central People's Government shall assist or authorize the Government of the Hong Kong Special Administrative Region to conclude visa abolition agreements with foreign states or regions.

Art 13

Article 156

The Hong Kong Special Administrative Region may, as necessary, establish official or semi-official economic and trade missions in foreign countries and shall report the establishment of such missions to the Central People's Government for the record.

Art 13

第一百五十七條

外國在香港特別行政區設立領事機構或其他官方、半官方機構，須經中央人民政府批准。

已同中華人民共和國建立正式外交關係的國家在香港設立的領事機構和其他官方機構，可予保留。

尚未同中華人民共和國建立正式外交關係的國家在香港設立的領事機構和其他官方機構，可根據情況允許保留或改為半官方機構。

尚未為中華人民共和國承認的國家，只能在香港特別行政區設立民間機構。

Article 157

The establishment of foreign consular and other official or semi-official missions in the Hong Kong Special Administrative Region shall require the approval of the Central People's Government.

Art 13

Consular and other official missions established in Hong Kong by states which have formal diplomatic relations with the People's Republic of China may be maintained.

According to the circumstances of each case, consular and other official missions established in Hong Kong by states which have no formal diplomatic relations with the People's Republic of China may be permitted either to remain or be changed to semi-official missions.

States not recognized by the People's Republic of China may only establish non-governmental institutions in the Region.

第八章 本法的解釋和修改

第一百五十八條

本法的解釋權屬於全國人民代表大會常務委員會。

全國人民代表大會常務委員會授權香港特別行政區法院在審理案件時對本法關於香港特別行政區自治範圍內的條款自行解釋。

香港特別行政區法院在審理案件時對本法的其他條款也可解釋。但如香港特別行政區法院在審理案件時需要對本法關於中央人民政府管理的事務或中央和香港特別行政區關係的條款進行解釋，而該條款的解釋又影響到案件的判決，在對該案件作出不可上訴的終局判決前，應由香港特別行政區終審法院請全國人民代表大會常務委員會對有關條款作出解釋。如全國人民代表大會常務委員會作出解釋，香港特別行政區法院在引用該條款時，應以全國人民代表大會常務委員會的解釋為準。但在此以前作出的判決不受影響。

全國人民代表大會常務委員會在對本法進行解釋前，徵詢其所屬的香港特別行政區基本法委員會的意見。

Inst 25 (p 332),
Inst 26 (p 340),
Inst 27 (p 348),
Inst 28 (p 354),
Inst 29 (p 368)

Art 80, 81

Inst 28 (p 354)

Inst 4 (p 192)

Chapter VIII: Interpretation and Amendment of the Basic Law

Article 158

The power of interpretation of this Law shall be vested in the Standing Committee of the National People's Congress.

The Standing Committee of the National People's Congress shall authorize the courts of the Hong Kong Special Administrative Region to interpret on their own, in adjudicating cases, the provisions of this Law which are within the limits of the autonomy of the Region.

The courts of the Hong Kong Special Administrative Region may also interpret other provisions of this Law in adjudicating cases. However, if the courts of the Region, in adjudicating cases, need to interpret the provisions of this Law concerning affairs which are the responsibility of the Central People's Government, or concerning the relationship between the Central Authorities and the Region, and if such interpretation will affect the judgments on the cases, the courts of the Region shall, before making their final judgments which are not appealable, seek an interpretation of the relevant provisions from the Standing Committee of the National People's Congress through the Court of Final Appeal of the Region. When the Standing Committee makes an interpretation of the provisions concerned, the courts of the Region, in applying those provisions, shall follow the interpretation of the Standing Committee. However, judgments previously rendered shall not be affected.

The Standing Committee of the National People's Congress shall consult its Committee for the Basic Law of the Hong Kong Special Administrative Region before giving an interpretation of this Law.

Inst 25 (p 333),
Inst 26 (p 341),
Inst 27 (p 349),
Inst 28 (p 355),
Inst 29 (p 369)

Art 80, 81

Inst 28 (p 355)

Inst 4 (p 193)

第一百五十九條

本法的修改權屬於全國人民代表大會。

　　本法的修改提案權屬於全國人民代表大會常務委員會、國務院和香港特別行政區。香港特別行政區的修改議案，須經香港特別行政區的全國人民代表大會代表三分之二多數、香港特別行政區立法會全體議員三分之二多數和香港特別行政區行政長官同意後，交由香港特別行政區出席全國人民代表大會的代表團向全國人民代表大會提出。

Inst 4 (p 192)

　　本法的修改議案在列入全國人民代表大會的議程前，先由香港特別行政區基本法委員會研究並提出意見。

序言

　　本法的任何修改，均不得同中華人民共和國對香港既定的基本方針政策相抵觸。

Article 159

The power of amendment of this Law shall be vested in the National People's Congress.

The power to propose bills for amendments to this Law shall be vested in the Standing Committee of the National People's Congress, the State Council and the Hong Kong Special Administrative Region. Amendment bills from the Hong Kong Special Administrative Region shall be submitted to the National People's Congress by the delegation of the Region to the National People's Congress after obtaining the consent of two-thirds of the deputies of the Region to the National People's Congress, two-thirds of all the members of the Legislative Council of the Region, and the Chief Executive of the Region.

Before a bill for amendment to this Law is put on the agenda of the National People's Congress, the Committee for the Basic Law of the Hong Kong Special Administrative Region shall study it and submit its views.

Inst 4 (p 193)

No amendment to this Law shall contravene the established basic policies of the People's Republic of China regarding Hong Kong.

Preamble

第九章　附　則

第一百六十條

Art 8,
Inst 7 (p 202)

香港特別行政區成立時，香港原有法律除由全國人民代表大會常務委員會宣布為同本法抵觸者外，採用為香港特別行政區法律，如以後發現有的法律與本法抵觸，可依照本法規定的程序修改或停止生效。

Art 120–122

　　在香港原有法律下有效的文件、證件、契約和權利義務，在不抵觸本法的前提下繼續有效，受香港特別行政區的承認和保護。

Chapter IX: Supplementary Provisions

Article 160

Upon the establishment of the Hong Kong Special Administrative Region, the laws previously in force in Hong Kong shall be adopted as laws of the Region except for those which the Standing Committee of the National People's Congress declares to be in contravention of this Law. If any laws are later discovered to be in contravention of this Law, they shall be amended or cease to have force in accordance with the procedure as prescribed by this Law.

Art 8, Inst 7 (p 203)

Documents, certificates, contracts, and rights and obligations valid under the laws previously in force in Hong Kong shall continue to be valid and be recognized and protected by the Hong Kong Special Administrative Region, provided that they do not contravene this Law.

Art 120–122

附件一 香港特別行政區行政長官的產生辦法[*]

Art 45–46,
Inst 3 (p 186),
Inst 8 (p 222),
Inst 10 (p 236),
Inst 11 (p 246),
Inst 13 (p 260),
Inst 18 (p 302)

（1990年4月4日第七屆全國人民代表大會第三次會議通過，
2010年8月28日第十一屆全國人民代表大會常務委員會
第十六次會議批准修正[#]，2021年3月30日第十三屆
全國人民代表大會常務委員會第二十七次會議修訂[##]）

一、 行政長官由一個具有廣泛代表性、符合香港
特別行政區實際情況、體現社會整體利益的
選舉委員會根據本法選出，由中央人民政府
任命。

二、 選舉委員會委員共1,500人，由下列各界人士
組成：[#]

第一界別：工商、金融界 　　　　300人

註：

[*] 本文件的中文文本轉載自《中華人民共和國全國人民代表大會常務委員會公
報（2021年第四號）》。

[#] 參閱《中華人民共和國香港特別行政區基本法附件一香港特別行政區行政長
官的產生辦法修正案》（2010年8月28日第十一屆全國人民代表大會常務委員
會第十六次會議批准）（見文件十一之附件，頁250）。

[##] 參閱《全國人民代表大會關於完善香港特別行政區選舉制度的決定》（2021
年3月11日第十三屆全國人民代表大會第四次會議通過）（見文件十八，頁
302）。

Annex I: Method for the Selection of the Chief Executive of the Hong Kong Special Administrative Region

Art 45–46,
Inst 3 (p 187),
Inst 8 (p 223),
Inst 10 (p 237),
Inst 11 (p 247),
Inst 13 (p 261),
Inst 18 (p 303)

(Adopted at the Third Session of the Seventh National People's Congress
on 4 April 1990, amended, as approved at the Sixteenth Meeting
of the Standing Committee of the Eleventh National People's Congress
on 28 August 2010[#], and amended at the Twenty-Seventh Meeting
of the Standing Committee of the Thirteenth National People's Congress
on 30 March 2021[##])

1. The Chief Executive shall be elected in accordance with this Law by an Election Committee which is broadly representative, suited to the actual situation of the Hong Kong Special Administrative Region (HKSAR), and represents the overall interests of society, and shall be appointed by the Central People's Government.

2. The Election Committee shall be composed of 1,500 members from the following sectors:[#]

   First Sector: Industrial, commercial and financial
   sectors   300

Note:

[#] *See* Amendment to Annex I to the Basic Law of the Hong Kong Special Administrative Region of the People's Republic of China Concerning the Method for the Selection of the Chief Executive of the Hong Kong Special Administrative Region (Approved at the Sixteenth Meeting of the Standing Committee of the Eleventh National People's Congress on 28 August 2010) (Appendix of Instrument 11, p. 251).

[##] *See* Decision of the National People's Congress on Improving the Electoral System of the Hong Kong Special Administrative Region (Adopted at the Fourth Session of the Thirteenth National People's Congress on 11 March 2021) (Instrument 18, p. 303).

第二界別：專業界　　　　　　　300人

第三界別：基層、勞工和宗教等界　300人

第四界別：立法會議員、

　　　　　地區組織代表等界　　300人

第五界別：香港特別行政區

　　　　　全國人大代表、香港特別行政區

　　　　　全國政協委員和有關全國性團體

　　　　　香港成員的代表界　　300人

選舉委員會委員必須由香港特別行政區永久性居民擔任。

選舉委員會每屆任期五年。

三、　選舉委員會各個界別的劃分及名額如下：

第一界別設十八個界別分組：

Inst 18 (p 304)

工業界（第一）　　　　　　17席

工業界（第二）　　　　　　17席

紡織及製衣界　　　　　　　17席

商界（第一）　　　　　　　17席

商界（第二）　　　　　　　17席

商界（第三）　　　　　　　17席

金融界　　　　　　　　　　17席

金融服務界　　　　　　　　17席

保險界　　　　　　　　　　17席

地產及建造界　　　　　　　17席

Second Sector: The professions	300
Third Sector: Grassroots, labour, religious and other sectors	300
Fourth Sector: Members of the Legislative Council, representatives of district organisations and other organisations	300
Fifth Sector: HKSAR deputies to the National People's Congress (NPC), HKSAR members of the National Committee of the Chinese People's Political Consultative Conference (CPPCC), and representatives of Hong Kong members of relevant national organisations	300

Members of the Election Committee must be permanent residents of the HKSAR.

The term of office of the Election Committee shall be five years.

3. The delimitation of and the number of seats allocated to each sector of the Election Committee are as follows:

The First Sector shall be composed of the following 18 subsectors:

Inst 18 (p 305)

Industrial (first)	17
Industrial (second)	17
Textiles and garment	17
Commercial (first)	17
Commercial (second)	17
Commercial (third)	17
Finance	17
Financial services	17
Insurance	17
Real estate and construction	17

航運交通界	17席
進出口界	17席
旅遊界	17席
酒店界	16席
飲食界	16席
批發及零售界	17席
香港僱主聯合會	15席
中小企業界	15席

第二界別設十個界別分組：

科技創新界	30席
工程界	30席
建築測量都市規劃及園境界	30席
會計界	30席
法律界	30席
教育界	30席
體育演藝文化及出版界	30席
醫學及衛生服務界	30席
中醫界	30席
社會福利界	30席

第三界別設五個界別分組：

漁農界	60席
勞工界	60席
基層社團	60席

Transport	17
Import and export	17
Tourism	17
Hotel	16
Catering	16
Wholesale and retail	17
Employers' Federation of Hong Kong	15
Small and medium enterprises	15

The Second Sector shall be composed of the following
10 subsectors:

Technology and innovation	30
Engineering	30
Architectural, surveying, planning and landscape	30
Accountancy	30
Legal	30
Education	30
Sports, performing arts, culture and publication	30
Medical and health services	30
Chinese medicine	30
Social welfare	30

The Third Sector shall be composed of the following
five subsectors:

Agriculture and fisheries	60
Labour	60
Grassroots associations	60

同鄉社團　　　　　　　　　　　60席

宗教界　　　　　　　　　　　　60席

第四界別設五個界別分組：

立法會議員　　　　　　　　　　90席

鄉議局　　　　　　　　　　　　27席

港九分區委員會及地區撲滅罪行委員
　會、地區防火委員會委員的代表　76席
"新界"分區委員會及地區撲滅罪行委
　員會、地區防火委員會委員的代表　80席

內地港人團體的代表　　　　　　27席

第五界別設兩個界別分組：

香港特別行政區全國人大代表和
　香港特別行政區全國政協委員　　190席
有關全國性團體香港成員的代表　110席

四、　　選舉委員會以下列方式產生：

（一）　香港特別行政區全國人大代表、香港特別
　　　　行政區全國政協委員、全國人民代表大會常
　　　　務委員會香港特別行政區基本法委員會香
　　　　港委員、立法會議員、大學校長或者學校董
　　　　事會或者校務委員會主席，以及工程界（15
　　　　席）、建築測量都市規劃及園境界（15席）、

Associations of Chinese fellow townsmen	60
Religious	60

The Fourth Sector shall be composed of the following
five subsectors:

Members of the Legislative Council	90
Heung Yee Kuk	27
Representatives of members of Area Committees, District Fight Crime Committees, and District Fire Safety Committees of Hong Kong Island and Kowloon	76
Representatives of members of Area Committees, District Fight Crime Committees, and District Fire Safety Committees of the New Territories	80
Representatives of associations of Hong Kong residents in the Mainland	27

The Fifth Sector shall be composed of the following
two subsectors:

HKSAR deputies to the NPC and HKSAR members of the CPPCC National Committee	190
Representatives of Hong Kong members of relevant national organisations	110

4. The Election Committee shall be constituted in the following manner:

(1) HKSAR deputies to the NPC, HKSAR members of the CPPCC National Committee, Hong Kong members of the Committee for the Basic Law of the HKSAR under the NPC Standing Committee, members of the Legislative Council, university presidents or chairpersons of the board of governors or the council of universities, and responsible persons of statutory bodies, advisory bodies and relevant associations of the subsectors of engineering (15), architectural, surveying, planning and landscape (15),

教育界（5席）、醫學及衛生服務界（15席）、社會福利界（15席）等界別分組的法定機構、諮詢組織及相關團體負責人，是相應界別分組的選舉委員會委員。

除第五界別外，香港特別行政區全國人大代表和香港特別行政區全國政協委員也可以在其有密切聯繫的選舉委員會其他界別分組登記為委員。如果香港特別行政區全國人大代表或者香港特別行政區全國政協委員登記為選舉委員會其他界別分組的委員，則其計入相應界別分組的名額，該界別分組按照本款第三項規定產生的選舉委會委員的名額相應減少。香港特別行政區全國人大代表和香港特別行政區全國政協委員登記為選舉委員會有關界別分組的委員後，在該屆選舉委員會任期內，根據上述規定確定的選舉委員會各界別分組按照本款第一、二、三項規定產生的委員的名額維持不變。

(二)　宗教界界別分組的選舉委員會委員由提名產生；科技創新界界別分組的部分委員（15席）在中國科學院、中國工程院香港院士中提名產生；會計界界別分組的部分委員（15席）在國家財政部聘任的香港會計諮詢專家中提名產生；法律界界別分組的部分委員（9席）在中國法學會香港理事中提名產生；體育演藝文化及出版界界別分組的部分委員（15席）由

education (5), medical and health services (15) and social welfare (15) shall be Election Committee members of the corresponding subsectors.

An HKSAR deputy to the NPC or an HKSAR member of the CPPCC National Committee may choose to register as an Election Committee member in a subsector other than one in the Fifth Sector with which he or she has a substantial connection. If an HKSAR deputy to the NPC or an HKSAR member of the CPPCC National Committee is registered as an Election Committee member in a subsector other than one in the Fifth Sector, his or her seat shall be counted as one in that subsector and the number of members to be returned by that subsector in accordance with paragraph (3) of this subsection shall be reduced accordingly. After the registration of HKSAR deputies to the NPC and HKSAR members of the CPPCC National Committee as Election Committee members of the relevant subsectors, the number of members to be returned by those subsectors in accordance with paragraphs (1), (2) and (3) of this subsection, as determined by the provision in this sub-paragraph, shall remain unchanged within the term of office of the Election Committee.

(2) Election Committee members of the religious subsector shall be nominated; 15 members of the technology and innovation subsector shall be nominated from among Hong Kong academicians of the Chinese Academy of Sciences and the Chinese Academy of Engineering;15 members of the accountancy subsector shall be nominated from among Hong Kong Accounting Advisors appointed by the Ministry of Finance;9 members of the legal subsector shall be nominated from among Hong Kong members of the Council of the China Law Society;15 members of the sports, performing arts, culture and publication subsector shall be

中國香港體育協會暨奧林匹克委員會、中國文學藝術界聯合會香港會員總會和香港出版總會分別提名產生；中醫界界別分組的部分委員（15席）在世界中醫藥學會聯合會香港理事中提名產生；內地港人團體的代表界別分組的委員（27席）由各內地港人團體提名產生。

（三）　　除本款第一、二項規定的選舉委員會委員外，其他委員由相應界別分組的合資格團體選民選出。各界別分組的合資格團體選民由法律規定的具有代表性的機構、組織、團體或企業構成。除香港特別行政區選舉法列明者外，有關團體和企業須獲得其所在界別分組相應資格後持續運作三年以上方可成為該界別分組選民。第四界別的鄉議局、港九分區委員會及地區撲滅罪行委員會、地區防火委員會委員的代表、"新界"分區委員會及地區撲滅罪行委員會、地區防火委員會委員的代表和第五界別的有關全國性團體香港成員的代表等界別分組的選舉委員會委員，可由個人選民選出。選舉委員會委員候選人須獲得其所在界別分組5個選民的提名。每個選民

nominated respectively by the Sports Federation and Olympic Committee of Hong Kong, China, China Federation of Literary and Art Circles Hong Kong Member Association and Hong Kong Publishing Federation;15 members of the Chinese medicine subsector shall be nominated from among Hong Kong members of the Council of the World Federation of Chinese Medicine Societies; and The 27 members of the subsector of representatives of associations of Hong Kong residents in the Mainland shall be nominated by such associations.

(3) Election Committee members of a subsector, except for those specified in paragraphs (1) and (2) of this subsection, shall be elected by eligible corporate voters for the corresponding subsector. Eligible corporate voters for subsectors shall be composed of institutions, organisations, associations or enterprises which are representative and specified by law. Unless specified in the electoral law of the HKSAR, an association or enterprise may become a corporate voter for a subsector only if it has been operating for not less than three years after acquiring relevant qualifications for that subsector. Election Committee members of subsectors --the Heung Yee Kuk, representatives of members of Area Committees, District Fight Crime Committees, and District Fire Safety Committees of Hong Kong Island and Kowloon, and representatives of members of Area Committees, District Fight Crime Committees, and District Fire Safety Committees of the New Territories in the Fourth Sector and representatives of Hong Kong members of relevant national organisations in the Fifth Sector may be elected by individual voters. A candidate for Election Committee member of a subsector shall be nominated by five voters for the subsector. The number of candidates each voter for a subsector may

可提名不超過其所在界別分組選舉委員會委員名額的候選人。選舉委員會各界別分組選民根據提名的名單，以無記名投票選舉產生該界別分組的選舉委員會委員。

上款規定涉及的選舉委員會委員的具體產生辦法，包括有關界別分組的法定機構、諮詢組織、相關團體和合資格團體選民的界定、候選人提名辦法、投票辦法等，由香港特別行政區以選舉法規定。

五、　選舉委員會設召集人制度，負責必要時召集選舉委員會會議，辦理有關事宜。總召集人由擔任國家領導職務的選舉委員會委員擔任，總召集人在選舉委員會每個界別各指定若干名召集人。

六、　行政長官候選人須獲得不少於188名選舉委員會委員的提名，且上述五個界別中每個界別參與提名的委員須不少於15名。每名選舉委員會委員只可提出一名候選人。[#]

註：

[#] 參閱《中華人民共和國香港特別行政區基本法附件一香港特別行政區行政長官的產生辦法修正案》（2010年8月28日第十一屆全國人民代表大會常務委員會第十六次會議批准）（見文件十一之附件，頁250）。

nominate shall not exceed the number of seats allocated to the subsector. Voters for a subsector of the Election Committee shall elect Election Committee members of that subsector from the list of nominations by secret ballot.

The specific method for returning the Election Committee members referred to in the preceding subsection, including the definition of statutory bodies, advisory bodies, relevant associations and eligible corporate voters for relevant subsectors, the method for nomination of candidates and the method for voting shall be prescribed by the electoral law of the HKSAR.

5. There shall be a system of conveners for the Election Committee. The conveners shall be responsible for convening meetings of the Election Committee as necessary and handle relevant matters. A chief convener shall be an Election Committee member who holds an office of state leadership. The chief convener shall designate a number of conveners for each sector of the Election Committee.

6. A candidate for the office of Chief Executive shall be nominated by not less than 188 members of the Election Committee, with not less than 15 members from each of the five sectors. Each Election Committee member may nominate one candidate only.#

Note:

See Amendment to Annex I to the Basic Law of the Hong Kong Special Administrative Region of the People's Republic of China Concerning the Method for the Selection of the Chief Executive of the Hong Kong Special Administrative Region (Approved at the Sixteenth Meeting of the Standing Committee of the Eleventh National People's Congress on 28 August 2010) (Appendix of Instrument 11, p. 251).

七、 選舉委員會根據提名的名單,經一人一票無記名投票選出行政長官候任人,行政長官候任人須獲得超過750票。具體選舉辦法由香港特別行政區以選舉法規定。

八、 香港特別行政區候選人資格審查委員會負責審查並確認選舉委員會委員候選人和行政長官候選人的資格。香港特別行政區維護國家安全委員會根據香港特別行政區政府警務處維護國家安全部門的審查情況,就選舉委員會委員候選人和行政長官候選人是否符合擁護中華人民共和國香港特別行政區基本法、效忠中華人民共和國香港特別行政區的法定要求和條件作出判斷,並就不符合上述法定要求和條件者向香港特別行政區候選人資格審查委員會出具審查意見書。

對香港特別行政區候選人資格審查委員會根據香港特別行政區維護國家安全委員會的審查意見書作出的選舉委員會委員候選人和行政長官候選人資格確認的決定,不得提起訴訟。

九、 香港特別行政區應當採取措施,依法規管操縱、破壞選舉的行為。

7. The Election Committee shall elect the Chief Executive designate from the list of nominations by secret ballot on a one-person-one-vote basis. The Chief Executive designate must obtain more than 750 votes. The specific election method shall be prescribed by the electoral law of the HKSAR.

8. The Candidate Eligibility Review Committee of the HKSAR shall be responsible for reviewing and confirming the eligibility of candidates for Election Committee members and for the office of Chief Executive. The Committee for Safeguarding National Security of the HKSAR shall, on the basis of the review by the department for safeguarding national security of the Police Force of the HKSAR, make findings as to whether a candidate for Election Committee member or for the office of Chief Executive meets the legal requirements and conditions of upholding the Basic Law of the Hong Kong Special Administrative Region of the People's Republic of China and swearing allegiance to the Hong Kong Special Administrative Region of the People's Republic of China, and issue an opinion to the Candidate Eligibility Review Committee of the HKSAR in respect of a candidate who fails to meet such legal requirements and conditions.

    No legal proceedings may be instituted in respect of a decision made by the Candidate Eligibility Review Committee of the HKSAR on the eligibility of a candidate for Election Committee member or for the office of Chief Executive pursuant to the opinion of the Committee for Safeguarding National Security of the HKSAR.

9. The HKSAR shall, in accordance with the law, take measures against acts of manipulating or undermining election.

十、　　全國人民代表大會常務委員會依法行使本辦法的修改權。全國人民代表大會常務委員會作出修改前，以適當形式聽取香港社會各界意見。

十一、　依據本辦法產生的選舉委員會任期開始時，依據原辦法產生的選舉委員會任期即告終止。

十二、　本辦法自2021年3月31日起施行。原附件一及有關修正案不再施行。

10. The NPC Standing Committee exercises in accordance with the law the power to amend this Method. Prior to making any amendment, the NPC Standing Committee shall solicit views of various sectors of Hong Kong by appropriate means.

11. The term of office of the Election Committee constituted under the Method previously in force shall terminate upon the commencement of term of office of the Election Committee constituted under this Method.

12. This Method shall come into force on 31 March 2021. Annex I and its amendment previously in force shall cease to apply.

Art 68,
Inst 3 (p 186),
Inst 8 (p 222),
Inst 10 (p 236),
Inst 12 (p 254),
Inst 13 (p 260),
Inst 16 (p 292),
Inst 17 (p 296),
Inst 18 (p 302)

附件二　香港特別行政區立法會的產生辦法和
表決程序*

(1990年4月4日第七屆全國人民代表大會第三次會議通過，
2010年8月28日第十一屆全國人民代表大會常務委員會
第十六次會議備案修正#，2021年3月30日第十三屆
全國人民代表大會常務委員會第二十七次會議修訂) ##

一、　　　香港特別行政區立法會議員每屆90人，組成
如下：#

選舉委員會選舉的議員	40人
功能團體選舉的議員	30人
分區直接選舉的議員	20人

註：

* 本文件的中文文本轉載自《中華人民共和國全國人民代表大會常務委員會公報（2021年第四號）》。

\# 參閱《中華人民共和國香港特別行政區基本法附件二香港特別行政區立法會的產生辦法和表決程序修正案》（2010年8月28日第十一屆全國人民代表大會常務委員會第十六次會議予以備案）（見文件十二之附件，頁258）。

\## 參閱《全國人民代表大會關於完善香港特別行政區選舉制度的決定》（2021年3月11日第十三屆全國人民代表大會第四次會議通過）（見文件十八，頁302）。

Annex II: Method for the Formation of the Legislative Council of the Hong Kong Special Administrative Region and Its Voting Procedures*

Art 68,
Inst 3 (p 187),
Inst 8 (p 223),
Inst 10 (p 237),
Inst 12 (p 255),
Inst 13 (p 261),
Inst 16 (p 293),
Inst 17 (p 297),
Inst 18 (p 303)

(Adopted at the Third Session of the Seventh National People's Congress on 4 April 1990, amended, as approved at the Sixteenth Meeting of the Standing Committee of the Eleventh National People's Congress on 28 August 2010#, and amended at the Twenty-Seventh Meeting of the Standing Committee of the Thirteenth National People's Congress on 30 March 2021)##

1. The Legislative Council of the Hong Kong Special Administrative Region (HKSAR) shall be composed of 90 members for each term. The composition of the Legislative Council shall be as follows:#

    Members returned by the Election Committee   40

    Members returned by functional constituencies   30

    Members returned by geographical constituencies through direct elections   20

Note:

See Amendment to Annex II to the Basic Law of the Hong Kong Special Administrative Region of the People's Republic of China Concerning the Method for the Formation of the Legislative Council of the Hong Kong Special Administrative Region and Its Voting Procedures (Recorded at the Sixteenth Meeting of the Standing Committee of the Eleventh National People's Congress on 28 August 2010) (Appendix of Instrument 12, p. 259).

See Decision of the National People's Congress on Improving the Electoral System of the Hong Kong Special Administrative Region (Adopted at the Fourth Session of the Thirteenth National People's Congress on 11 March 2021) (Instrument 18, p. 303).

上述選舉委員會即本法附件一規定的選舉委員會。

二、 選舉委員會選舉的議員候選人須獲得不少於10名、不多於20名選舉委員會委員的提名，且每個界別參與提名的委員不少於2名、不多於4名。任何合資格選民均可被提名為候選人。每名選舉委員會委員只可提出一名候選人。

選舉委員會根據提名的名單進行無記名投票，每一選票所選的人數等於應選議員名額的有效，得票多的40名候選人當選。

三、 功能團體選舉設以下二十八個界別：

漁農界

鄉議局

工業界（第一）

工業界（第二）

紡織及製衣界

商界（第一）

商界（第二）

商界（第三）

金融界

金融服務界

保險界

The above-mentioned Election Committee refers to the one provided for in Annex I to this Law.

2.　Candidates for members of the Legislative Council returned by the Election Committee shall be nominated by at least 10 but no more than 20 members of the Election Committee, with at least 2 but no more than 4 members from each sector. Any eligible voter in an election of the Legislative Council may be nominated as a candidate. Each Election Committee member may nominate one candidate only.

The Election Committee shall elect members of the Legislative Council from the list of nominations by secret ballot. A ballot paper is valid only if the number of candidates voted for is equal to the number of members of the Legislative Council to be returned. The 40 candidates who obtain the highest numbers of votes shall be elected.

3.　There shall be 28 functional constituencies for election of members of the Legislative Council:

　　Agriculture and fisheries

　　Heung Yee Kuk

　　Industrial (first)

　　Industrial (second)

　　Textiles and garment

　　Commercial (first)

　　Commercial (second)

　　Commercial (third)

　　Finance

　　Financial services

　　Insurance

　　地產及建造界

　　航運交通界

　　進出口界

　　旅遊界

　　飲食界

　　批發及零售界

　　科技創新界

　　工程界

　　建築測量都市規劃及園境界

　　會計界

　　法律界

　　教育界

　　體育演藝文化及出版界

　　醫療衛生界

　　社會福利界

　　勞工界

　　香港特別行政區全國人大代表香港特別
　　　　行政區全國政協委員及有關全國性
　　　　團體代表界

其中，勞工界選舉產生三名議員，其他界別
各選舉產生一名議員。

Real estate and construction

Transport

Import and export

Tourism

Catering

Wholesale and retail

Technology and innovation

Engineering

Architectural, surveying, planning and landscape

Accountancy

Legal

Education

Sports, performing arts, culture and publication

Medical and health services

Social welfare

Labour

HKSAR deputies to the National People's Congress
(NPC), HKSAR members of the National
Committee of the Chinese People's Political
Consultative Conference (CPPCC), and
representatives of relevant national organisations

Three members shall be returned by the labour functional
constituency, and one member shall be returned by each
of the other functional constituencies.

以下界別的議員，由個人選民選出。

鄉議局

工程界

建築測量都市規劃及園境界

會計界

法律界

教育界

醫療衛生界

社會福利界

香港特別行政區全國人大代表香港特別
　　行政區全國政協委員及有關全國性
　　團體代表界

其他界別的議員由合資格團體選民選舉產
生，各界別的合資格團體選民由法律規定的
具有代表性的機構、組織、團體或企業構成。
除香港特別行政區選舉法明者外，有關團
體和企業須獲得其所在界別相應資格後持續
運作三年以上方可成為該界別選民。

Members of the Legislative Council returned by the following functional constituencies shall be elected by individual voters:

Heung Yee Kuk

Engineering

Architectural, surveying, planning and landscape

Accountancy

Legal

Education

Medical and health services

Social welfare

HKSAR deputies to the NPC, HKSAR members of the CPPCC National Committee and representatives of relevant national organisations

Members of the Legislative Council returned by the other functional constituencies shall be elected by eligible corporate voters. Eligible corporate voters for functional constituencies shall be composed of institutions, organisations, associations or enterprises which are representative and specified by law. Unless specified in the electoral law of the HKSAR, an association or enterprise may become a corporate voter for a functional constituency only if it has been operating for not less than three years after acquiring relevant qualifications for that functional constituency.

候選人須獲得所在界別不少於10個、不多於
20個選民和選舉委員會每個界別不少於2名、
不多於4名委員的提名。每名選舉委員會委員
在功能團體選舉中只可提出一名候選人。

各界別選民根據提名的名單，以無記名投票
選舉產生該界別立法會議員。

各界別有關法定團體的劃分、合資格團體選
民的界定、選舉辦法由香港特別行政區以選
舉法規定。

四、　　　分區直接選舉設立十個選區，每個選區選舉
產生兩名議員。

候選人須獲得所在選區不少於100個、不多
於200個選民和選舉委員會每個界別不少於
2名、不多於4名委員的提名。每名選舉委員
會委員在分區直接選舉中只可提出一名候選
人。

選民根據提名的名單以無記名投票選擇一名
候選人，得票多的兩名候選人當選。

A candidate for a functional constituency shall be nominated by at least 10 but no more than 20 voters for the functional constituency as well as at least 2 but no more than 4 members from each sector of the Election Committee. Each Election Committee member may nominate one candidate only for the election of members of the Legislative Council returned by functional constituencies.

Voters for a functional constituency shall elect Legislative Council member for that functional constituency from the list of nominations by secret ballot.

The delimitation of corporate bodies and the definition of eligible corporate voters for functional constituencies, and the election method shall be prescribed by the electoral law of the HKSAR.

4. There shall be 10 geographical constituencies for returning members of the Legislative Council through direct elections. Two members shall be returned by each geographical constituency.

A candidate for a geographical constituency shall be nominated by at least 100 but no more than 200 voters for the geographical constituency as well as at least 2 but no more than 4 members from each sector of the Election Committee. Each Election Committee member may nominate one candidate only for direct election of members of the Legislative Council returned by geographical constituencies.

For each geographical constituency, a voter may vote for one candidate on the list of nominations by secret ballot. The two candidates who obtain the highest numbers of votes shall be elected.

選區劃分、投票辦法由香港特別行政區以選舉法規定。

五、　　香港特別行政區候選人資格審查委員會負責審查並確認立法會議員候選人的資格。香港特別行政區維護國家安全委員會根據香港特別行政區政府警務處維護國家安全部門的審查情況，就立法會議員候選人是否符合擁護中華人民共和國香港特別行政區基本法、效忠中華人民共和國香港特別行政區的法定要求和條件作出判斷，並就不符合上述法定要求和條件者向香港特別行政區候選人資格審查委員會出具審查意見書。

對香港特別行政區候選人資格審查委員會根據香港特別行政區維護國家安全委員會的審查意見書作出的立法會議員候選人資格確認的決定，不得提起訴訟。

六、　　香港特別行政區應當採取措施，依法規管操縱、破壞選舉的行為。

The delineation of geographical constituencies and the voting method shall be prescribed by the electoral law of the HKSAR.

5.   The Candidate Eligibility Review Committee of the HKSAR shall be responsible for reviewing and confirming the eligibility of candidates for members of the Legislative Council. The Committee for Safeguarding National Security of the HKSAR shall, on the basis of the review by the department for safeguarding national security of the Police Force of the HKSAR, make findings as to whether a candidate for member of the Legislative Council meets the legal requirements and conditions of upholding the Basic Law of the Hong Kong Special Administrative Region of the People's Republic of China and swearing allegiance to the Hong Kong Special Administrative Region of the People's Republic of China, and issue an opinion to the Candidate Eligibility Review Committee of the HKSAR in respect of a candidate who fails to meet such legal requirements and conditions.

No legal proceedings may be instituted in respect of a decision made by the Candidate Eligibility Review Committee of the HKSAR on the eligibility of a candidate for member of the Legislative Council pursuant to the opinion of the Committee for Safeguarding National Security of the HKSAR.

6.   The HKSAR shall, in accordance with the law, take measures against acts of manipulating or undermining election.

七、 除本法另有規定外，香港特別行政區立法會對法案和議案的表決採取下列程序：

政府提出的法案，如獲得出席會議的全體議員的過半數票，即為通過。

Art 74

立法會議員個人提出的議案、法案和對政府法案的修正案均須分別經選舉委員會選舉產生的議員和功能團體選舉、分區直接選舉產生的議員兩部分出席會議議員各過半數通過。

八、 全國人民代表大會常務委員會依法行使本辦法和法案、議案的表決程序的修改權。全國人民代表大會常務委員會作出修改前，以適當形式聽取香港社會各界意見。

九、 本辦法和法案、議案的表決程序自2021年3月31日起施行。原附件二及有關修正案不再施行。

7. Unless otherwise provided for in this Law, the Legislative Council shall adopt the following procedures for voting on bills and motions:

The passage of bills introduced by the government shall require a simple majority of votes of the members of the Legislative Council present.

The passage of motions, bills or amendments to government bills introduced by individual members of the Legislative Council shall require a simple majority of votes of each of the two groups of members present, i.e. members returned by the Election Committee, and those returned by functional constituencies and by geographical constituencies through direct elections.

Art 74

8. The NPC Standing Committee exercises in accordance with the law the power to amend this Method and the procedures for voting on bills and motions. Prior to making any amendment, the NPC Standing Committee shall solicit views of various sectors of Hong Kong by appropriate means.

9. This Method and the procedures for voting on bills and motions shall come into force on 31 March 2021. Annex II and its amendment previously in force shall cease to apply.

Art 18,
Inst 19 (p 312),
Inst 20 (p 316),
Inst 21 (p 318),
Inst 22 (p 320),
Inst 23 (p 322)

附件三　在香港特別行政區實施的全國性法律[*]

下列全國性法律，自一九九七年七月一日起由香港特別行政區在當地公布或立法實施。

一、　　《關於中華人民共和國國都、紀年、國歌、國旗的決議》

二、　　《關於中華人民共和國國慶日的決議》

三、　　《中央人民政府公布中華人民共和國國徽的命令》附：國徽圖案、説明、使用辦法

註：

[*] 關於對列於附件三的法律作出的增減，請參閱：

　　a.《全國人民代表大會常務委員會關於〈中華人民共和國香港特別行政區基本法〉附件三所列全國性法律增減的決定》（1997年7月1日第八屆全國人民代表大會常務委員會第二十六次會議通過）（見文件十九，頁312）；

　　b.《全國人民代表大會常務委員會關於增加〈中華人民共和國香港特別行政區基本法〉附件三所列全國性法律的決定》（1998年11月4日通過）（見文件二十，頁316）；

　　c.《全國人民代表大會常務委員會關於增加〈中華人民共和國香港特別行政區基本法〉附件三所列全國性法律的決定》（2005年10月27日通過）（見文件二十一，頁318）。

　　d.《全國人民代表大會常務委員會關於增加〈中華人民共和國香港特別行政區基本法〉附件三所列全國性法律的決定》（2017年11月4日第十二屆全國人民代表大會常務委員會第三十次會議通過）（見文件二十二，頁320）；及

Art 18,
Inst 19 (p 313),
Inst 20 (p 317),
Inst 21 (p 319),
Inst 22 (p 321),
Inst 23 (p 323)

Annex III: National Laws to be Applied in the Hong Kong Special Administrative Region*

The following national laws shall be applied locally with effect from 1 July 1997 by way of promulgation or legislation by the Hong Kong Special Administrative Region:

1. Resolution on the Capital, Calendar, National Anthem and National Flag of the People's Republic of China

2. Resolution on the National Day of the People's Republic of China

3. Order on the National Emblem of the People's Republic of China Proclaimed by the Central People's Government Attached: Design of the national emblem, notes of explanation and instructions for use

Note:
* For addition to and deletion from the list of laws in Annex III, please *see*:

a. Decision of the Standing Committee of the National People's Congress on adding to and deleting from the list of the National Laws in Annex III to the Basic Law of the Hong Kong Special Administrative Region of the People's Republic of China (Adopted at the Twenty-sixth Meeting of the Standing Committee of the Eighth National People's Congress on 1 July 1997) (see Instrument 19, p. 313);

b. Decision of the Standing Committee of the National People's Congress on adding a law to the list of the National Laws in Annex III to the Basic Law of the Hong Kong Special Administrative Region of the People's Republic of China (Adopted on 4 November 1998) (see Instrument 20, p. 317);

c. Decision of the Standing Committee of the National People's Congress on adding a law to the list of the National Laws in Annex III to the Basic Law of the Hong Kong Special Administrative Region of the People's Republic of China (Adopted on 27 October 2005) (see Instrument 21, p. 319).

d. Decision of the Standing Committee of the National People's Congress on adding a law to the list of the national laws in Annex III to the Basic Law of the Hong Kong Special Administrative Region of the People's Republic of China (Adopted at the Thirtieth Meeting of the Standing Committee of the Twelfth National People's Congress on 4 November 2017) (see Instrument 22, p. 321); and

四、　　《中華人民共和國政府關於領海的聲明》

五、　　《中華人民共和國國籍法》

六、　　《中華人民共和國外交特權與豁免條例》

註：

e.《全國人民代表大會常務委員會關於增加〈中華人民共和國香港特別行政區基本法〉附件三所列全國性法律的決定》（2020年6月30日第十三屆全國人民代表大會常務委員會第二十次會議通過）（見文件二十三，頁322）。

4.   Declaration of the Government of the People's Republic of China on the Territorial Sea

5.   Nationality Law of the People's Republic of China

6.   Regulations of the People's Republic of China Concerning Diplomatic Privileges and Immunities

Note:
  e. Decision of the Standing Committee of the National People's Congress on the addition to the list of national laws in Annex III to the Basic Law of the Hong Kong Special Administrative Region of the People's Republic of China (Adopted at the Twentieth Session of the Standing Committee of the Thirteenth National People's Congress on 30 June 2020) (see Instrument 23, p. 323).

香港特別行政區區旗圖案

香港特別行政區區徽圖案

The Design of the Regional Flag
of the Hong Kong Special Administrative Region

The Design of the Regional Emblem
of the Hong Kong Special Administrative Region

中華人民共和國國務院令第221號

Inst 2 (p 184)

根據1990年4月4日第七屆全國人民代表大會第三次會議通過的《全國人民代表大會關於設立香港特別行政區的決定》,《中華人民共和國香港特別行政區行政區域圖》已經1997年5月7日國務院第56次常務會議通過,現予公布。

　　附:中華人民共和國香港特別行政區行政區域界線文字表述

李鵬

總理

一九九七年七月一日

Order of the State Council of the People's Republic of China No. 221

It is hereby promulgated that in accordance with the Decision of the National People's Congress on the Establishment of the Hong Kong Special Administrative Region adopted at the Third Session of the Seventh National People's Congress on 4 April 1990, the map of the administrative division of the Hong Kong Special Administrative Region of the People's Republic of China was approved at the 56th Executive Meeting of the State Council on 7 May 1997.

Inst 2 (p 185)

Enclosure: Description of the boundary of the administrative division of the Hong Kong Special Administrative Region of the People's Republic of China

LI Peng
Premier
1 July 1997

Note:

This English translation is prepared by Security Bureau, Government of the Hong Kong Special Administrative Region. It is for reference only and has no legislative effect.

附

中華人民共和國香港特別行政區
行政區域界線文字表述

區域界線由陸地部分和海上部分組成。

一、陸地部分

陸地部分由以下三段組成:

(一) 沙頭角鎮段

1. 由沙頭角碼頭底部東角 (1號點,北緯 22°32'37.21",東經114°13'34.85") 起至新樓街東側並行的排水溝入海口處,再沿排水溝中心線至該線與中英街中心線的交點 (2號點,北緯 22°32'45.42",東經114°13'32.40");

2. 由2號點起沿中英街中心線至步步街與中英街兩街中心線的交點 (3號點,北緯22°32'52.26",東經114°13'36.91");

3. 由3號點起以直線連接沙頭角河橋西側河中心橋墩底部的西端 (4號點,北緯22°32'52.83",東經114°13'36.86")。

Enclosure

Description of the Boundary
of the Administrative Division
of the Hong Kong Special Administrative Region
of the People's Republic of China

The boundary comprises a land and sea sector.

I. The Land Sector

The land sector comprises three sections as follows:

(1) Sha Tau Kok Town

1. The boundary starts at the eastern corner of the base of the Sha Tau Kok pier ("Point 1", Latitude 22°32'37.21" North, Longitude 114°13'34.85" East). From there, it runs directly to the mouth of the ditch running along the eastern side of San Lau Street. It then follows the centre line of the ditch, as far as the point where that line meets the centre line of Chung Ying Street ("Point 2", Latitude 22°32'45.42" North, Longitude 114°13'32.40" East).

2. From Point 2, the boundary follows the centre line of Chung Ying Street as far as the point where that line meets the centre line of Bubu Street ("Point 3", Latitude 22°32'52.26" North, Longitude 114°13'36.91" East).

3. From Point 3, the boundary follows a straight line to the western tip of the base of the foundation of Sha Tau Kok River Bridge in the middle of the river ("Point 4", Latitude 22°32'52.83" North, Longitude 114°13'36.86" East).

（二）沙頭角鎮至伯公坳段

由4號點起沿沙頭角河中心線逆流而上經伯公坳東側山谷谷底至該坳鞍部中心止（5號點，北緯22°33'23.49"，東經114°12'24.25"）。

（三）伯公坳至深圳河入海段

由伯公坳鞍部起沿該坳西側主山谷谷底至深圳河伯公坳源頭，再沿深圳河中心線直至深圳灣（亦稱后海灣）河口處止。

深圳河治理後，以新河中心線作為區域界線。

二、海上部分

海上部分由以下三段組成：

（一）深圳灣海域段

由深圳河入海口起，沿南航道中央至84號航燈標（亦稱"B"號航燈標）（6號點，北緯22°30'36.23"，東經113°59'42.20"），再與以下兩點直線連成：

1. 深圳灣83號航燈標（亦稱"A"號航燈標）（7號點，北緯22°28'20.49"，東經113°56'52.10"）；

(2) Sha Tau Kok Town to Pak Kung Au

From Point 4, the boundary runs upstream along the centre line of the Sha Tau Kok River and thence along the bottom line of the valley east of Pak Kung Au until it reaches the middle of the Pak Kung Au saddle point ("Point 5", Latitude 22°33'23.49" North, Longitude 114°12'24.25" East).

(3) Pak Kung Au to the Mouth of the Shenzhen River

The boundary runs from Point 5 along the bottom line of the main valley west of Pak Kung Au as far as the source of the Shenzhen River at Pak Kung Au. It continues along the centre line of the Shenzhen River to the mouth of the river at Shenzhen Bay (otherwise known as Deep Bay).

After the realignment of the Shenzhen River, the boundary will follow the new centre line of the river.

II. The Sea Sector

The sea sector comprises three sections as follows:

(1) Shenzhen Bay

From the mouth of the Shenzhen River, the boundary runs along the middle of the southern navigable channel as far as Beacon 84 (otherwise known as "B" Beacon) ("Point 6", Latitude 22°30'36.23" North, Longitude 113°59'42.20" East). From there, it follows straight lines in sequence through the following two points:

1. Beacon 83 (otherwise known as "A" Beacon) in Shenzhen Bay ("Point 7", Latitude 22°28'20.49" North, Longitude 113°56'52.10" East); and

2. 上述7號點與內伶仃島南端的東角咀的聯線與東經113°52'08.8"經線的交點（8號點，北緯22°25'43.7"，東經113°52'08.8"）。

（二）南面海域段

由8號點起與以下13點直線連成：

1. 由8號點沿東經113°52'08.8"經線向南延伸至北緯22°20'處（9號點，北緯22°20'，東經113°52'08.8"）；

2. 大澳北面海岸線最突出部向西北1海里處（10號點，北緯22°16'23.2"，東經113°50'50.6"）；

3. 大澳西面海岸線最突出部向西北1海里處（11號點，北緯22°16'03.8"，東經113°50'20.4"）；

4. 雞公山西南面海岸線最突出部向西北1海里處（12號點，北緯22°14'21.4"，東經113°49'35.0"）；

5. 大嶼山雞翼角西面海岸線最突出部向西1海里處（13號點，北緯22°13'01.4"，東經113°49'01.6"）；

2. "Point 8", (Latitude 22°25'43.7" North, Longitude 113°52'08.8" East), defined as the point where the line between Point 7 and Dongjiaozui at the southernmost tip of Neilingding Island intersects the meridian line of Longitude 113°52'08.8" East.

(2) Southern Sea Section

From Point 8, the boundary follows a series of straight lines sequentially through the following thirteen points:

1. The boundary first runs southwards along the meridian line of Longitude 113°52'08.8" East until it reaches Latitude 22°20' North ("Point 9", Latitude 22°20' North, Longitude 113°52'08.8" East). The boundary runs thence in sequence to:

2. "Point 10" (Latitude 22°16'23.2" North, Longitude 113°50'50.6" East), defined as the point one nautical mile northwest of the most northerly point on the coastline of Tai O;

3. "Point 11" (Latitude 22°16'03.8" North, Longitude 113°50'20.4" East), defined as the point one nautical mile northwest of the most westerly point on the coastline of Tai O;

4. "Point 12" (Latitude 22°14'21.4" North, Longitude 113°49'35.0" East), defined as the point one nautical mile northwest of the tip of the protruding point on the Lantau coastline southwest of Kai Kung Shan;

5. "Point 13" (Latitude 22°13'01.4" North, Longitude 113°49'01.6" East), defined as the point one nautical mile west of the most westerly point on Kai Yet Kok off Lantau Island;

6. 大嶼山分流角西南面海岸線最突出部向西南1海里處（14號點，北緯22°11'01.9"，東經113°49'56.6"）；

7. 索罟群島大鴉洲南面海岸線最突出部與大蜘洲銀角咀北面海岸線最突出部間的中點（15號點，北緯22°08'33.1"，東經113°53'47.6"）；

8. 索罟群島頭顱洲南面海岸線最突出部向南1海里處（16號點，北緯22°08'12.2"，東經113°55'20.6"）；

9. 以索罟群島頭顱洲南面海岸線最突出部為中心之1海里半徑與北緯22°08'54.5"緯線在東面的交點（17號點，北緯22°08'54.5"，東經113°56'22.4"）；

10. 以蒲台群島墨洲西南面海岸線最突出部為中心之1海里半徑與北緯22°08'54.5"緯線在西面的交點（18號點，北緯22°08'54.5"，東經114°14'09.6"）；

11. 蒲台島南角咀正南1海里處（19號點，北緯22°08'18.8"，東經114°15'18.6"）；

6. "Point 14" (Latitude 22°11'01.9" North, Longitude 113°49'56.6" East), defined as the point one nautical mile southwest of the most southwesterly point on the coastline at Fan Lau Kok on Lantau Island;

7. "Point 15" (Latitude 22°08'33.1" North, Longitude 113°53'47.6" East), defined as the mid-point of a straight line between the most southerly point on the coastline of Tai A Chau in the Soko Islands and the tip of the protruding point at Yinjiaozui on the northern coastline of Dazhizhou;

8. "Point 16" (Latitude 22°08'12.2" North, Longitude 113°55'20.6" East), defined as the point one nautical mile south of the most southerly point on the coastline of Tau Lo Chau in the Soko Islands;

9. "Point 17" (Latitude 22°08'54.5" North, Longitude 113°56'22.4" East), defined as the eastern point of intersection between the parallel of Latitude 22°08'54.5" North and an arc sector of one nautical mile radius centred on the most southerly point on the coastline of Tau Lo Chau in the Soko Islands;

10. "Point 18" (Latitude 22°08'54.5" North, Longitude 114°14'09.6" East), defined as the western point of intersection between the parallel of Latitude 22°08'54.5" North and an arc sector of one nautical mile radius centred on the most southwesterly point on the coastline of Mat Chau in the Po Toi Islands;

11. "Point 19" (Latitude 22°08'18.8" North, Longitude 114°15'18.6" East), defined as the point one nautical mile due south of Nam Kok Tsui on Po Toi Island;

12. 以蒲台島大角頭東南面海岸線最突出部為中
    心之1海里半徑與北緯22°08'54.5"緯線在東
    面的交點（20號點，北緯22°08'54.5"，東經
    114°17'02.4"）；

13. 北緯22°08'54.5"，東經114°30'08.8"（21號點）。

（三）大鵬灣海域段

由21號點與以下10點和1號點直線連成：

1. 北緯22°21'54.5"，東經114°30'08.8"（22號點）；

2. 大鹿灣北面海岸線最突出至石牛洲導航
   燈間的中點（23號點，北緯22°28'07.4"，東經
   114°27'17.6"）；

3. 水頭沙西南海岸線最突出部至平洲島更樓
   石間的中點（24號點，北緯22°32'41.9"，東經
   114°27'18.5"）；

4. 秤頭角至平洲島的洲尾角間的中點（25號點，北
   緯22°33'43.2"，東經114°26'02.3"）；

5. 背仔角海岸線最突出部至白沙洲北面海岸線最
   突出部間的中點（26號點，北緯22°34'06.0"，東
   經114°19'58.7"）；

12. "Point 20" (Latitude 22°08'54.5" North, Longitude
   114°17'02.4" East), defined as the eastern point of
   intersection between the parallel of Latitude 22°08'54.5"
   North and an arc sector of one nautical mile radius
   centred on the most southeasterly point at Tai Kok Tau
   on Po Toi Island;

13. "Point 21", defined by the coordinates Latitude
   22°08'54.5" North, Longitude 114°30'08.8" East.

(3) Mirs Bay

From Point 21, the boundary then runs in sequential straight
lines through the following ten points, then back to Point 1:

1. "Point 22", defined by the coordinates Latitude
   22°21'54.5" North, Longitude 114°30'08.8" East;

2. "Point 23" (Latitude 22°28'07.4" North, Longitude
   114°27'17.6" East), defined as the mid-point of a straight
   line between the tip of the protruding point on the
   coastline north of Daluwan and the beacon on Shek Ngau
   Chau;

3. "Point 24" (Latitude 22°32'41.9" North, Longitude
   114°27'18.5" East), defined as the mid-point of a straight
   line between the tip of the protruding point on the
   coastline southwest of Shuitousha and Kang Lau Shek
   on Ping Chau Island;

4. "Point 25" (Latitude 22°33'43.2" North, Longitude
   114°26'02.3" East), defined as the mid-point of a straight
   line between Chengtoujiao and Chau Mei Kok on Ping
   Chau Island;

5. "Point 26" (Latitude 22°34'06.0" North, Longitude
   114°19'58.7" East), defined as the mid-point of a straight
   line between the tip of the protruding point on the
   coastline at Beizaijiao and the most northerly point on
   the coastline of Round Island;

6. 正角咀海岸線最突出部至吉澳雞公頭東面海岸線最突出部間的中點（27號點，北緯22°34'00.0"，東經114°18'32.7"）；

7. 塘元涌海岸線最突出部至吉澳北面海岸線最突出部間的中點（28號點，北緯22°33'55.8"，東經114°16'33.7"）；

8. 恩上南小河入海口處至長排頭間的中點（29號點，北緯22°33'20.6"，東經114°14'55.2"）；

9. 官路下小河入海口處至三角咀間的中點（30號點，北緯22°33'02.6"，東經114°14'13.4"）；

10. 1號點正東方向至對岸間的中點（31號點，北緯22°32'37.2"，東經114°14'01.1"）。

註：上述坐標值採用WGS84坐標系。

6. "Point 27" (Latitude 22°34'00.0" North, Longitude 114°18'32.7" East), defined as the mid-point of a straight line between the tip of the protruding point on the coastline at Zhengjiaozui and the most easterly point on the coastline at Kai Kung Tau on Crooked Island;

7. "Point 28" (Latitude 22°33'55.8" North, Longitude 114°16'33.7" East), defined as the mid-point of a straight line between the tip of the protruding point on the coastline at Tangyuanchong and the most northerly point on the coastline of Crooked Island;

8. "Point 29" (Latitude 22°33'20.6" North, Longitude 114°14'55.2" East), defined as the mid-point of a straight line between the point where the stream south of Enshang meets the sea and Cheung Pai Tau;

9. "Point 30" (Latitude 22°33'02.6" North, Longitude 114°14'13.4" East), defined as the mid-point of a straight line between the point where the stream at Guanluxia meets the sea and Sam Kuk Tsui; and

10. "Point 31" (Latitude 22°32'37.2" North, Longitude 114°14'01.1" East), defined as the mid-point of a straight line running due east from Point 1 to the opposite shoreline.

Note: The above geographical coordinates are represented by WGS84.

1:500 000

中華人民共和國香港特別行政區行政區圖

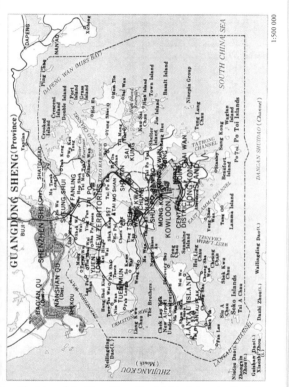

The Map of the Hong Kong Special Administrative Region
of the People's Republic of China

全國人民代表大會和全國人民代表大會常務委員會決定

Decisions of the National People's Congress
and the Standing Committee
of the National People's Congress

文件一

全國人民代表大會關於
《中華人民共和國香港特別行政區基本法》
的決定

（1990年4月4日第七屆全國人民代表大會第三次會議通過）

Anx I (p 124),
Anx II (p 142),
Anx III (p 156)

第七屆全國人民代表大會第三次會議通過《中華人民共和國香港特別行政區基本法》，包括附件一：《香港特別行政區行政長官的產生辦法》，附件二：《香港特別行政區立法會的產生辦法和表決程序》，附件三：《在香港特別行政區實施的全國性法律》，以及香港特別行政區區旗和區徽圖案。《中華人民共和國憲法》第三十一條規定："國家在必要時得設立特別行政區。在特別行政區內實行的制度按照具體情況由全國人民代表大會以法律規定。"香港特別行政區基本法是根據

Instrument 1

Decision of the National People's Congress on the Basic Law of the Hong Kong Special Administrative Region of the People's Republic of China

(Adopted at the Third Session
of the Seventh National People's Congress on 4 April 1990)

The Third Session of the Seventh National People's Congress adopts the Basic Law of the Hong Kong Special Administrative Region of the People's Republic of China, including Annex I: Method for the Selection of the Chief Executive of the Hong Kong Special Administrative Region, Annex II: Method for the Formation of the Legislative Council of the Hong Kong Special Administrative Region and Its Voting Procedures, Annex III: National Laws to be Applied in the Hong Kong Special Administrative Region, and the designs of the regional flag and regional emblem of the Hong Kong Special Administrative Region. Article 31 of the Constitution of the People's Republic of China provides: "The State may establish special administrative regions when necessary. The systems to be instituted in special administrative regions shall be prescribed by law enacted by the National People's Congress in the light of the specific conditions." The Basic Law of the Hong Kong Special Administrative Region is constitutional as it is enacted in accordance with the

Anx I (p 125),
Anx II (p 143),
Anx III (p 157)

Note:

This English translation is reproduced from "The Laws of the People's Republic of China 1990–1992" compiled by the Legislative Affairs Commission of the Standing Committee of the National People's Congress of the People's Republic of China. It is for reference only and has no legislative effect.

《中華人民共和國憲法》、按照香港的具體情況制定的,是符合憲法的。香港特別行政區設立後實行的制度、政策和法律,以香港特別行政區基本法為依據。

　　《中華人民共和國香港特別行政區基本法》自1997年7月1日起實施。

Constitution of the People's Republic of China and in the light of the specific conditions of Hong Kong. The systems, policies and laws to be instituted after the establishment of the Hong Kong Special Administrative Region shall be based on the Basic Law of the Hong Kong Special Administrative Region.

Preamble

The Basic Law of the Hong Kong Special Administrative Region of the People's Republic of China shall be put into effect as of 1 July 1997.

文件二

全國人民代表大會關於
設立香港特別行政區的決定

(1990年4月4日第七屆全國人民代表大會第三次會議通過)

第七屆全國人民代表大會第三次會議根據《中華人民共和國憲法》第三十一條和第六十二條第十三項的規定，決定：

一、 自1997年7月1日起設立香港特別行政區。

二、 香港特別行政區的區域包括香港島、九龍半島，以及所轄的島嶼和附近海域。香港特別行政區的行政區域圖由國務院另行公布。

Order No. 221
(p 162)

Instrument 2

Decision of the National People's Congress on the Establishment of the Hong Kong Special Administrative Region

(Adopted at the Third Session
of the Seventh National People's Congress on 4 April 1990)

In accordance with the provisions of Article 31 and sub-paragraph 13 of Article 62 of the Constitution of the People's Republic of China, the Third Session of the Seventh National People's Congress decides:

1. The Hong Kong Special Administrative Region is to be established on 1 July 1997.

2. The area of the Hong Kong Special Administrative Region covers the Hong Kong Island, the Kowloon Peninsula, and the islands and adjacent waters under its jurisdiction. The map of the administrative division of the Hong Kong Special Administrative Region will be published by the State Council separately.

*Order No. 221
(p 163)*

Note:

This English translation is reproduced from "The Laws of the People's Republic of China 1990–1992" compiled by the Legislative Affairs Commission of the Standing Committee of the National People's Congress of the People's Republic of China. It is for reference only and has no legislative effect.

文件三

全國人民代表大會關於香港特別行政區
第一屆政府和立法會產生辦法的決定

（1990年4月4日第七屆全國人民代表大會第三次會議通過）

一、 香港特別行政區第一屆政府和立法會根據體現
   國家主權、平穩過渡的原則產生。

二、 在1996年內，全國人民代表大會設立香港特別行
   政區籌備委員會，負責籌備成立香港特別行政
   區的有關事宜，根據本決定規定第一屆政府和立
   法會的具體產生辦法。籌備委員會由內地和不少
   於50%的香港委員組成，主任委員和委員由全國
   人民代表大會常務委員會委任。

Instrument 3

Decision of the National People's Congress on the Method for the Formation of the First Government and the First Legislative Council of the Hong Kong Special Administrative Region

(Adopted at the Third Session
of the Seventh National People's Congress on 4 April 1990)

1. The first Government and the first Legislative Council of the Hong Kong Special Administrative Region shall be formed in accordance with the principles of State sovereignty and smooth transition.

2. Within the year 1996, the National People's Congress shall establish a Preparatory Committee for the Hong Kong Special Administrative Region, which shall be responsible for preparing the establishment of the Hong Kong Special Administrative Region and shall prescribe the specific method for the formation of the first Government and the first Legislative Council in accordance with this Decision. The Preparatory Committee shall be composed of mainland members and of Hong Kong members who shall constitute not less than 50 per cent of its membership. Its chairman and members shall be appointed by the Standing Committee of the National People's Congress.

Note:
   This English translation is reproduced from "The Laws of the People's Republic of China 1990–1992" compiled by the Legislative Affairs Commission of the Standing Committee of the National People's Congress of the People's Republic of China. It is for reference only and has no legislative effect.

三、 香港特別行政區籌備委員會負責籌組香港特別
行政區第一屆政府推選委員會（以下簡稱推選委
員會）。

Art 24

推選委員會全部由香港永久性居民組成，必須具
有廣泛代表性，成員包括全國人民代表大會香港
地區代表、香港地區全國政協委員的代表、香港
特別行政區成立前曾在香港行政、立法、諮詢機
構任職並有實際經驗的人士和各階層、界別中具
有代表性的人士。

推選委員會由400人組成，比例如下：

工商、金融界	25%
專業界	25%
勞工、基層、宗教等界	25%
原政界人士、香港地區全國人大代表、 香港地區全國政協委員的代表	25%

3. The Preparatory Committee for the Hong Kong Special
    Administrative Region shall be responsible for preparing
    the establishment of the Selection Committee for the
    First Government of the Hong Kong Special
    Administrative Region (hereinafter referred to as the
    Selection Committee).

    The Selection Committee shall be composed entirely of   *Art 24*
    permanent residents of Hong Kong and must be broadly
    representative. It shall include Hong Kong deputies to
    the National People's Congress, representatives of Hong
    Kong members of the National Committee of the
    Chinese People's Political Consultative Conference,
    persons with practical experience who have served in
    Hong Kong's executive, legislative and advisory organs
    prior to the establishment of the Hong Kong Special
    Administrative Region, and persons representative of
    various strata and sectors of society.

    The Selection Committee shall be composed of 400
    members in the following proportions:

Industrial, commercial and financial sectors	25%
The professions	25%
Labour, grass-roots, religious and other sectors	25%
Former political figures, Hong Kong deputies to the National People's Congress, and representatives of Hong Kong members of the National Committee of the Chinese People's Political Consultative Conference	25%

四、 推選委員會在當地以協商方式、或協商後提名選
舉，推舉第一任行政長官人選，報中央人民政府

Art 45, 46

任命。第一任行政長官的任期與正常任期相同。

五、 第一屆香港特別行政區政府由香港特別行政區
行政長官按香港特別行政區基本法規定負責籌
組。

六、 香港特別行政區第一屆立法會由60人組成，其中
分區直接選舉產生議員20人，選舉委員會選舉
產生議員10人，功能團體選舉產生議員30人。原
香港最後一屆立法局的組成如符合本決定和香
港特別行政區基本法的有關規定，其議員擁護中
華人民共和國香港特別行政區基本法、願意效忠
中華人民共和國香港特別行政區並符合香港特
別行政區基本法規定條件者，經香港特別行政
區籌備委員會確認，即可成為香港特別行政區第
一屆立法會議員。

香港特別行政區第一屆立法會議員的任期為兩
年。

4. The Selection Committee shall recommend the candidate for the first Chief Executive through local consultations or through nomination and election after consultations, and report the recommended candidate to the Central People's Government for appointment. The term of office of the first Chief Executive shall be the same as the regular term.

Art 45, 46

5. The Chief Executive of the Hong Kong Special Administrative Region shall be responsible for preparing the formation of the first Government of the Region in accordance with the Basic Law of the Hong Kong Special Administrative Region.

6. The first Legislative Council of the Hong Kong Special Administrative Region shall be composed of 60 members, with 20 members returned by geographical constituencies through direct elections, 10 members returned by an election committee, and 30 members returned by functional constituencies. If the composition of the last Hong Kong Legislative Council before the establishment of the Hong Kong Special Administrative Region is in conformity with the relevant provisions of this Decision and the Basic Law of the Hong Kong Special Administrative Region, those of its members who uphold the Basic Law of the Hong Kong Special Administrative Region of the People's Republic of China and pledge allegiance to the Hong Kong Special Administrative Region of the People's Republic of China, and who meet the requirements set forth in the Basic Law of the Region may, upon confirmation by the Preparatory Committee, become members of the first Legislative Council of the Region.

The term of office of members of the first Legislative Council of the Hong Kong Special Administrative Region shall be two years.

文件四

全國人民代表大會關於批准
香港特別行政區基本法起草委員會關於
設立全國人民代表大會常務委員會
香港特別行政區基本法委員會的建議的決定

(1990年4月4日第七屆全國人民代表大會第三次會議通過)

第七屆全國人民代表大會第三次會議決定：

一、 批准香港特別行政區基本法起草委員會關於設立全國人民代表大會常務委員會香港特別行政區基本法委員會的建議。

二、 在《中華人民共和國香港特別行政區基本法》實施時，設立全國人民代表大會常務委員會香港特別行政區基本法委員會。

Instrument 4

Decision of the National People's Congress Approving the Proposal by the Drafting Committee for the Basic Law of the Hong Kong Special Administrative Region on the Establishment of the Committee for the Basic Law of the Hong Kong Special Administrative Region Under the Standing Committee of the National People's Congress

(Adopted at the Third Session
of the Seventh National People's Congress on 4 April 1990)

The Third Session of the Seventh National People's Congress decides:

1. to approve the proposal by the Drafting Committee for the Basic Law of the Hong Kong Special Administrative Region on the Establishment of the Committee for the Basic Law of the Hong Kong Special Administrative Region under the Standing Committee of the National People's Congress; and

2. to establish the Committee for the Basic Law of the Hong Kong Special Administrative Region under the Standing Committee of the National People's Congress when the Basic Law of the Hong Kong Special Administrative Region of the People's Republic of China is put into effect.

Note:

This English translation is reproduced from "The Laws of the People's Republic of China 1990–1992" compiled by the Legislative Affairs Commission of the Standing Committee of the National People's Congress of the People's Republic of China. It is for reference only and has no legislative effect.

附

香港特別行政區基本法起草委員會
關於設立全國人民代表大會常務委員會
香港特別行政區基本法委員會的建議

一、 名稱：全國人民代表大會常務委員會香港特別行政區基本法委員會。

二、 隸屬關係：是全國人民代表大會常務委員會下設的工作委員會。

Art 17, 18, 158, 159

三、 任務：就有關香港特別行政區基本法第十七條、第十八條、第一百五十八條、第一百五十九條實施中的問題進行研究，並向全國人民代表大會常務委員會提供意見。

Art 24

四、 組成：成員十二人，由全國人民代表大會常務委員會任命內地和香港人士各六人組成，其中包括法律界人士，任期五年。香港委員須由在外國無居留權的香港特別行政區永久性居民中的中國公民擔任，由香港特別行政區行政長官、立法會主席和終審法院首席法官聯合提名，報全國人民代表大會常務委員會任命。

Appendix

Proposal by the Drafting Committee for the Basic Law of the Hong Kong Special Administrative Region on the Establishment of the Committee for the Basic Law of the Hong Kong Special Administrative Region Under the Standing Committee of the National People's Congress

1. Name: The Committee for the Basic Law of the Hong Kong Special Administrative Region under the Standing Committee of the National People's Congress.

2. Affiliation: To be a working committee under the Standing Committee of the National People's Congress.

3. Function: To study questions arising from the implementation of Articles 17, 18, 158 and 159 of the Basic Law of the Hong Kong Special Administrative Region and submit its views thereon to the Standing Committee of the National People's Congress. *Art 17, 18, 158, 159*

4. Composition: Twelve members, six from the mainland and six from Hong Kong, including persons from the legal profession, appointed by the Standing Committee of the National People's Congress for a term of office of five years. Hong Kong members shall be Chinese citizens who are permanent residents of the Hong Kong Special Administrative Region with no right of abode in any foreign country and shall be nominated jointly by the Chief Executive, President of the Legislative Council and Chief Justice of the Court of Final Appeal of the Region for appointment by the Standing Committee of the National People's Congress. *Art 24*

文件五

全國人民代表大會常務委員會關於 《中華人民共和國香港特別行政區基本法》 英文本的決定

(1990年6月28日通過)

第七屆全國人民代表大會常務委員會第十四次會議決定：全國人民代表大會法律委員會主持審定的《中華人民共和國香港特別行政區基本法》英譯本為正式英文本，和中文本同樣使用；英文本中的用語的含義如果有與中文本有出入的，以中文本為準。

Instrument 5

Decision of the Standing Committee of the National People's Congress on the English Text of the Basic Law of the Hong Kong Special Administrative Region of the People's Republic of China

(Adopted on 28 June 1990)

The 14th Meeting of the Standing Committee of the Seventh National People's Congress decides: the English translation of the Basic Law of the Hong Kong Special Administrative Region of the People's Republic of China, examined and approved under the aegis of the Law Committee of the National People's Congress, shall be the official English text and shall be equally authentic as the Chinese text. In case of any discrepancy in the meaning of wording between the English text and the Chinese text, the Chinese text shall prevail.

Note:

This English translation is reproduced from "The Laws of the People's Republic of China 1990–1992" compiled by the Legislative Affairs Commission of the Standing Committee of the National People's Congress of the People's Republic of China. It is for reference only and has no legislative effect.

文件六

全國人民代表大會常務委員會關於
鄭耀棠等32名全國人大代表所提議案的決定

(1994年8月31日第八屆全國人民代表大會常務委員會
第九次會議通過)

第八屆全國人民代表大會常務委員會第九次會議根據全
國人大法律委員會的審議報告,審議了第八屆全國人大第
二次會議主席團交付法律委員會審議的鄭耀棠等32名全
國人大代表提出的議案。

Inst 3 (p 190)

　　會議認為,港英最後一屆立法局、市政局和區域市政
局、區議會於1997年6月30日終止。英國政府單方面決定的
有關港英最後一屆立法局、市政局和區域市政局、區議會
的選舉安排,違反中英聯合聲明,不符合《中華人民共和
國香港特別行政區基本法》和《全國人民代表大會關於香
港特別行政區第一屆政府和立法會產生辦法的決定》。會
議決定:由香港特別行政區籌備委員會根據《全國人民代

Instrument 6

Decision of the Standing Committee of the National People's Congress on the Proposal Submitted by Zheng Yaotang and Other Thirty-one Deputies to the National People's Congress

(Adopted at the Ninth Meeting of the Standing Committee of the Eighth National People's Congress on August 31, 1994)

The Ninth Meeting of the Standing Committee of the Eighth National People's Congress has, in accordance with the deliberation report of the Law Committee of the National People's Congress, deliberated the proposal submitted by Zheng Yaotang and other thirty-one deputies to the National People's Congress referred to the Law Committee by the Presidium of the Second Session of the Eighth National People's Congress.

The Meeting holds that the last Legislative Council, Urban Council, District Urban Council and District Legislature of the British Hong Kong Government shall terminate on June 30, 1997 and that the election arrangements for the last Legislative Council, Urban Council, District Urban Council and District Legislature of the British Hong Kong Government decided unilaterally by the British Government violate the Sino-British Joint Declaration and contravene the Basic Law of the Hong Kong Special Administrative Region of the People's Republic of China and the Decision of the National People's Congress on the Method for the Formation of the First Government and the First Legislative Council of the Hong Kong Special Administrative Region. The Meeting decides that the Preparatory Committee for the Hong Kong Special Administrative Region shall, in

Inst 3 (p 191)

表大會關於香港特別行政區第一屆政府和立法會產生辦法的決定》，負責籌備成立香港特別行政區的有關事宜，規定香港特別行政區第一屆立法會的具體產生辦法，組建香港特別行政區第一屆立法會。根據《中華人民共和國香港特別行政區基本法》，香港特別行政區的區域組織的職權和組成方法由香港特別行政區的法律規定。

Art 97–98

accordance with the Decision of the National People's Congress on the Methods for the Formation of the First Government and the First Legislative Council of the Hong Kong Special Administrative Region, be responsible for relevant affairs in the preparation for the establishment of the Hong Kong Special Administrative Region, prescribe the specific methods for the formation of the First Legislative Council of the Hong Kong Special Administrative Region and organize the First Legislative Council of the Hong Kong Special Administrative Region, and that according to the Basic Law of the Hong Kong Special Administrative Region of the People's Republic of China, the powers and functions of the district organizations in the Hong Kong Special Administrative Region and the method for their formation shall be prescribed by laws of the Hong Kong Special Administrative Region.

Art 97–98

文件七

Art 160

全國人民代表大會常務委員會關於根據 《中華人民共和國香港特別行政區基本法》 第一百六十條處理香港原有法律的決定

(1997年2月23日第八屆全國人民代表大會常務委員會 第二十四次會議通過)

Art 8, 160

《中華人民共和國香港特別行政區基本法》(以下簡稱 《基本法》) 第一百六十條規定:"香港特別行政區成立 時,香港原有法律除由全國人民代表大會常務委員會宣布 為同本法抵觸者外,採用為香港特別行政區法律,如以後 發現有的法律與本法抵觸,可依照本法規定的程序修改 或停止生效。"第八條規定:"香港原有法律,即普通法、 衡平法、條例、附屬立法和習慣法,除同本法相抵觸或經

Instrument 7

Art 160

Decision of the Standing Committee of the National People's Congress Concerning the Handling of the Laws Previously in Force in Hong Kong in accordance with Article 160 of the Basic Law of the Hong Kong Special Administrative Region of the People's Republic of China

(Adopted at the Twenty-fourth Meeting of the Standing Committee of the Eighth National People's Congress on 23 February 1997)

Art 8, 160

It is provided in Article 160 of the Basic Law of the Hong Kong Special Administrative Region of the People's Republic of China (hereinafter referred to as the Basic Law for short) that "Upon the establishment of the Hong Kong Special Administrative Region, the laws previously in force in Hong Kong shall be adopted as laws of the Region except for those which the Standing Committee of the National People's Congress declares to be in contravention of this Law. If any laws are later discovered to be in contravention of this Law, they shall be amended or cease to have force in accordance with the procedure as prescribed by this Law." Article 8 of the Basic Law stipulates: "The Laws previously in force in Hong Kong, that is, the common law, rules of equity, ordinances, subordinate legislation and customary law, shall be

Note:

This English translation is reproduced from "The Laws of the People's Republic of China 1997" compiled by the Legislative Affairs Commission of the Standing Committee of the National People's Congress of the People's Republic of China. It is for reference only and has no legislative effect.

香港特別行政區的立法機關作出修改者外，予以保留。"
第八屆全國人民代表大會常務委員會第二十四次會議根
據上述規定，審議了香港特別行政區籌備委員會關於處
理香港原有法律問題的建議，決定如下：

Art 8

一、 香港原有法律，包括普通法、衡平法、條例、附
屬立法和習慣法，除同《基本法》抵觸者外，採
用為香港特別行政區法律。

二、 列於本決定附件一的香港原有的條例及附屬立
法抵觸《基本法》，不採用為香港特別行政區法
律。

三、 列於本決定附件二的香港原有的條例及附屬立
法的部分條款抵觸《基本法》，抵觸的部分條款
不採用為香港特別行政區法律。

maintained, except for any that contravene this Law or are subject to any amendment by the legislature of the Hong Kong Special Administrative Region." In accordance with the provisions mentioned above, the Standing Committee of the Eighth National People's Congress at its 24th Meeting deliberated the proposal of the Preparatory Committee for the Hong Kong Special Administrative Region on handling the laws previously in force in Hong Kong and adopted the decision as follows:

1. The laws previously in force in Hong Kong, including the common law, rules of equity, ordinances, subordinate legislation and customary law, shall be adopted as laws of the Hong Kong Special Administrative Region, except for any that contravene the Basic Law.

   Art 8

2. The ordinances and subordinate legislation previously in force in Hong Kong, listed in Appendix I of this Decision, which are in contravention of the Basic Law shall not be adopted as laws of the Hong Kong Special Administrative Region.

3. Since some provisions of the ordinances and subordinate legislation, which are previously in force in Hong Kong and listed in Appendix II of this Decision, contravene the Basic Law, they shall not be adopted as provisions of laws of the Hong Kong Special Administrative Region.

文件七

四、 採用為香港特別行政區法律的香港原有法律，
自1997年7月1日起，在適用時，應作出必要的變
更、適應、限制或例外，以符合中華人民共和
國對香港恢復行使主權後香港的地位和《基本法》
的有關規定，如《新界土地（豁免）條例》在適用
時應符合上述原則。

Art 160

除符合上述原則外，原有的條例或附屬立法中：

(一) 規定與香港特別行政區有關的外交事務
的法律，如與在香港特別行政區實施的
全國性法律不一致，應以全國性法律為
準，並符合中央人民政府享有的國際權
利和承擔的國際義務。

Art 13, 18

(二) 任何給予英國或英聯邦其它國家或地區
特權待遇的規定，不予保留，但有關香
港與英國或英聯邦其它國家或地區之間
互惠性規定，不在此限。

4.   The laws previously in force in Hong Kong, which have been adopted as laws of the Hong Kong Special Administrative Region, shall be applied as of 1 July 1997 with such modifications, adaptations restrictions and exceptions as may be necessary for making them conform with the status of Hong Kong after the People's Republic of China resumes the exercise of sovereignty over it and with the relevant provisions of the Basic Law, for example, the New Territories Land (Exemption) Ordinance shall be applied in accordance with the principle mentioned above. *Art 160*

In addition to the above-mentioned principle, the following provisions shall be conformed with when applying the provisions of the ordinances and subordinate legislation previously in force:

(1)   Where the provisions relating to the diplomatic affairs of the Hong Kong Special Administrative Region are found inconsistent with the national laws coming into effect in the Hong Kong Special Administrative Region, the national laws shall prevail, and the provisions shall be made in keeping with the international rights enjoyed by the Central People's Government and the international obligations it undertakes. *Art 13, 18*

(2)   No provisions which accord privileges to the United Kingdom or any other countries or regions of the British Commonwealth shall be maintained with the exception of the reciprocity provisions in connection with Hong Kong and the United Kingdom or any other countries or regions of the British Commonwealth.

(三) 有關英國駐香港軍隊的權利、豁免及義務的規定，凡不抵觸《基本法》和《中華人民共和國香港特別行政區駐軍法》的規定者，予以保留，適用於中華人民共和國中央人民政府派駐香港特別行政區的軍隊。

Art 9

(四) 有關英文的法律效力高於中文的規定，應解釋為中文和英文都是正式語文。

(五) 在條款中引用的英國法律的規定，如不損害中華人民共和國的主權和不抵觸《基本法》的規定，在香港特別行政區對其作出修改前，作為過渡安排，可繼續參照適用。

五、 在符合第四條規定的條件下，採用為香港特別行政區法律的香港原有法律，除非文意另有所指，對其中的名稱或詞句的解釋或適用，須遵循本決定附件三所規定的替換原則。

(3)   The provisions regarding the rights, immunities and obligations of the British troops stationed in Hong Kong shall be maintained provided that they do not contravene the provisions of the Basic Law and the Law of the People's Republic of China on Garrisoning the Hong Kong Special Administrative Region and shall be applicable to the troops stationed in Hong Kong by the Central People's Government of the People's Republic of China.

(4)   The provision that the English language is superior to the Chinese language in terms of legal effect shall be construed as that both the Chinese and English language are the official languages.   *Art 9*

(5)   If the provisions in the British laws that are quoted in Hong Kong ordinances and subordinate legislation do not jeopardize the sovereignty of the People's Republic of China or contravene the provisions of the Basic Law, they may, as a transitional arrangement, continue to be applied mutatis mutandis before they are amended by the Hong Kong Special Administrative Region.

5.   On condition that the provisions in Article 4 are conformed with, the substitution rules prescribed in Appendix III of this Decision shall be followed when interpreting or applying the words and expressions in the laws previously in force in Hong Kong which are adopted as laws of the Hong Kong Special Administrative Region, except that they mean otherwise.

六、 採用為香港特別行政區法律的香港原有法律，如以後發現與《基本法》相抵觸者，可依照《基本法》規定的程序修改或停止生效。

附件一

香港原有法律中下列條例及附屬立法抵觸《基本法》，不採用為香港特別行政區法律：

1. 《受託人（香港政府證券）條例》（香港法例第77章）；

2. 《英國法律應用條例》（香港法例第88章）；

3. 《英國以外婚姻條例》（香港法例第180章）；

4. 《華人引渡條例》（香港法例第235章）；

5. 《香港徽幟（保護）條例》（香港法例第315章）；

6. 《國防部大臣（產業承繼）條例》（香港法例第193章）；

7. 《皇家香港軍團條例》（香港法例第199章）；

8. 《強制服役條例》（香港法例第246章）；

6. If the laws previously in force in Hong Kong which are adopted as laws of the Hong Kong Special Administrative Region are later discovered to be in contravention of the Basic Law, they may be amended or cease to have force in accordance with the procedure as prescribed by the Basic Law.

Appendix 1

The following ordinances and subordinate legislation in the laws previously in force in Hong Kong are in contravention of the Basic Law and therefore shall not be adopted as laws of the Hong Kong Special Administrative Region:

1. Trustees (Hong Kong Government Securities) Ordinance (Cap. 77);
2. Application of English Law Ordinance (Cap. 88);
3. Foreign Marriage Ordinance (Cap. 180);
4. Chinese Extradition Ordinance (Cap. 235);
5. Colony Armorial Bearings (Protection) Ordinance (Cap. 315);
6. Secretary of State for Defence (Succession to Property) Ordinance (Cap. 193);
7. Royal Hong Kong Regiment Ordinance (Cap. 199);
8. Compulsory Service Ordinance (Cap. 246);

9. 《陸軍及皇家空軍法律服務處條例》(香港法例第286章);

10. 《英國國籍(雜項規定)條例》(香港法例第186章);

11. 《1981年英國國籍法(相應修訂)條例》(香港法例第373章);

12. 《選舉規定條例》(香港法例第367章);

13. 《立法局(選舉規定)條例》(香港法例第381章);

14. 《選區分界及選舉事務委員會條例》(香港法例第432章)。

附件二

香港原有法律中下列條例及附屬立法的部分條款抵觸《基本法》,不採用為香港特別行政區法律:

1. 《人民入境條例》(香港法例第115章)第2條中有關"香港永久性居民"的定義和附表一"香港永久性居民"的規定;

2. 任何為執行在香港適用的英國國籍法所作出的規定;

3. 《市政局條例》(香港法例第101章)中有關選舉的規定;

9. Army and Royal Air Force Legal Services Ordinance (Cap. 286);

10. British Nationality (Miscellaneous Provisions) Ordinance (Cap. 186);

11. British Nationality Act 1981 (Consequential Amendments) Ordinance (Cap. 373);

12. Electoral Provisions Ordinance (Cap. 367);

13. Legislative Council (Electoral Provisions) Ordinance (Cap. 381);

14. Boundary and Election Commission Ordinance (Cap. 432).

Appendix 2

Some provisions of the following ordinances and subordinate legislation in the laws previously in force in Hong Kong are in contravention of the Basic Law and therefore shall not be adopted as provisions of laws of the Hong Kong Special Administrative Region:

1. The provisions regarding the definition of "Hong Kong permanent resident" in s2 and the provisions regarding "the Hong Kong permanent resident" in Schedule 1 of the Immigration Ordinance (Cap. 115);

2. Any provisions made for implementing the British Nationality Act applicable in Hong Kong;

3. Provisions for election in the Urban Council Ordinance (Cap. 101);

4. 《區域市政局條例》(香港法例第385章)中有關選舉的規定;

5. 《區議會條例》(香港法例第366章)中有關選舉的規定;

6. 《舞弊及非法行為條例》(香港法例第288章)中的附屬立法A《市政局、區域市政局以及區議會選舉費用令》和附屬立法C《立法局決議》;

7. 《香港人權法案條例》(香港法例第383章)第2條第(3)款有關該條例的解釋及應用目的的規定,第3條有關"對先前法例的影響"和第4條有關"日後的法例的釋義"的規定;

8. 《個人資料(私隱)條例》(香港法例第486章)第3條第(2)款有關該條例具有凌駕地位的規定;

9. 1992年7月17日以來對《社團條例》(香港法例第151章)的重大修改;

10. 1995年7月27日以來對《公安條例》(香港法例第245章)的重大修改。

4. Provisions for election in the Regional Council Ordinance (Cap. 385);

5. Provisions for election in the District Boards Ordinance (Cap. 366);

6. Subsidiary legislation A: "Urban Council, Regional Council and District Boards Election Expenses Order" and subsidiary legislation C: "Resolution of the Legislative Council" in the Corrupt and Illegal Practices Ordinance (Cap. 288);

7. The provisions in s2(3) regarding the purpose of this ordinance for the purpose of its interpretation and application, in s3 regarding the effect on pre-existing legislation and in s4 regarding interpretation of subsequent legislation in the Hong Kong Bill of Rights Ordinance (Cap. 383);

8. The provisions in s3 (2) that the ordinance acquires an overriding position in the Personal Data (Privacy) Ordinance (Cap. 486);

9. Major amendments to the Societies Ordinance (Cap. 151) made since 17 July 1992; and

10. Major amendments to the Public Ordinance (Cap. 245) made since 27 July 1995.

附件三

採用為香港特別行政區法律的香港原有法律中的名稱或
詞句在解釋或適用時一般須遵循以下替換原則：

Art 1, 12

1.　任何提及"女王陛下"、"王室"、"英國政府"及
"國務大臣"等相類似名稱或詞句的條款，如該
條款內容是關於香港土地所有權或涉及《基本
法》所規定的中央管理的事務和中央與香港特
別行政區的關係，則該等名稱或詞句應相應地
解釋為中央或中國的其它主管機關，其它情況下
應解釋為香港特別行政區政府。

2.　任何提及"女王會同樞密院"或"樞密院"的條
款，如該條款內容是關於上訴權事項，則該等名
稱或詞句應解釋為香港特別行政區終審法院，
其它情況下，依第1項規定處理。

Appendix 3

The words and expressions in the laws previously in force in Hong Kong which are adopted as laws of the Hong Kong Special Administrative Region, when construed or applied, shall be subject to the following substitution rules:

Art 1, 12

1. Any reference to "Her Majesty", "Crown", "The British Government, U.K." and "Secretary of State" and other similar names or expressions, if the provision relates to the ownership of the land in Hong Kong or involves the affairs within the responsibilities of the Central Authorities and relationship between the Central Authorities and the Region as prescribed by the Basic Law, shall be construed correspondingly as a reference to the Central Authorities or other competent organs, and under other circumstances, as the Government of the Hong Kong Special Administrative Region;

2. Any reference to "Her Majesty in Council" or "Privy Council", if the provision relates to the matter of right of appeal, shall be construed as a reference to the Court of Final Appeal of the Hong Kong Special Administrative Region, and under other circumstances, shall be dealt with in accordance with Item 1;

3. 任何冠以"皇家"的政府機構或半官方機構的名稱應刪去"皇家"字樣，並解釋為香港特別行政區相應的機構。

4. 任何"本殖民地"的名稱應解釋為香港特別行政區；任何有關香港領域的表述應依照國務院頒布的香港特別行政區行政區域圖作出相應解釋後適用。

5. 任何"最高法院"及"高等法院"等名稱或詞句應相應地解釋為高等法院及高等法院原訟法庭。

6. 任何"總督"、"總督會同行政局"、"布政司"、"律政司"、"首席按察司"、"政務司"、"憲制事務司"、"海關總監"及"按察司"等名稱或詞句應相應地解釋為香港特別行政區行政長官、行政長官會同行政會議、政務司長、律政司長、終審法院首席法官或高等法院首席法官、民政事務局局長、政制事務局局長、海關關長及高等法院法官。

3. Any reference to the government organs or semi-official organs with the word "Royal" in their names shall be construed as reference to the corresponding organs of the Hong Kong Special Administrative Region with the word "Royal" being deleted;

4. Any reference to "the colony" shall be construed as a reference to the Hong Kong Special Administrative Region; any description of the territory of Hong Kong shall be applicable after being correspondingly interpreted in accordance with the administrative division map of the Hong Kong Special Administrative Region promulgated by the State Council;

5. Any reference to "the Supreme Court" and "High Court" shall be correspondingly construed as a reference to the High Court and the Court of First Instance of the High Court;

6. Any reference to "the Governor", "Governor in Council", "Chief Secretary", "Attorney General", "Chief Justice", "Secretary for Home Affairs", "Secretary for Constitutional Affairs", "Commissioner of Customs and Excise", and "justices" shall be correspondingly construed as a reference to the Chief Executive, Chief Executive in Council, Secretary of the Department of Administration, Secretary of the Department of Justice, Chief Justice of the Court of Final Appeal or Chief Judge of High Court, Secretary for Home Affairs, Secretary for Constitutional Affairs, Commissioner of Customs and Excise, and judges of the High Court of the Hong Kong Special Administrative Region;

7. 在香港原有法律中文文本中,任何有關立法局、司法機關或行政機關及其人員的名稱或詞句應相應地依照《基本法》的有關規定進行解釋和適用。

8. 任何提及"中華人民共和國"和"中國"等相類似名稱或詞句的條款,應解釋為包括台灣、香港和澳門在內的中華人民共和國;任何單獨或同時提及大陸、台灣、香港和澳門的名稱或詞句的條款,應相應地將其解釋為中華人民共和國的一個組成部分。

9. 任何提及"外國"等相類似名稱或詞句的條款,應解釋為中華人民共和國以外的任何國家或地區,或者根據該項法律或條款的內容解釋為"香港特別行政區以外的任何地方";任何提及"外籍人士"等相類似名稱或詞句的條款,應解釋為中華人民共和國公民以外的任何人士。

10. 任何提及"本條例的條文不影響亦不得視為影響女王陛下、其儲君或其繼位人的權利"的規定,應解釋為"本條例的條文不影響亦不得視為影響中央或香港特別行政區政府根據《基本法》和其他法律的規定所享有的權利"。

7. Any reference to the Legislative Council, Judiciary or the Executive Authorities and their staff in the Chinese text of the laws previously in force in Hong Kong shall be construed or applied correspondingly in accordance with the relevant provisions of the Basic Law;

8. Any reference to "the People's Republic of China" and "China" or other similar names or expressions shall be construed as a reference to the People's Republic of China including Taiwan, Hong Kong and Macao; any reference to the Mainland, Taiwan, Hong Kong and Macao, separately or together, shall be correspondingly construed as a reference to a component part of the People's Republic of China;

9. Any reference to "foreign country or foreign State" and other similar words or expressions shall be construed as a reference to any country or region other than the People's Republic of China or, in accordance with the contents of the law or the provision, shall be construed as a reference to "any place other than the Hong Kong Special Administrative Region"; and any reference to "foreign national" or other similar words or expressions shall be construed as a reference to any person other than the citizen of the People's Republic of China; and

10. Any reference to "Nothing in this ordinance shall affect or be deemed to affect the rights of Her Majesty the Queen, Her Heirs or Successors" shall be construed as a reference to "Nothing in this ordinance shall affect or be deemed to affect the rights enjoyed by the Central Government or the Government of the Hong Kong Special Administrative Region in accordance with the provisions of the Basic Law and other enactments."

文件八

全國人民代表大會常務委員會關於
香港特別行政區2007年行政長官和
2008年立法會產生辦法有關問題的決定

(2004年4月26日第十屆全國人民代表大會常務委員會
第九次會議通過)

第十屆全國人民代表大會常務委員會第九次會議審議了
香港特別行政區行政長官董建華2004年4月15日提交的
《關於香港特別行政區2007年行政長官和2008年立法會
產生辦法是否需要修改的報告》，並在會前徵詢了香港特
別行政區全國人大代表、全國政協委員和香港各界人士、

Instrument 8

Art 45, 68

Decision of the Standing Committee of the National People's Congress on Issues Relating to the Methods for Selecting the Chief Executive of the Hong Kong Special Administrative Region in the Year 2007 and for Forming the Legislative Council of the Hong Kong Special Administrative Region in the Year 2008

(Adopted at the Ninth Meeting of the Standing Committee of
the Tenth National People's Congress on 26 April 2004)

At its 9th Meeting, the Standing Committee of the Tenth National People's Congress examined the Report on Whether There Is a Need to Amend the Methods for Selecting the Chief Executive of the Hong Kong Special Administrative Region in 2007 and for Forming the Legislative Council of the Hong Kong Special Administrative Region in 2008, submitted by Tung Chee-hwa, the Chief Executive of the Hong Kong Special Administrative Region, on 15 April 2004 and, before the meeting, had consulted deputies to the National People's Congress and members of the National Committee of the Chinese People's Political Consultative Conference from the Hong Kong Special Administrative Region, people from different sectors of Hong Kong, Hong Kong members of the Committee for the Basic Law of the Hong Kong Special Administrative

Note:

全國人大常委會香港特別行政區基本法委員會香港委員、香港特別行政區政府政制發展專責小組的意見，同時徵求了國務院港澳事務辦公室的意見。全國人大常委會在審議中充分注意到近期香港社會對2007年以後行政長官和立法會的產生辦法的關注，其中包括一些團體和人士希望2007年行政長官和2008年立法會全部議員由普選產生的意見。

Art 45, 68　　會議認為，《中華人民共和國香港特別行政區基本法》（以下簡稱香港基本法）第四十五條和第六十八條已明確規定，香港特別行政區行政長官和立法會的產生辦法應根據香港特別行政區的實際情況和循序漸進的原則而規定，最終達至行政長官由一個有廣泛代表性的提名委員會按民主程序提名後普選產生、立法會全部議員由普選產生的目標。香港特別行政區行政長官和立法會的產生辦法應符合香港基本法的上述原則和規定。有關香港特別行政區行政長官和立法會產生辦法的任何改變，都應遵循

Region under the Standing Committee of the National People's Congress, and the Constitutional Development Task Force of the Government of the Hong Kong Special Administrative Region, and had, at the same time, sought the advice of the Hong Kong and Macao Affairs Office of the State Council. In the course of examination, the Standing Committee of the National People's Congress paid full attention to the recent concerns of the Hong Kong community about the methods for selecting the Chief Executive and for forming the Legislative Council after the year 2007, including the views of some bodies and public figures that they wish to see the selection of the Chief Executive by universal suffrage in the year 2007 and the election of all the members of the Legislative Council by universal suffrage in the year 2008.

The participants hold that the provisions in Articles 45 and 68 of *Art 45, 68* the Basic Law of the Hong Kong Special Administrative Region of the People's Republic of China (hereinafter referred to as the Basic Law of Hong Kong, in short) already expressly stipulate that the methods for selecting the Chief Executive and for forming the Legislative Council shall be prescribed in the light of the actual situation in the Hong Kong Special Administrative Region and in accordance with the principle of gradual and orderly progress, and that the ultimate aims are the selection of the Chief Executive by universal suffrage upon nomination by a broadly representative nominating committee in accordance with democratic procedures and the election of all the members of the Legislative Council by universal suffrage. The methods for selecting the Chief Executive of the Hong Kong Special Administrative Region and for forming the Legislative Council of the Hong Kong Special Administrative Region shall conform to the principles and provisions of the Basic Law of Hong Kong mentioned above. Any change relating to the methods for selecting the Chief Executive of the Hong Kong Special Administrative Region and for forming the Legislative Council of

與香港社會、經濟、政治的發展相協調,有利於社會各階層、各界別、各方面的均衡參與,有利於行政主導體制的有效運行,有利於保持香港的長期繁榮穩定等原則。

Inst 3
(p 188, 190)

　　會議認為,香港特別行政區成立以來,香港居民所享有的民主權利是前所未有的。第一任行政長官由400人組成的推選委員會選舉產生,第二任行政長官由800人組成的選舉委員會選舉產生;立法會60名議員中分區直選產生的議員已由第一屆立法會的20名增加到第二屆立法會的24名,今年9月產生的第三屆立法會將達至30名。香港實行民主選舉的歷史不長,香港居民行使參與推選特別行政區行政長官的民主權利,至今不到7年。香港回歸祖國以來,立法會中分區直選議員的數量已有相當幅度的增加,在達至分區直選議員和功能團體選舉的議員各佔一半的格局後,對香港社會整體運作的影響,尤其是對行政主導體制的影響尚有待實踐檢驗。加之目前香港社會各界對於2007年以後行政長官和立法會的產生辦法如何確定仍存

the Hong Kong Special Administrative Region shall conform to the principles that it is compatible with the social, economic and political development of Hong Kong and that it is conducive to the balanced participation of all strata, sectors and groups of the society, to the effective operation of the executive-led system, and to the maintenance of long-term prosperity and stability of Hong Kong.

The participants hold that since the establishment of the Hong Kong Special Administrative Region, Hong Kong residents have enjoyed democratic rights that they had never had before. The first Chief Executive was elected by the Selection Committee, which was composed of 400 members. The second Chief Executive was elected by the Election Committee, which was composed of 800 members. Out of the 60 members of the Legislative Council, the number of members returned by geographical constituencies through direct elections has increased from 20 in the Legislative Council in the first term to 24 in the Legislative Council in the second term and will reach 30 in the Legislative Council in the third term to be formed in September this year. Hong Kong does not have a long history of practising democratic elections, and it is not seven years yet since Hong Kong residents exercised the democratic right to participate in the selection of the Chief Executive of the Special Administrative Region. Since the return of Hong Kong to the motherland, the number of members of the Legislative Council returned by geographical constituencies through direct elections has increased by a fairly wide margin. When the setup is such that half of the members are returned by geographical constituencies through direct elections and the other half by functional constituencies, the impact on the operation of the Hong Kong society as a whole, especially the impact on the executive-led system, remains to be tested through practice. Moreover, at present, different sectors of the Hong Kong society have considerable differences on how to determine the methods for selecting the Chief Executive and

Inst 3
(p 189, 191)

227

Art 45, 68

在較大分歧,尚未形成廣泛共識。在此情況下,實現香港基本法第四十五條規定的行政長官由一個有廣泛代表性的提名委員會按民主程序提名後普選產生和香港基本法第六十八條規定的立法會全部議員由普選產生的條件還不具備。

Inst 26 (p 340)

鑑此,全國人大常委會依據香港基本法的有關規定和《全國人民代表大會常務委員會關於〈中華人民共和國香港特別行政區基本法〉附件一第七條和附件二第三條的解釋》,對香港特別行政區2007年行政長官和2008年立法會的產生辦法決定如下:

一、 2007年香港特別行政區第三任行政長官的選舉,不實行由普選產生的辦法。2008年香港特別行政區第四屆立法會的選舉,不實行全部議員由普選產生的辦法,功能團體和分區直選產生的議

for forming the Legislative Council after the year 2007 and have not come to a broad consensus. Such being the case, the conditions do not yet exist for the selection of the Chief Executive by universal suffrage upon nomination by a broadly representative nominating committee in accordance with democratic procedures, as provided for in Article 45 of the Basic Law of Hong Kong, or for the election of all the members of the Legislative Council by universal suffrage, as provided for in Article 68 of the Basic Law of Hong Kong. *Art 45, 68*

In view of the above and pursuant to the relevant provisions of the Basic Law of Hong Kong and the Interpretation by the Standing Committee of the National People's Congress of Annex I (7) and Annex II (III) to the Basic Law of the Hong Kong Special Administrative Region of the People's Republic of China, the Standing Committee of the National People's Congress makes the following decision on the methods for selecting the Chief Executive of the Hong Kong Special Administrative Region in the year 2007 and for forming the Legislative Council of the Hong Kong Special Administrative Region in the year 2008: *Inst 26 (p 341)*

(1) The election of the third Chief Executive of the Hong Kong Special Administrative Region to be held in the year 2007 shall not be conducted by means of universal suffrage. The election of the Legislative Council of the Hong Kong Special Administrative Region in the fourth term in the year 2008 shall not be conducted by means of an election of all the members by universal suffrage, the ratio between the members returned by functional constituencies and the members returned by geographical constituencies through direct elections, who shall respectively occupy half of the seats, is to remain

Anx I (p 124),
Anx II (p 142),
Inst 26 (p 340)

員各佔半數的比例維持不變，立法會對法案、議案的表決程序維持不變。

二、 在不違反本決定第一條的前提下，2007年香港特別行政區第三任行政長官的具體產生辦法和2008年香港特別行政區第四屆立法會的具體產生辦法，可按照香港基本法第四十五條、第六十八條的規定和附件一第七條、附件二第三條的規定作出符合循序漸進原則的適當修改。

Art 45, 68

會議認為，按照香港基本法的規定，在香港特別行政區根據實際情況，循序漸進地發展民主，是中央堅定不移的一貫立場。隨着香港社會各方面的發展和進步，經過香港特別行政區政府和香港居民的共同努力，香港特別行政區的民主制度一定能夠不斷地向前發展，最終達至香港基本法規定的行政長官由一個有廣泛代表性的提名委員會按民主程序提名後普選產生和立法會全部議員由普選產生的目標。

unchanged, and the procedures for voting on bills and motions in the Legislative Council are to remain unchanged.

Anx I (p 125),
Anx II (p 143),
Inst 26 (p 341)

(2) On the premise that Decision (1) is not contravened, appropriate amendments that conform to the principle of gradual and orderly progress may be made to the specific method for selecting the third Chief Executive of the Hong Kong Special Administrative Region in the year 2007 and the specific method for forming the Legislative Council of the Hong Kong Special Administrative Region in the fourth term in the year 2008, in accordance with the provisions of Articles 45 and 68 of the Basic Law of Hong Kong and the provisions of Annex I (7) and Annex II (III) to the Basic Law of Hong Kong.

The participants hold that developing democracy in the Hong Kong Special Administrative Region in the light of the actual situation and in a gradual and orderly manner according to the provisions of the Basic Law of Hong Kong has been the unswerving, consistent position of the Central Authorities. Along with the development and progress in all aspects of the Hong Kong society and through the joint endeavors of the Government of the Hong Kong Special Administrative Region and Hong Kong residents, the democratic system of the Hong Kong Special Administrative Region will certainly progress incessantly, and ultimately attain the aims of selecting the Chief Executive by universal suffrage upon nomination by a broadly representative nominating committee in accordance with democratic procedures and electing all the members of the Legislative Council by universal suffrage, as provided for in the Basic Law of Hong Kong.

Art 45, 68

文件九

全國人民代表大會常務委員會關於授權香港特別行政區對深圳灣口岸港方口岸區實施管轄的決定

（2006年10月31日第十屆全國人民代表大會常務委員會第二十四次會議通過）

第十屆全國人民代表大會常務委員會第二十三次會議審議了國務院關於提請審議授權香港特別行政區對深圳灣口岸港方口岸區實施管轄的議案，第二十四次會議審議了關於授權香港特別行政區對深圳灣口岸港方口岸區實施管轄的決定（草案）。會議認為，為了緩解內地與香港特別行政區交往日益增多帶來的陸路通關壓力，適應深圳市與香港特別行政區之間交通運輸和便利通關的客觀要求，

Instrument 9

Decision of the Standing Committee of the National People's Congress on Empowering the Hong Kong Special Administrative Region to Exercise Jurisdiction over the Shenzhen Bay Port Hong Kong Port Area

(Adopted at the 24th Meeting of the Standing Committee
of the Tenth National People's Congress on October 31, 2006)

At its 23rd Meeting, the Standing Committee of the Tenth National People's Congress discussed the proposal, submitted for deliberation by the State Council, on empowering the Hong Kong Special Administrative Region to exercise jurisdiction over the Shenzhen Bay Port Hong Kong Port Area, and at its 24th Meeting, the Standing Committee discussed the draft decision on empowering the Hong Kong Special Administrative Region to exercise jurisdiction over the Shenzhen Bay Port Hong Kong Port Area. The participants deem that it is necessary to set up the Shenzhen Bay Port Hong Kong Port Area to be exclusively used for the inspection and clearance of personnel, means of transportation and goods, in order to slacken the strain on the overland clearance caused by the daily increase in the exchange between the mainland and the Hong Kong Special Administrative Region, to meet the objective need of transportation and

促進內地和香港特別行政區之間的人員交流和經貿往來，推動兩地經濟共同發展，在深圳灣口岸內設立港方口岸區，專用於人員、交通工具、貨物的通關查驗，是必要的。全國人民代表大會常務委員會決定：

一、 授權香港特別行政區自深圳灣口岸啟用之日起，對該口岸所設港方口岸區依照香港特別行政區法律實施管轄。

香港特別行政區對深圳灣口岸港方口岸區實行禁區式管理。

二、 深圳灣口岸港方口岸區的範圍，由國務院規定。

三、 深圳灣口岸港方口岸區土地使用期限，由國務院依照有關法律的規定確定。

convenient clearance between Shenzhen City and the Hong Kong Special Administrative Region , to promote personnel exchange, economic contact and trade between the mainland and the Hong Kong Special Administrative Region, and to push forward the joint economic development of the two regions. The Standing Committee of the National People's Congress has made the decision as follows:

1. It empowers the Hong Kong Special Administrative Region to exercise, in accordance with the laws of Hong Kong Special Administrative Region, jurisdiction over the Shenzhen Bay Port Hong Kong Port Area, beginning from the date the port is put to use.

   The Hong Kong Special Administrative Region shall carry out out-of-bounds administration over the Shenzhen Bay Port Hong Kong Port Area.

2. The scope of the Shenzhen Bay Port Hong Kong Port Area shall be defined by the State Council.

3. The term of land use of the Shenzhen Bay Port Hong Kong Port Area shall be determined by the State Council in accordance with the provisions of relevant laws.

文件十

全國人民代表大會常務委員會
關於香港特別行政區2012年行政長官和
立法會產生辦法及有關普選問題的決定

(2007年12月29日第十屆全國人民代表大會
常務委員會第三十一次會議通過)

第十屆全國人民代表大會常務委員會第三十一次會議審議了香港特別行政區行政長官曾蔭權2007年12月12日提交的《關於香港特別行政區政制發展諮詢情況及2012年行政長官和立法會產生辦法是否需要修改的報告》。會議認為，2012年香港特別行政區第四任行政長官的具體產生辦法和第五屆立法會的具體產生辦法可以作出適當修改；

Instrument 10

Decision of the Standing Committee of the National People's Congress on Issues Relating to the Methods for Selecting the Chief Executive of the Hong Kong Special Administrative Region and for Forming the Legislative Council of the Hong Kong Special Administrative Region in the Year 2012 and on Issues Relating to Universal Suffrage

Art 45, 68

(Adopted by the Standing Committee of the Tenth National People's Congress at its Thirty-first Meeting on 29 December 2007)

At its 31st Meeting, the Standing Committee of the Tenth National People's Congress deliberated the Report on the Public Consultation on Constitutional Development and on Whether There is a Need to Amend the Methods for Selecting the Chief Executive of the Hong Kong Special Administrative Region and for Forming the Legislative Council of the Hong Kong Special Administrative Region in 2012, submitted by Tsang Yam-kuen, the Chief Executive of the Hong Kong Special Administrative Region, on 12 December 2007. It is held at the Meeting that appropriate amendments may be made to the specific method for selecting the fourth Chief Executive and the specific method for forming the fifth term Legislative Council of the Hong Kong

Note:
This English translation is reproduced from "The Laws of the People's Republic of China 2007" compiled by the Legislative Affairs Commission of the Standing Committee of the National People's Congress of the People's Republic of China. It is for reference only and has no legislative effect.

2017年香港特別行政區第五任行政長官的選舉可以實行由普選產生的辦法；在行政長官由普選產生以後，香港特別行政區立法會的選舉可以實行全部議員由普選產生的辦法。全國人民代表大會常務委員會根據《中華人民共和國香港特別行政區基本法》的有關規定和《全國人民代表大會常務委員會關於〈中華人民共和國香港特別行政區基本法〉附件一第七條和附件二第三條的解釋》決定如下：

一、 2012年香港特別行政區第四任行政長官的選舉，不實行由普選產生的辦法。2012年香港特別行政區第五屆立法會的選舉，不實行全部議員由普選產生的辦法，功能團體和分區直選產生的議員各佔半數的比例維持不變，立法會對法案、議案的表決程序維持不變。在此前提下，2012年

Inst 26 (p 340)

Special Administrative Region in the year 2012; that the election of the fifth Chief Executive of the Hong Kong Special Administrative Region in year 2017 may be implemented by the method of universal suffrage; that after the Chief Executive is selected by universal suffrage, the election of the Legislative Council of the Hong Kong Special Administrative Region may be implemented by the method of electing all the members by universal suffrage. Pursuant to the relevant provisions of the Basic Law of the Hong Kong Special Administrative Region of the People's Republic of China and the Interpretation by the Standing Committee of the National People's Congress of Article 7 of Annex I and Article III of Annex II to the Basic Law of the Hong Kong Special Administrative Region of the People's Republic of China, the Standing Committee of the National People's Congress hereby makes the following decision:

Inst 26 (p 341)

1. The election of the fourth Chief Executive of the Hong Kong Special Administrative Region in the year 2012 shall not be implemented by the method of universal suffrage. The election of the fifth term Legislative Council of the Hong Kong Special Administrative Region in year 2012 shall not be implemented by the method of electing all the members by universal suffrage. The half-and-half ratio between members returned by functional constituencies and members returned by geographical constituencies through direct elections shall remain unchanged. The procedures for voting on bills and motions in the Legislative Council shall remain unchanged. Subject to the aforementioned, appropriate amendments conforming to the principle of gradual and orderly progress may be made to the specific method for selecting the fourth Chief Executive of the Hong Kong Special Administrative Region in the year 2012 and the specific method for forming the fifth term Legislative

香港特別行政區第四任行政長官的具體產生辦法和2012年香港特別行政區第五屆立法會的具體產生辦法，可按照《中華人民共和國香港特別行政區基本法》第四十五條、第六十八條的規定和附件一第七條、附件二第三條的規定作出符合循序漸進原則的適當修改。

二、 在香港特別行政區行政長官實行普選前的適當時候，行政長官須按照香港基本法的有關規定和《全國人民代表大會常務委員會關於〈中華人民共和國香港特別行政區基本法〉附件一第七條和附件二第三條的解釋》，就行政長官產生辦法的修改問題向全國人民代表大會常務委員會提出報告，由全國人民代表大會常務委員會確定。修改行政長官產生辦法的法案及其修正案，應由香港特別行政區政府向立法會提出，經立法會全體議員三分之二多數通過，行政長官同意，報全國人民代表大會常務委員會批准。

Council of the Hong Kong Special Administrative Region in the year 2012 in accordance with the provisions of Articles 45 and 68, and those of Article 7 of Annex I and Article III of Annex II to the Basic Law of the Hong Kong Special Administrative Region of the People's Republic of China. *Inst 45, 68, Inst 26 (p 341)*

2. At an appropriate time prior to the selection of the Chief Executive of the Hong Kong Special Administrative Region by universal suffrage, the Chief Executive shall make a report to the Standing Committee of the National People's Congress as regards the issue of amending the method for selecting the Chief Executive in accordance with the relevant provisions of the Hong Kong Basic Law and the Interpretation by the Standing Committee of the National People's Congress of Article 7 of Annex I and Article III of Annex II to the Basic Law of the Hong Kong Special Administrative Region of the People's Republic of China; a determination thereon shall be made by the Standing Committee of the National People's Congress. The bills on the amendments to the method for selecting the Chief Executive and the proposed amendments to such bills shall be introduced by the Government of the Hong Kong Special Administrative Region to the Legislative Council; such amendments must be made with the endorsement of a two-thirds majority of all the members of the Legislative Council and the consent of the Chief Executive and they shall be reported to the Standing Committee of the National People's Congress for approval. *Inst 26 (p 341)* *Art 159*

Inst 26 (p 340)

三、 在香港特別行政區立法會全部議員實行普選前的適當時候，行政長官須按照香港基本法的有關規定和《全國人民代表大會常務委員會關於〈中華人民共和國香港特別行政區基本法〉附件一第七條和附件二第三條的解釋》，就立法會產生辦法的修改問題以及立法會表決程序是否相應作出修改的問題向全國人民代表大會常務委員會提出報告，由全國人民代表大會常務委員會確定。修改立法會產生辦法和立法會法案、議案表決程序的法案及其修正案，應由香港特別行政區政府向立法會提出，經立法會全體議員三分之二多數通過，行政長官同意，報全國人民代表大會常務委員會備案。

Inst 26 (p 341)

3. At an appropriate time prior to the election of all the members of the Legislative Council of the Hong Kong Special Administrative Region by universal suffrage, the Chief Executive shall make a report to the Standing Committee of the National People's Congress as regards the issue of amending the method for forming the Legislative Council and the issue of whether any corresponding amendment should be made to the procedures for voting on bills and motions in the Legislative Council in accordance with the relevant provisions of the Hong Kong Basic Law and the Interpretation by the Standing Committee of the National People's Congress of Article 7 of Annex I and Article III of Annex II to the Basic Law of the Hong Kong Special Administrative Region of the People's Republic of China; a determination thereon shall be made by the Standing Committee of the National People's Congress. The bills on the amendments to the method for forming the Legislative Council and its procedures for voting on bills and motions and the proposed amendments to such bills shall be introduced by the Government of the Hong Kong Special Administrative Region to the Legislative Council; such amendments must be made with the endorsement of a two-thirds majority of all the members of the Legislative Council and the consent of the Chief Executive and they shall be reported to the Standing Committee of the National People's Congress for the record.

Inst 8 (p 222)

四、 香港特別行政區行政長官的產生辦法、立法會
的產生辦法和法案、議案表決程序如果未能依
照法定程序作出修改，行政長官的產生辦法繼
續適用上一任行政長官的產生辦法，立法會的
產生辦法和法案、議案表決程序繼續適用上一
屆立法會的產生辦法和法案、議案表決程序。

Art 45

會議認為，根據香港基本法第四十五條的規定，在香
港特別行政區行政長官實行普選產生的辦法時，須組成一
個有廣泛代表性的提名委員會。提名委員會可參照香港基
本法附件一有關選舉委員會的現行規定組成。提名委員會
須按照民主程序提名產生若干名行政長官候選人，由香港
特別行政區全體合資格選民普選產生行政長官人選，報中
央人民政府任命。

會議認為，經過香港特別行政區政府和香港市民的共
同努力，香港特別行政區的民主制度一定能夠不斷向前發
展，並按照香港基本法和本決定的規定，實現行政長官和
立法會全部議員由普選產生的目標。

4.   If no amendment is made to the method for selecting the Chief Executive, the method for forming the Legislative Council or its procedures for voting on bills and motions in accordance with the legal procedures, the method for selecting the Chief Executive used for the preceding term shall continue to apply, and the method for forming the Legislative Council and the procedures for voting on bills and motions used for the preceding term shall continue to apply.

Inst 8 (p 223)

It is held at the Meeting that in accordance with the provisions of Article 45 of the Hong Kong Basic Law, in selecting the Chief Executive of the Hong Kong Special Administrative Region by the method of universal suffrage, a broadly representative nominating committee shall be formed. The nominating committee may be formed with reference to the current provisions regarding the Election Committee in Annex I to the Hong Kong Basic Law. The nominating committee shall in accordance with democratic procedures nominate a certain number of candidates for the office of the Chief Executive, who is to be elected through universal suffrage by all registered electors of the Hong Kong Special Administrative Region, and to be appointed by the Central People's Government.

Art 45

It is held at the Meeting that with the joint efforts of the Government of the Hong Kong Special Administrative Region and the people of Hong Kong, the democratic system of the Hong Kong Special Administrative Region will definitely make progress continuously, and that the aim of the selection of the Chief Executive and the election of all the members of the Legislative Council by universal suffrage will be realized in accordance with the Hong Kong Basic Law and this Decision.

文件十一

Art 45,
Anx I (p 124)

全國人民代表大會常務委員會關於批准 《中華人民共和國香港特別行政區基本法 附件一香港特別行政區行政長官的 產生辦法修正案》的決定

(2010年8月28日第十一屆全國人民代表大會
常務委員會第十六次會議通過)

Anx I (p 124),
Inst 10 (p 236),
Inst 26 (p 340)

第十一屆全國人民代表大會常務委員會第十六次會議決定：

　　根據《中華人民共和國香港特別行政區基本法》附件一、《全國人民代表大會常務委員會關於〈中華人民共和國香港特別行政區基本法〉附件一第七條和附件二第三條的解釋》和《全國人民代表大會常務委員會關於香港特

Instrument 11

Decision of the Standing Committee of the National People's Congress on Approving the Amendment to Annex I to the Basic Law of the Hong Kong Special Administrative Region of the People's Republic of China Concerning the Method for the Selection of the Chief Executive of the Hong Kong Special Administrative Region

Art 45, Anx I (p 125)

(Adopted at the Sixteenth Meeting of the Standing Committee of the Eleventh National People's Congress on 28 August 2010)

At its 16th Meeting, the Standing Committee of the Eleventh National People's Congress decides as follows:

Anx I (p 125), Inst 10 (p 236), Inst 26 (p 341)

In accordance to Annex I to the Basic Law of the Hong Kong Special Administrative Region of the People's Republic of China, the Interpretation by the Standing Committee of the National People's Congress of Article 7 of Annex I and Article III of Annex II to the Basic Law of the Hong Kong Special Administrative Region of the People's Republic of China and the Decision of the Standing Committee of the National People's Congress on Issues Relating to the Methods for the Selection of the Chief Executive of the Hong Kong Special Administrative Region and for Forming the Legislative Council of the Hong Kong Special

---

Note:

This English translation is reproduced from "The Laws of the People's Republic of China 2010" compiled by the Legislative Affairs Commission of the Standing Committee of the National People's Congress of the People's Republic of China. It is for reference only and has no legislative effect.

別行政區2012年行政長官和立法會產生辦法及有關普選問題的決定》，批准香港特別行政區提出的《中華人民共和國香港特別行政區基本法附件一香港特別行政區行政長官的產生辦法修正案》。

《中華人民共和國香港特別行政區基本法附件一香港特別行政區行政長官的產生辦法修正案》自批准之日起生效。

Administrative Region in the Year 2012 and on Issues Relating to Universal Suffrage, the Amendment to Annex I to the Basic Law of the Hong Kong Special Administrative Region of the People's Republic of China Concerning the Method for the Selection of the Chief Executive of the Hong Kong Special Administrative Region proposed by the Hong Kong Special Administrative Region is hereby approved.

The Amendment to Annex I to the Basic Law of the Hong Kong Special Administrative Region of the People's Republic of China Concerning the Method for the Selection of the Chief Executive of the Hong Kong Special Administrative Region shall come into effect as of the date of approval.

附

中華人民共和國香港特別行政區基本法附件一 香港特別行政區行政長官的產生辦法修正案

(2010年8月28日第十一屆全國人民代表大會
常務委員會第十六次會議批准)

一、 二〇一二年選舉第四任行政長官人選的選舉委
員會共1200人,由下列各界人士組成:

工商、金融界	300人
專業界	300人
勞工、社會服務、宗教等界	300人

Appendix

Amendment to Annex I to the Basic Law of the Hong Kong Special Administrative Region of the People's Republic of China Concerning the Method for the Selection of the Chief Executive of the Hong Kong Special Administrative Region

(Approved at the Sixteenth Meeting of the Standing Committee of the Eleventh National People's Congress on 28 August 2010)

1. The Election Committee for electing the fourth-term Chief Executive in 2012 shall be composed of 1200 members from the following sectors:

Industrial, commercial and financial sectors	300
The professions	300
Labour, social services, religious and other sectors	300

立法會議員、區議會議員的代表、
　　鄉議局的代表、香港特別行政區全
　　國人大代表、香港特別行政區全國
　　政協委員的代表　　　　　　　300人
選舉委員會每屆任期五年。

二、不少於一百五十名的選舉委員可聯合提名行政
　　長官候選人。每名委員只可提出一名候選人。

Members of the Legislative Council,
representatives of members of the District
Councils, representatives of the Heung Yee
Kuk, Hong Kong deputies to the National
People's Congress, and representatives of
Hong Kong members of the National
Committee of the Chinese People's Political
Consultative Conference   300

The term of office of the Election Committee shall be
five years.

2.   Candidates for the office of Chief Executive may be
     nominated jointly by not less than 150 members of the
     Election Committee. Each member may nominate only
     one candidate.

文件十二

文件十二

Anx II (p 142),
Inst 10 (p 236),
Inst 26 (p 340)

全國人民代表大會常務委員會公告
〔十一屆〕第十五號

根據《中華人民共和國香港特別行政區基本法》附件二、《全國人民代表大會常務委員會關於〈中華人民共和國香港特別行政區基本法〉附件一第七條和附件二第三條的解釋》和《全國人民代表大會常務委員會關於香港特別行政區2012年行政長官和立法會產生辦法及有關普選問題的決定》，全國人民代表大會常務委員會對《中華人民共和國香港特別行政區基本法附件二香港特別行政區立法會的產生辦法和表決程序修正案》予以備案，現予公布。

Instrument 12

Proclamation of the Standing Committee of the National People's Congress (Eleventh National People's Congress) No. 15

Anx II (p 143),
Inst 10 (p 237),
Inst 26 (p 341)

It is promulgated that pursuant to Annex II to the Basic Law of the Hong Kong Special Administrative Region of the People's Republic of China, "The Interpretation by the Standing Committee of the National People's Congress of Article 7 of Annex I and Article III of Annex II to the Basic Law of the Hong Kong Special Administrative Region of the People's Republic of China" and the "Decision of the Standing Committee of the National People's Congress on Issues Relating to the Methods for Selecting the Chief Executive of the Hong Kong Special Administrative Region and for Forming the Legislative Council of the Hong Kong Special Administrative Region in the Year 2012 and on Issues Relating to Universal Suffrage", the "Amendment to Annex II to the Basic Law of the Hong Kong Special Administrative Region of the People's Republic of China Concerning the Method for the Formation of the Legislative Council of the Hong Kong Special Administrative Region and Its Voting Procedures" is recorded by the Standing Committee of the National People's Congress.

Note:

This English translation is prepared by the Department of Justice, Government of the Hong Kong Special Administrative Region. It is for reference only and has no legislative effect.

　　《中華人民共和國香港特別行政區基本法附件二香港特別行政區立法會的產生辦法和表決程序修正案》自公布之日起生效。

　　特此公告。

全國人民代表大會常務委員會

2010年8月28日

The "Amendment to Annex II to the Basic Law of the Hong Kong Special Administrative Region of the People's Republic of China Concerning the Method for the Formation of the Legislative Council of the Hong Kong Special Administrative Region and Its Voting Procedures" comes into effect on the date of promulgation.

This proclamation is hereby made.

Standing Committee of the National People's Congress
28 August 2010

附

中華人民共和國香港特別行政區基本法附件二
香港特別行政區立法會的產生辦法和
表決程序修正案

(2010年8月28日第十一屆全國人民代表大會
常務委員會第十六次會議予以備案)

二〇一二年第五屆立法會共70名議員,其組成如下:

功能團體選舉的議員	35人
分區直接選舉的議員	35人

Appendix

Amendment to Annex II to the Basic Law of the Hong Kong Special Administrative Region of the People's Republic of China Concerning the Method for the Formation of the Legislative Council of the Hong Kong Special Administrative Region and Its Voting Procedures

Anx II (p 143)

(Recorded at the Sixteenth Meeting of the Standing Committee of the Eleventh National People's Congress on 28 August 2010)

The fifth-term Legislative Council in the year 2012 shall be composed of 70 members, and the composition shall be as follows:

Members returned by functional constituencies	35
Members returned by geographical constituencies through direct elections	35

Note:

This English translation is reproduced from "The Laws of the People's Republic of China 2010" compiled by the Legislative Affairs Commission of the Standing Committee of the National People's Congress of the People's Republic of China. It is for reference only and has no legislative effect.

文件十三

全國人民代表大會常務委員會關於
香港特別行政區行政長官普選問題和
2016年立法會產生辦法的決定

Art 45, 68
Anx I (p 124),
Anx II (p 142),
Inst 10 (p 236),
Inst 11 (p 246)

（2014年8月31日第十二屆全國人民代表大會
常務委員會第十次會議通過）

第十二屆全國人民代表大會常務委員會第十次會議審議了香港特別行政區行政長官梁振英2014年7月15日提交的《關於香港特別行政區2017年行政長官及2016年立法會產生辦法是否需要修改的報告》，並在審議中充分考慮了香港社會的有關意見和建議。

Inst 10 (p 236)

會議指出，2007年12月29日第十屆全國人民代表大會常務委員會第三十一次會議通過的《全國人民代表大會常務委員會關於香港特別行政區2012年行政長官和立法會產生辦法及有關普選問題的決定》規定，2017年香港特

Instrument 13

Decision of the Standing Committee of the National People's Congress on Issues Relating to the Selection of the Chief Executive of the Hong Kong Special Administrative Region by Universal Suffrage and on the Method for Forming the Legislative Council of the Hong Kong Special Administrative Region in the Year 2016

Art 45, 68
Anx I (p 125),
Anx II (p 143),
Inst 10 (p 236),
Inst 11 (p 246)

(Adopted at the Tenth Session of the Standing Committee
of the Twelfth National People's Congress on 31 August 2014)

The Standing Committee of the Twelfth National People's Congress considered at its Tenth Session the Report on whether there is a need to amend the methods for selecting the Chief Executive of the Hong Kong Special Administrative Region in 2017 and for forming the Legislative Council of the Hong Kong Special Administrative Region in 2016 submitted by Leung Chun-ying, the Chief Executive of the Hong Kong Special Administrative Region, on 15 July 2014. In the course of deliberation, the relevant views and suggestions of the Hong Kong community were given full consideration.

The Session points out that according to the Decision of the Standing Committee of the National People's Congress on Issues Relating to the Methods for Selecting the Chief Executive of the Hong Kong Special Administrative Region and for Forming the Legislative Council of the Hong Kong Special Administrative Region in the Year 2012 and on Issues Relating to Universal

Inst 10 (p 236)

Note:
    This English translation is for reference only and has no legislative effect.

Inst 26 (p 340)

別行政區第五任行政長官的選舉可以實行由普選產生的辦法；在行政長官實行普選前的適當時候，行政長官須按照香港基本法的有關規定和《全國人民代表大會常務委員會關於〈中華人民共和國香港特別行政區基本法〉附件一第七條和附件二第三條的解釋》，就行政長官產生辦法的修改問題向全國人民代表大會常務委員會提出報告，由全國人民代表大會常務委員會確定。2013年12月4日至2014年5月3日，香港特別行政區政府就2017行政長官產生辦法和2016年立法會產生辦法進行了廣泛、深入的公眾諮詢。諮詢過程中，香港社會普遍希望2017年實現行政長官由普選產生，並就行政長官普選辦法必須符合香港基本法和全國人大常委會有關決定、行政長官必須由愛國愛港人士擔任等重要原則形成了廣泛共識。對於2017年行政長官普選辦法和2016年立法會產生辦法，香港社會提出了各種意見和建議。在此基礎上，香港特別行政區行政長官

Suffrage adopted by the Standing Committee of the Tenth National People's Congress at its Thirty-first Session on 29 December 2007, the election of the fifth Chief Executive of the Hong Kong Special Administrative Region in the year 2017 may be implemented by the method of universal suffrage; at an appropriate time prior to the selection of the Chief Executive of the Hong Kong Special Administrative Region by universal suffrage, the Chief Executive shall make a report to the Standing Committee of the National People's Congress as regards the issue of amending the method for selecting the Chief Executive in accordance with the relevant provisions of the Hong Kong Basic Law and the Interpretation by the Standing Committee of the National People's Congress of Article 7 of Annex I and Article III of Annex II to the Basic Law of the Hong Kong Special Administrative Region of the People's Republic of China, and a determination thereon shall be made by the Standing Committee of the National People's Congress. From 4 December 2013 to 3 May 2014, the Government of the Hong Kong Special Administrative Region conducted an extensive and in-depth public consultation on the methods for selecting the Chief Executive in 2017 and for forming the Legislative Council in 2016. In the course of consultation, the Hong Kong community generally expressed the hope to see the selection of the Chief Executive by universal suffrage in 2017, and broad consensus was reached on important principles such as: the method for selecting the Chief Executive by universal suffrage shall comply with the Hong Kong Basic Law and the relevant Decisions of the Standing Committee of the National People's Congress and the Chief Executive shall be a person who loves the country and loves Hong Kong. With respect to the methods for selecting the Chief Executive by universal suffrage in 2017 and for forming the Legislative Council in 2016, the Hong Kong community put forward various views and suggestions. It was on this basis that

Inst 26 (p 341)

Inst 26 (p 340)

就2017年行政長官和2016年立法會產生辦法修改問題向全國人大常委會提出報告。會議認為，行政長官的報告符合香港基本法、全國人大常委會關於香港基本法附件一第七條和附件二第三條的解釋以及全國人大常委會有關決定的要求，全面、客觀地反映了公眾諮詢的情況，是一個積極、負責、務實的報告。

Art 45

會議認為，實行行政長官普選，是香港民主發展的歷史性進步，也是香港特別行政區政治體制的重大變革，關係到香港長期繁榮穩定，關係到國家主權、安全和發展利益，必須審慎、穩步推進。香港特別行政區行政長官普選源於香港基本法第四十五條第二款的規定，即"行政長官的產生辦法根據香港特別行政區的實際情況和循序漸進的原則而規定，最終達至由一個有廣泛代表性的提名委員會按民主程序提名後普選產生的目標。"制定行政長官普

the Chief Executive of the Hong Kong Special Administrative Region made a report to the Standing Committee of the National People's Congress on issues relating to amending the methods for selecting the Chief Executive in 2017 and for forming the Legislative Council in 2016. The Session is of the view that the report complies with the requirements of the Hong Kong Basic Law, the Interpretation by the Standing Committee of the National People's Congress of Article 7 of Annex I and Article III of Annex II to the Hong Kong Basic Law and the relevant Decisions of the Standing Committee of the National People's Congress, and reflects comprehensively and objectively the views collected during the public consultation; and is thus a positive, responsible and pragmatic report.

Inst 26 (p 341)

The Session is of the view that implementing universal suffrage for the selection of the Chief Executive represents a historic progress in Hong Kong's democratic development and a significant change in the political structure of the Hong Kong Special Administrative Region. Since the long-term prosperity and stability of Hong Kong and the sovereignty, security and development interests of the country are at stake, there is a need to proceed in a prudent and steady manner. The selection of the Chief Executive of the Hong Kong Special Administrative Region by universal suffrage has its origin in Paragraph 2 of Article 45 of the Hong Kong Basic Law: "The method for selecting the Chief Executive shall be specified in the light of the actual situation in the Hong Kong Special Administrative Region and in accordance with the principle of gradual and orderly progress. The ultimate aim is the selection of the Chief Executive by universal suffrage upon nomination by a broadly representative nominating committee in accordance with democratic procedures." The formulation of the method for selecting the Chief Executive by universal suffrage must strictly comply with the relevant provisions of the Hong Kong Basic Law, accord with

Art 45

選辦法，必須嚴格遵循香港基本法有關規定，符合"一國兩制"的原則，符合香港特別行政區的法律地位，兼顧社會各階層的利益，體現均衡參與，有利於資本主義經濟發展，循序漸進地發展適合香港實際情況的民主制度。鑒於香港社會對如何落實香港基本法有關行政長官普選的規定存在較大爭議，全國人大常委會對正確實施香港基本法和決定行政長官產生辦法負有憲制責任，有必要就行政長官普選辦法的一些核心問題作出規定，以促進香港社會凝聚共識，依法順利實現行政長官普選。

Art 43

會議認為，按照香港基本法的規定，香港特別行政區行政長官既要對香港特別行政區負責，也要對中央人民政府負責，必須堅持行政長官由愛國愛港人士擔任的原則。這是"一國兩制"方針政策的基本要求，是行政長官的法律地位和重要職責所決定的，是保持香港長期繁榮穩定，

the principle of "one country, two systems", and befit the legal status of the Hong Kong Special Administrative Region. It must meet the interests of different sectors of the society, achieve balanced participation, be conducive to the development of the capitalist economy, and make gradual and orderly progress in developing a democratic system that suits the actual situation in Hong Kong. Given the divergent views within the Hong Kong community on how to implement the Hong Kong Basic Law provisions on universal suffrage for selecting the Chief Executive, and in light of the constitutional responsibility of the Standing Committee of the National People's Congress for the proper implementation of the Hong Kong Basic Law and for deciding on the method for the selection of the Chief Executive, the Standing Committee of the National People's Congress finds it necessary to make provisions on certain core issues concerning the method for selecting the Chief Executive by universal suffrage, so as to facilitate the building of consensus within the Hong Kong community and the attainment of universal suffrage for the selection of the Chief Executive smoothly and in accordance with law.

The Session is of the view that since the Chief Executive of the Hong Kong Special Administrative Region shall be accountable to both the Hong Kong Special Administrative Region and the Central People's Government in accordance with the provisions of the Hong Kong Basic Law, the principle that the Chief Executive has to be a person who loves the country and loves Hong Kong must be upheld. This is a basic requirement of the policy of "one country, two systems". It is determined by the legal status as well as important functions and duties of the Chief Executive, and is called for by the actual need to maintain long-term prosperity and stability of Hong Kong and uphold the sovereignty, security and development interests of the country. The method for selecting the Chief Executive by universal

Art 43

維護國家主權、安全和發展利益的客觀需要。行政長官普選辦法必須為此提供相應的制度保障。

Anx II (p 142),
Inst 10 (p 236)

會議認為，2012年香港特別行政區第五屆立法會產生辦法經過修改後，已經向擴大民主的方向邁出了重大步伐。香港基本法附件二規定的現行立法會產生辦法和表決程序不作修改，2016年第六屆立法會產生辦法和表決程序繼續適用現行規定，符合循序漸進地發展適合香港實際情況的民主制度的原則，符合香港社會的多數意見，也有利於香港社會各界集中精力優先處理行政長官普選問題，從而為行政長官實行普選後實現立法會全部議員由普選產生的目標創造條件。

Inst 10 (p 236),
Inst 26 (p 340)

鑒此，全國人民代表大會常務委員會根據《中華人民共和國香港特別行政區基本法》、《全國人民代表大會常務委員會關於〈中華人民共和國香港特別行政區基本法〉附件一第七條和附件二第三條的解釋》和《全國人民代表大會常務委員會關於香港特別行政區2012年行政長官和立法會產生辦法及有關普選問題的決定》的有關規定，決定如下：

suffrage must provide corresponding institutional safeguards for this purpose.

The Session is of the view that the amendments made to the method for forming the fifth term Legislative Council in 2012 represented major strides towards the direction of enhancing democracy. The existing formation method and voting procedures for the Legislative Council as prescribed in Annex II to the Hong Kong Basic Law will not be amended, and will continue to apply in respect of the sixth term Legislative Council in 2016. This is consistent with the principle of gradual and orderly progress in developing a democratic system that suits Hong Kong's actual situation and conforms to the majority view in the Hong Kong community. It also helps the various sectors of the Hong Kong community to focus their efforts on addressing the issues concerning universal suffrage for selecting the Chief Executive first, thus creating the conditions for attaining the aim of electing all the members of the Legislative Council by universal suffrage after the implementation of universal suffrage for the selection of the Chief Executive.

Anx II (p 143), Inst 10 (p 237)

Accordingly, pursuant to the relevant provisions of the Basic Law of the Hong Kong Special Administrative Region of the People's Republic of China, the Interpretation by the Standing Committee of the National People's Congress of Article 7 of Annex I and Article III of Annex II to the Basic Law of the Hong Kong Special Administrative Region of the People's Republic of China and the Decision of the Standing Committee of the National People's Congress on Issues Relating to the Methods for Selecting the Chief Executive of the Hong Kong Special Administrative Region and for Forming the Legislative Council of the Hong Kong Special Administrative Region in the Year 2012 and on Issues Relating to Universal Suffrage, the Standing Committee of the National People's Congress makes the following decision:

Inst 10 (p 237), Inst 26 (p 341)

一、 從2017年開始，香港特別行政區行政長官選舉可以實行由普選產生的辦法。

二、 香港特別行政區行政長官選舉實行由普選產生的辦法時：

Inst 10 (p 236)

    （一）　須組成一個有廣泛代表性的提名委員會。提名委員會的人數、構成和委員產生辦法按照第四任行政長官選舉委員會的人數、構成和委員產生辦法而規定。

    （二）　提名委員會按民主程序提名產生二至三名行政長官候選人。每名候選人均須獲得提名委員會全體委員半數以上的支持。

    （三）　香港特別行政區合資格選民均有行政長官選舉權，依法從行政長官候選人中選出一名行政長官人選。

Art 45

    （四）　行政長官人選經普選產生後，由中央人民政府任命。

I.   Starting from 2017, the selection of the Chief Executive of the Hong Kong Special Administrative Region may be implemented by the method of universal suffrage.

II. When the selection of the Chief Executive of the Hong Kong Special Administrative Region is implemented by the method of universal suffrage:

    (1)   A broadly representative nominating committee shall be formed. The provisions for the number of members, composition and formation method of the nominating committee shall be made in accordance with the number of members, composition and formation method of the Election Committee for the Fourth Chief Executive. *Inst 10 (p 237)*

    (2)   The nominating committee shall nominate two to three candidates for the office of Chief Executive in accordance with democratic procedures. Each candidate must have the endorsement of more than half of all the members of the nominating committee.

    (3)   All eligible electors of the Hong Kong Special Administrative Region have the right to vote in the election of the Chief Executive and elect one of the candidates for the office of Chief Executive in accordance with law.

    (4)   The Chief Executive-elect, after being selected through universal suffrage, will have to be appointed by the Central People's Government. *Art 45*

Anx I (p 124),
Art 159

三、 行政長官普選的具體辦法依照法定程序通過修改《中華人民共和國香港特別行政區基本法》附件一《香港特別行政區行政長官的產生辦法》予以規定。修改法案及其修正案應由香港特別行政區政府根據香港基本法和本決定的規定,向香港特別行政區立法會提出,經立法會全體議員三分之二多數通過,行政長官同意,報全國人民代表大會常務委員會批准。

Inst 10 (p 236)

四、 如行政長官普選的具體辦法未能經法定程序獲得通過,行政長官的選舉繼續適用上一任行政長官的產生辦法。

Anx II (p 142),
Inst 10 (p 236),
Inst 26 (p 340)

五、 香港基本法附件二關於立法會產生辦法和表決程序的現行規定不作修改,2016年香港特別行政區第六屆立法會產生辦法和表決程序,繼續適用第五屆立法會產生辦法和法案、議案表決程序。在行政長官由普選產生以後,香港特別行政區立法會的選舉可以實行全部議員由普選產生的辦法。在立法會實行普選前的適當時候,由普選產生的行政長官按照香港基本法的有關規定和《全國人民代表大會常務委員會關於〈中華

III. The specific method of universal suffrage for selecting the Chief Executive shall be prescribed in accordance with legal procedures through amending Annex I to the Basic Law of the Hong Kong Special Administrative Region of the People's Republic of China: The Method for the Selection of the Chief Executive of the Hong Kong Special Administrative Region. The bill on the amendments and the proposed amendments to such bill shall be introduced by the Hong Kong Special Administrative Region Government to the Legislative Council of the Hong Kong Special Administrative Region in accordance with the Hong Kong Basic Law and the provisions of this Decision. Such amendments shall obtain the endorsement of a two-thirds majority of all the members of the Legislative Council and the consent of the Chief Executive before being submitted to the Standing Committee of the National People's Congress for approval.

Anx I (p 125)

IV. If the specific method of universal suffrage for selecting the Chief Executive is not adopted in accordance with legal procedures, the method used for selecting the Chief Executive for the preceding term shall continue to apply.

Inst 10 (p 236)

V. The existing formation method and voting procedures for the Legislative Council as prescribed in Annex II to the Hong Kong Basic Law will not be amended. The formation method and procedures for voting on bills and motions of the fifth term Legislative Council will continue to apply to the sixth term Legislative Council of the Hong Kong Special Administrative Region in 2016. After the election of the Chief Executive by universal suffrage, the election of all the members of the Legislative Council of the Hong Kong Special

Anx II (p 143),
Inst 10 (p 237),
Inst 26 (p 341)

人民共和國香港特別行政區基本法〉附件一第
七條和附件二第三條的解釋》,就立法會產生辦
法的修改問題向全國人民代表大會常務委員會
提出報告,由全國人民代表大會常務委員會確
定。

　　會議強調,堅定不移地貫徹落實"一國兩制"、"港人
治港"、高度自治方針政策,嚴格按照香港基本法辦事,穩
步推進2017年行政長官由普選產生,是中央的一貫立場。
希望香港特別行政區政府和香港社會各界依照香港基本
法和本決定的規定,共同努力,達至行政長官由普選產生
的目標。

Administrative Region may be implemented by the method of universal suffrage. At an appropriate time prior to the election of the Legislative Council by universal suffrage, the Chief Executive elected by universal suffrage shall submit a report to the Standing Committee of the National People's Congress in accordance with the relevant provisions of the Hong Kong Basic Law and the Interpretation by the Standing Committee of the National People's Congress of Article 7 of Annex I and Article III of Annex II to the Basic Law of the Hong Kong Special Administrative Region of the People's Republic of China as regards the issue of amending the method for forming the Legislative Council. A determination thereon shall be made by the Standing Committee of the National People's Congress.

The Session stresses that it is the consistent position of the Central Authorities to implement resolutely and firmly the principles of "one country, two systems", "Hong Kong people administering Hong Kong" and a high degree of autonomy, strictly adhere to the Hong Kong Basic Law and steadily take forward the selection of the Chief Executive by universal suffrage in 2017. It is hoped that the Hong Kong Special Administrative Region Government and all sectors of the Hong Kong community will act in accordance with the provisions of the Hong Kong Basic Law and this Decision and jointly work towards the attainment of the aim of selecting the Chief Executive by universal suffrage.

文件十四

全國人民代表大會常務委員會關於批准 《內地與香港特別行政區關於在廣深港高鐵 西九龍站設立口岸實施"一地兩檢"的 合作安排》的決定

（2017年12月27日第十二屆全國人民代表大會常務委員會
第三十一次會議通過）

第十二屆全國人民代表大會常務委員會第三十一次會議
審議了國務院關於提請審議《關於批准〈內地與香港特別
行政區關於在廣深港高鐵西九龍站設立口岸實施"一地兩
檢"的合作安排〉的決定（草案）》的議案。全國人民代表

Instrument 14

Decision of the Standing Committee of the National People's Congress on Approving the Co-operation Arrangement between the Mainland and the Hong Kong Special Administrative Region on the Establishment of the Port at the West Kowloon Station of the Guangzhou-Shenzhen-Hong Kong Express Rail Link for Implementing Co-location Arrangement

---

(Adopted at the Thirty-first Session of the Standing Committee of the Twelfth National People's Congress on 27 December 2017)

The Standing Committee of the Twelfth National People's Congress examined at its Thirty-first Session the motion submitted by the State Council requesting examination of the Draft Decision on Approving the Co-operation Arrangement between the Mainland and the Hong Kong Special Administrative Region on the Establishment of the Port at the West Kowloon Station of the Guangzhou-Shenzhen-Hong Kong Express Rail Link for Implementing Co-location Arrangement. In the course of its examination, the Standing Committee of the National

---

Note:

This English translation is prepared by the Government of the Hong Kong Special Administrative Region. It is for reference only and has no legislative effect. In case of differences between the Chinese text and the English translation, the Chinese text prevails.

大會常務委員會在審議中充分考慮了香港特別行政區和內地各有關方面對廣深港高鐵連接口岸設置及通關查驗模式的意見。

會議認為，建設廣深港高鐵並實現香港特別行政區與全國高鐵網絡的互聯互通，有利於促進香港特別行政區與內地之間的人員往來和經貿活動，有利於深化香港特別行政區與內地的互利合作，有利於香港特別行政區更好地融入國家發展大局，對保持香港特別行政區長期繁榮穩定具有重要意義。為充分發揮高鐵高速高效優勢，使廣大乘客充分享受快捷便利的服務，確保廣深港高鐵香港段的運輸、經濟和社會效益，在廣深港高鐵香港特別行政區西九龍站（以下簡稱西九龍站）實施"一地兩檢"，設立內地口岸區，專門用於高鐵乘客及其隨身物品和行李的通關查驗，是必要的。

People's Congress has fully considered the views of relevant parties of the Hong Kong Special Administrative Region and the Mainland concerning the establishment of the port juxtaposed at the Guangzhou-Shenzhen-Hong Kong Express Rail Link and the mode of conducting clearance and inspection.

The Session is of the view that the construction of the Guangzhou-Shenzhen-Hong Kong Express Rail Link and the realization of the inter-connection and mutual access between the Hong Kong Special Administrative Region and the national high-speed rail network are conducive to promoting interactions between the people of, and economic and trade activities between, the Hong Kong Special Administrative Region and the Mainland; conducive to the deepening of mutually beneficial cooperation between the Hong Kong Special Administrative Region and the Mainland; and conducive to the Hong Kong Special Administrative Region's further integration into the macro picture of national development. These have great significance for maintaining the long-term prosperity and stability of the Hong Kong Special Administrative Region. To fully unleash the high-speed rail's advantages of high speed and great efficiency, enable the vast number of passengers to fully enjoy fast and convenient service,and ensure the transport, economic and social benefits and efficiency of the Hong Kong Section of the Guangzhou-Shenzhen-Hong Kong Express Rail Link, it is necessary to implement co-location arrangement at the West Kowloon Station of the Guangzhou-Shenzhen-Hong Kong Express Rail Link in the Hong Kong Special Administrative Region ("West Kowloon Station") and to establish the Mainland Port Area for the specific purpose of conducting clearance and inspection on high-speed rail passengers and their personal belongings and luggage.

Art 154

　　會議認為,《合作安排》符合"一國兩制"方針,符合憲法和香港特別行政區基本法。根據憲法,香港特別行政區基本法授權香港特別行政區實行高度自治,包括實行單獨的出入境管理制度等。香港特別行政區政府與內地有關方面就在西九龍站設立口岸並實施"一地兩檢"的相關問題協商作出適當安排,是香港特別行政區依法行使高度自治權的具體體現。在西九龍站設立內地口岸區,不改變香港特別行政區行政區域範圍,不影響香港特別行政區依法享有的高度自治權,不減損香港特別行政區居民依法享有的權利和自由。出於在西九龍站實施"一地兩檢"的需要,《合作安排》對內地和香港特別行政區管轄權(包括司法管轄權)劃分和法律適用作出規定,並明確西九龍站內地口岸區視為處於內地,是適當的。內地派駐西九龍站內地

The Session is of the view that the Co-operation Arrangement is consistent with the principle of "one country, two systems" and is consistent with the Constitution and the Basic Law of the Hong Kong Special Administrative Region. Pursuant to the Constitution, the Basic Law of the Hong Kong Special Administrative Region authorizes the Hong Kong Special Administrative Region to exercise a high degree of autonomy, including implementing a separate immigration controls system etc. The making of an appropriate arrangement through consultation on issues relating to the establishment of a port at the West Kowloon Station and the implementation of co-location arrangement thereat by the Government of the Hong Kong Special Administrative Region with the relevant parties of the Mainland is a clear demonstration of the exercise of a high degree of autonomy by the Hong Kong Special Administrative Region in accordance with law. The establishment of the Mainland Port Area at the West Kowloon Station does not alter the boundary of the administrative division of the Hong Kong Special Administrative Region, does not affect the high degree of autonomy enjoyed by the Hong Kong Special Administrative Region in accordance with law, and does not undermine the rights and freedoms enjoyed by the residents of the Hong Kong Special Administrative Region in accordance with law. Out of the need to implement co-location arrangement at the West Kowloon Station, it is appropriate that the Co-operation Arrangement makes provisions for the delineation of jurisdiction (including jurisdiction of the courts) and the application of laws of the Mainland and the Hong Kong Special Administrative Region and expressly provides for the West Kowloon Station Mainland Port Area to be regarded as being situated in the Mainland. The authorities stationed by the Mainland at the West

Art 154

Art 7, 18　口岸區的機構依照內地法律履行職責,其範圍嚴格限制在
內地口岸區之內,不同於香港特別行政區基本法第十八條
規定的將全國性法律在整個香港特別行政區實施的情況。
西九龍站內地口岸區場地使用權的取得、期限和費用由香
港特別行政區政府與內地有關機構簽訂合同作出規定,
符合香港特別行政區基本法第七條關於香港特別行政區
土地所有權和使用管理的規定。在西九龍站實施"一地兩
檢",符合香港特別行政區基本法關於香港特別行政區
政府應當制定適當政策促進和協調各行業發展、提供適
當的經濟和法律環境促進經濟發展等規定,符合"一國兩
制"方針和香港特別行政區基本法的根本宗旨。

　　根據《中華人民共和國憲法》和《中華人民共和國香
港特別行政區基本法》,全國人民代表大會常務委員會決
定:

Kowloon Station Mainland Port Area will perform their duties and functions in accordance with the laws of the Mainland, strictly confined to the Mainland Port Area. This is different from the application of national laws in the entire Hong Kong Special Administrative Region under Article 18 of the Basic Law of the Hong Kong Special Administrative Region. The acquisition of the right to use the areas of the West Kowloon Station Mainland Port Area, the duration and the fees will be provided for in a contract to be entered into by the Government of the Hong Kong Special Administrative Region and the relevant Mainland authorities, and this is consistent with the provisions of Article 7 of the Basic Law of the Hong Kong Special Administrative Region regarding the ownership of the land of the Hong Kong Special Administrative Region and the management of its uses. The implementation of co-location arrangement at the West Kowloon Station is consistent with the requirements of the Basic Law of the Hong Kong Special Administrative Region that the Government of the Hong Kong Special Administrative Region should formulate appropriate policies to promote and co-ordinate the development of various trades and provide an appropriate economic and legal environment for promoting economic developments etc., and is consistent with the fundamental purposes of the "one country, two systems" principle and of the Basic Law of the Hong Kong Special Administrative Region.

Pursuant to the Constitution of the People's Republic of China and the Basic Law of the Hong Kong Special Administrative Region of the People's Republic of China, the Standing Committee of the National People's Congress decides as follows:

Art 7, 18

一、 批准2017年11月18日廣東省人民政府與香港特
別行政區政府簽署的《合作安排》,並確認《合
作安排》符合憲法和香港特別行政區基本法。

　香港特別行政區應當立法保障《合作安排》得
以落實。

二、 西九龍站內地口岸區的設立及具體範圍,由國務
院批准。

　西九龍站內地口岸區自啟用之日起,由內地依照
內地法律和《合作安排》實施管轄,並派駐出入
境邊防檢查機關、海關、檢驗檢疫機構、口岸綜
合管理機構和鐵路公安機關依法履行職責,上
述機構及其人員不在西九龍站內地口岸區以外
區域執法。

三、 西九龍站口岸啟用後,對《合作安排》如有修
改,由國務院批准,並報全國人民代表大會常務
委員會備案。

1. The Co-operation Arrangement signed by the People's Government of Guangdong Province and the Government of the Hong Kong Special Administrative Region on 18 November 2017 is hereby approved, and it is also hereby confirmed that the Co-operation Arrangement is consistent with the Constitution and the Basic Law of the Hong Kong Special Administrative Region.

   The Hong Kong Special Administrative Region should enact legislation to ensure the implementation of the Co-operation Arrangement.

2. The establishment of the West Kowloon Station Mainland Port Area and its specific area are to be approved by the State Council.

   The Mainland will exercise jurisdiction over the West Kowloon Station Mainland Port Area in accordance with the laws of the Mainland and the Co-operation Arrangement with effect from its commissioning date, and will station immigration inspection authority, customs authority, inspection and quarantine authority, integrated port administration authority and railway police authority thereat to perform duties and functions in accordance with law. The above mentioned authorities and their personnel shall not enforce the law in any area outside the West Kowloon Station Mainland Port Area.

3. After the commissioning of the West Kowloon Station Port, any amendment to the Co-operation Arrangement shall be approved by the State Council and shall be reported to the Standing Committee of the National People's Congress for record.

文件十五

全國人民代表大會關於建立
健全香港特別行政區維護國家安全的法律
制度和執行機制的決定

Art 23,
App 1 (p 378)

（2020年5月28日第十三屆全國人民代表大會第三次會議通過）

序言

第十三屆全國人民代表大會第三次會議審議了全國人民代表大會常務委員會關於提請審議《全國人民代表大會關於建立健全香港特別行政區維護國家安全的法律制度和執行機制的決定（草案）》的議案。會議認為，近年來，香港特別行政區國家安全風險凸顯，"港獨"、分裂國家、暴力恐怖活動等各類違法活動嚴重危害國家主權、統一和領土完整，一些外國和境外勢力公然干預香港事務，利用香港從事危害我國國家安全的活動。為了維護國家主權、安全、發展利益，堅持和完善"一國兩制"制度體系，維護香港長期繁榮穩定，保障香港居民合法權益，根據《中

Instrument 15

Decision of the National People's Congress on Establishing and Improving the Legal System and Enforcement Mechanisms for the Hong Kong Special Administrative Region to Safeguard National Security

Art 23,
App 1 (p 379)

(Adopted at the Third Session of the Thirteenth National People's Congress on 28 May 2020)

The Third Session of the Thirteenth National People's Congress (NPC) deliberated the motion regarding the request for examination of the "Draft Decision of the National People's Congress on Establishing and Improving the Legal System and Enforcement Mechanisms for the Hong Kong Special Administrative Region to Safeguard National Security" submitted by the Standing Committee of the NPC. The session considered that the risks for national security in the Hong Kong Special Administrative Region (HKSAR) have become notable in recent years. Various unlawful activities such as advocacy for "Hong Kong independence" as well as acts of secession, violence and terrorism, etc have seriously jeopardised national sovereignty, unity and territorial integrity. Certain foreign or external forces have flagrantly interfered in Hong Kong's affairs and utilised Hong Kong to carry out activities endangering national security. To safeguard national sovereignty, security and development interests, uphold and improve the "one country, two systems" regime, safeguard the long-term prosperity and stability of Hong Kong, and safeguard the legitimate rights and interests of Hong Kong residents, the NPC has made the following decision

Preamble

華人民共和國憲法》第三十一條和第六十二條第二項、第
十四項、第十六項的規定,以及《中華人民共和國香港特
別行政區基本法》的有關規定,全國人民代表大會作出如
下決定:

一、 國家堅定不移並全面準確貫徹"一國兩制"、
"港人治港"、高度自治的方針,堅持依法治
港,維護憲法和香港特別行政區基本法確定的
香港特別行政區憲制秩序,採取必要措施建立
健全香港特別行政區維護國家安全的法律制度
和執行機制,依法防範、制止和懲治危害國家安
全的行為和活動。

二、 國家堅決反對任何外國和境外勢力以任何方式
干預香港特別行政區事務,採取必要措施予以
反制,依法防範、制止和懲治外國和境外勢力利
用香港進行分裂、顛覆、滲透、破壞活動。

三、 維護國家主權、統一和領土完整是香港特別行
政區的憲制責任。香港特別行政區應當儘早完
成香港特別行政區基本法規定的維護國家安全
立法。香港特別行政區行政機關、立法機關、司
法機關應當依據有關法律規定有效防範、制止
和懲治危害國家安全的行為和活動。

四、 香港特別行政區應當建立健全維護國家安全的
機構和執行機制,強化維護國家安全執法力量,

pursuant to Articles 31, 62(2), 62(14) and 62(16) of the Constitution of the People's Republic of China (PRC) and the relevant provisions of the Basic Law of the HKSAR of the PRC: `Art 1, 12`

1. The country unswervingly, fully and faithfully implements the principles of "one country, two systems", "Hong Kong people administering Hong Kong" and a high degree of autonomy; upholds that Hong Kong be administered in strict accordance with the law; upholds the Constitution and the constitutional order in the HKSAR established by the Basic Law of the HKSAR; takes necessary measures to establish and improve the legal system and enforcement mechanisms for the HKSAR to safeguard national security, as well as to prevent, stop and punish in accordance with the law acts and activities endangering national security.

2. The country resolutely opposes interference in the HKSAR's affairs by any foreign or external forces in any form, and will take necessary countermeasures to prevent, stop and punish in accordance with the law activities of secession, subversion, infiltration and sabotage carried out by foreign or external forces in Hong Kong. `Art 23`

3. It is the HKSAR's constitutional responsibilities to safeguard national sovereignty, unity and territorial integrity. The HKSAR must complete the national security legislation stipulated in the Basic Law of the HKSAR at an earlier date. The HKSAR's administrative, legislative and judicial organs must, in accordance with relevant laws and regulations, effectively prevent, stop and punish acts and activities endangering national security.

4. The HKSAR must establish and improve the institutions and enforcement mechanisms for safeguarding national

加強維護國家安全執法工作。中央人民政府維護國家安全的有關機關根據需要在香港特別行政區設立機構，依法履行維護國家安全相關職責。

五、 香港特別行政區行政長官應當就香港特別行政區履行維護國家安全職責、開展國家安全教育、依法禁止危害國家安全的行為和活動等情況，定期向中央人民政府提交報告。

App 1 (p 378)

六、 授權全國人民代表大會常務委員會就建立健全香港特別行政區維護國家安全的法律制度和執行機制制定相關法律，切實防範、制止和懲治任何分裂國家、顛覆國家政權、組織實施恐怖活動等嚴重危害國家安全的行為和活動以及外國

Anx III (p 156)

Inst 23 (p 322)

和境外勢力干預香港特別行政區事務的活動。全國人民代表大會常務委員會決定將上述相關法律列入《中華人民共和國香港特別行政區基本法》附件三，由香港特別行政區在當地公佈實施。

七、 本決定自公佈之日起施行。

security, strengthen the enforcement forces for safeguarding national security, and step up enforcement to safeguard national security. When needed, relevant national security organs of the Central People's Government (CPG) will set up agencies in the HKSAR to fulfil relevant duties to safeguard national security in accordance with the law.

5. The Chief Executive of the HKSAR must regularly report to the CPG on the HKSAR's performance of the duty to safeguard national security, carry out national security education, and forbid acts and activities of endangering national security in accordance with the law, etc.

6. The NPC Standing Committee is entrusted to formulate relevant laws on establishing and improving the legal system and enforcement mechanisms for the HKSAR to safeguard national security, in order to effectively prevent, stop and punish acts and activities to split the country, subvert state power, organise and carry out terrorist activities and other behaviours that seriously endanger national security, as well as activities of foreign or external forces interfering in the affairs of the HKSAR. The NPC Standing Committee decides on including relevant laws into Annex III of the Basic Law of the HKSAR of the PRC to be promulgated and implemented by the HKSAR locally.

App 1 (p 379)

Anx III (p 157)

Inst 23 (p 323)

7. The decision shall go into effect as of the date of promulgation.

文件十六

全國人民代表大會常務委員會關於
香港特別行政區第六屆立法會
繼續履行職責的決定

（2020年8月11日第十三屆全國人民代表大會常務委員會
第二十一次會議通過）

第十三屆全國人民代表大會常務委員會第二十一次會議審議了《國務院關於提請全國人民代表大會常務委員會就香港特別行政區第六屆立法會繼續運作作出決定的議案》。上述議案是應香港特別行政區行政長官向中央人民政府報送的有關報告提出的。香港特別行政區行政長官會同行政會議因應當地新冠肺炎疫情的嚴峻形勢已決定將香港特別行政區第七屆立法會選舉推遲一年，在此情況下香港特別行政區立法機關將出現空缺。為維護香港特別行政區憲制秩序和法治秩序，確保香港特別行政區政府正

Art 69

Instrument 16

Decision of the Standing Committee of the National People's Congress on the Continuing Discharge of Duties by the Sixth Term Legislative Council of the Hong Kong Special Administrative Region

(Adopted at the Twenty-first Session of the Standing Committee of the Thirteenth National People's Congress on 11 August 2020)

The Standing Committee of the Thirteenth National People's Congress deliberated at its Twenty-first Session the motion submitted by the State Council requesting a decision by the Standing Committee of the National People's Congress on the continuing operation of the sixth term Legislative Council of the Hong Kong Special Administrative Region. The motion was moved following the relevant report submitted by the Chief Executive of the Hong Kong Special Administrative Region to the Central People's Government. In response to the severe local situation of the novel coronavirus epidemic, the Chief Executive of the Hong Kong Special Administrative Region in consultation with the Executive Council had decided to postpone the election for the seventh term Legislative Council of the Hong Kong Special Administrative Region for one year. As such, there will be a lacuna in the legislature of the Hong Kong Special Administrative Region. To safeguard the constitutional order and order of the rule of law in the Hong Kong Special Administrative Region and to ensure the normal governmental administration of the Government of the Hong Kong Special

Art 69

常施政和社會正常運行,根據《中華人民共和國憲法》和《中華人民共和國香港特別行政區基本法》的有關規定,全國人民代表大會常務委員會作出如下決定:

　　2020年9月30日後,香港特別行政區第六屆立法會繼續履行職責,不少於一年,直至香港特別行政區第七屆立法會任期開始為止。香港特別行政區第七屆立法會依法產生後,任期仍為四年。

　　現予公告。

Administrative Region and the normal operation of the society, the Standing Committee of the National People's Congress decides, pursuant to the relevant provisions of the Constitution of the People's Republic of China and the Basic Law of the Hong Kong Special Administrative Region of the People's Republic of China, as follows:

After 30 September 2020, the sixth term Legislative Council of the Hong Kong Special Administrative Region is to continue to discharge duties for not less than one year until the seventh term of office of the Legislative Council of the Hong Kong Special Administrative Region begins. After the seventh term Legislative Council of the Hong Kong Special Administrative Region is formed in accordance with the law, its term of office remains to be four years.

Art 69

The decision is hereby announced.

文件十七

全國人民代表大會常務委員會
關於香港特別行政區立法會
議員資格問題的決定

(2020年11月11日第十三屆全國人民代表大會常務委員會
第二十三次會議通過)

第十三屆全國人民代表大會常務委員會第二十三次會議審議了《國務院關於提請就香港特別行政區立法會議員資格問題作出決定的議案》。上述議案是應香港特別行政區行政長官的請求而提出的。會議認為，為了全面準確貫徹落實"一國兩制"方針和《中華人民共和國香港特別行

Instrument 17

Decision of the Standing Committee of the National People's Congress on Issues Relating to the Qualification of the Members of the Legislative Council of the Hong Kong Special Administrative Region

(Adopted at the Twenty Third Session of the Standing Committee of the Thirteenth National People's Congress on 11 November 2020)

The Standing Committee of the Thirteenth National People's Congress deliberated at its Twenty-third Session the motion submitted by the State Council requesting a decision on issues relating to the qualification of the members of the Legislative Council of the Hong Kong Special Administrative Region. The motion was moved following the request of the Chief Executive of the Hong Kong Special Administrative Region. The Session is of the view that it must be ensured that relevant public officers of the Hong Kong Special Administrative Region, including members of the Legislative Council, meet the legal requirements and conditions on upholding the Basic Law of the Hong Kong Special Administrative Region of the People's Republic of China and bearing allegiance to the Hong Kong Special Administrative Region of the People's Republic of China, in order to fully and faithfully implement the principle of "One Country, Two Systems" and the Basic Law of the Hong Kong Special

Note:

  This English translation is prepared by the Department of Justice, Government of the Hong Kong Special Administrative Region. It is for reference purposes and has no legislative effect.

政區基本法》，維護國家主權、安全和發展利益，維護香港長期繁榮穩定，必須確保香港特別行政區有關公職人員包括立法會議員符合擁護中華人民共和國香港特別行政區基本法、效忠中華人民共和國香港特別行政區的法定要求和條件。為此，全國人民代表大會常務委員會同意國務院2020年11月7日提出的議案，根據《中華人民共和國憲法》第五十二條、第五十四條、第六十七條第一項的規定和《中華人民共和國香港特別行政區基本法》、《全國人民代表大會關於建立健全香港特別行政區維護國家安全的法律制度和執行機制的決定》、《中華人民共和國香港特別行政區維護國家安全法》的有關規定以及《全國人民代表大會常務委員會關於〈中華人民共和國香港特別行政區基本法〉第一百零四條的解釋》、《全國人民代表大會常務委員會關於香港特別行政區第六屆立法會繼續履行職責的決定》，作出如下決定：

一、 香港特別行政區立法會議員，因宣揚或者支持"港獨"主張、拒絕承認國家對香港擁有並行使主權、尋求外國或者境外勢力干預香港特別行

Inst 15 (p 286)

Inst 23 (p 322)

Inst 26 (p 368)

Inst 16 (p 292)

Administrative Region of the People's Republic of China, safeguard national sovereignty, security and development interests and safeguard the long-term prosperity and stability of Hong Kong. Accordingly, the Standing Committee of the National People's Congress has approved the motion moved by the State Council on 7 November 2020 and made the following decision pursuant to Articles 52, 54 and 67(1) of the Constitution of the People's Republic of China, the Basic Law of the Hong Kong Special Administrative Region of the People's Republic of China, the Decision of the National People's Congress on Establishing and Improving the Legal System and Enforcement Mechanisms for the Hong Kong Special Administrative Region to Safeguard National Security, the relevant provisions of the Law of the People's Republic of China on Safeguarding National Security in the Hong Kong Special Administrative Region and the Interpretation of Article 104 of the Basic Law of the Hong Kong Special Administrative Region of the People's Republic of China by the Standing Committee of the National People's Congress, and the Decision of the Standing Committee of the National People's Congress on the Continuing Discharge of Duties by the Sixth Term Legislative Council of the Hong Kong Special Administrative Region:

Inst 15 (p 287)

Inst 23 (p 323)

Inst 29 (p 369)

Inst 16 (p 293)

1.   A member of the Legislative Council of the Hong Kong Special Administrative Region does not meet the legal requirements and conditions on upholding the Basic Law of the Hong Kong Special Administrative Region of the People's Republic of China and bearing allegiance to the Hong Kong Special Administrative Region of the People's Republic of China if the member advocates or supports "Hong Kong independence", refuses to recognize the People's Republic of China's sovereignty over Hong Kong and the exercise of the sovereignty, solicits intervention by foreign or external forces in the

政區事務，或者具有其他危害國家安全等行為，不符合擁護中華人民共和國香港特別行政區基本法、效忠中華人民共和國香港特別行政區的法定要求和條件，一經依法認定，即時喪失立法會議員的資格。

二、 本決定適用於在原定於2020年9月6日舉行的香港特別行政區第七屆立法會選舉提名期間，因上述情形被香港特別行政區依法裁定提名無效的第六屆立法會議員。

今後參選或者出任立法會議員的，如遇有上述情形，均適用本決定。

三、 依據上述規定喪失立法會議員資格的，由香港特別行政區政府宣布。

Hong Kong Special Administrative Region's affairs, or carries out other activities endangering national security. Once the member is decided as such in accordance with law, he or she is immediately disqualified from being a member of the Legislative Council.

2. This Decision is applicable to the members of the sixth term Legislative Council of the Hong Kong Special Administrative Region whose nominations were decided to be invalid in accordance with law by the Hong Kong Special Administrative Region due to the circumstances mentioned above during the nomination period of the election for the seventh term Legislative Council of the Hong Kong Special Administrative Region originally scheduled for 6 September 2020. This Decision is applicable to any person standing for an election in respect of or taking up the office of a member of the Legislative Council in future where the circumstances mentioned above apply.

3. The disqualification of the members of the Legislative Council of the Hong Kong Special Administrative Region pursuant to the above provisions is to be announced by the Government of the Hong Kong Special Administrative Region.

文件十八

Art 26,
Art 45,
Art 68

全國人民代表大會關於完善
香港特別行政區選舉制度的決定

（2021年3月11日第十三屆全國人民代表大會第四次會議通過）

Inst 15 (p 286)

第十三屆全國人民代表大會第四次會議審議了全國人民
代表大會常務委員會關於提請審議《全國人民代表大會
關於完善香港特別行政區選舉制度的決定（草案）》的議
案。會議認為，香港回歸祖國後，重新納入國家治理體系，
《中華人民共和國憲法》和《中華人民共和國香港特別行
政區基本法》共同構成香港特別行政區的憲制基礎。香港
特別行政區實行的選舉制度，包括行政長官和立法會的
產生辦法，是香港特別行政區政治體制的重要組成部分，
應當符合"一國兩制"方針，符合香港特別行政區實際情
況，確保愛國愛港者治港，有利於維護國家主權、安全、

註：

* 本文件的中文文本轉載自《中華人民共和國全國人民代表大會常務委員會公
  報（2021年第三號）》。

Instrument 18

Decision of the National People's Congress On Improving the Electoral System of the Hong Kong Special Administrative Region

Art 26,
Art 45,
Art 68

(Adopted at the Fourth Session of the Thirteenth National People's Congress on 11 March 2021)

The Fourth Session of the Thirteenth National People's Congress (NPC) deliberated the motion regarding the request for examination of the "Draft Decision of the National People's Congress On Improving the Electoral System of the Hong Kong Special Administrative Region" submitted by the Standing Committee of the NPC. The session considered that the return of Hong Kong to the motherland put the region once again under the overall governance system of the country, and the Constitution of the People's Republic of China (PRC) and the Basic Law of the Hong Kong Special Administrative Region (HKSAR) of the PRC jointly form the constitutional basis of the HKSAR. The electoral system of the HKSAR, which includes the methods for the selection of the Chief Executive and for the formation of the Legislative Council (LegCo), is an important part of the political structure of the HKSAR. It should conform to the policy of "one country, two systems", meet the realities in the HKSAR and serve to ensure that Hong Kong is administered by people who love the country and Hong Kong; be conducive to safeguarding national sovereignty, security, and development

Inst 15 (p 287)

Note:

This is an English translation of the original instrument in Chinese and is published for information.

發展利益,保持香港長期繁榮穩定。為完善香港特別行政區選舉制度,發展適合香港特別行政區實際情況的民主制度,根據《中華人民共和國憲法》第三十一條和第六十二條第二項、第十四項、第十六項的規定,以及《中華人民共和國香港特別行政區基本法》、《中華人民共和國香港特別行政區維護國家安全法》的有關規定,全國人民代表大會作出如下決定:

一、 完善香港特別行政區選舉制度,必須全面準確貫徹落實"一國兩制"、"港人治港"、高度自治的方針,維護《中華人民共和國憲法》和《中華人民共和國香港特別行政區基本法》確定的香港特別行政區憲制秩序,確保以愛國者為主體的"港人治港",切實提高香港特別行政區治理效能,保障香港特別行政區永久性居民的選舉權和被選舉權。

二、 香港特別行政區設立一個具有廣泛代表性、符合香港特別行政區實際情況、體現社會整體利益的選舉委員會。選舉委員會負責選舉行政長官候任人、立法會部分議員,以及提名行政長官候選人、立法會議員候選人等事宜。

interests of the country and maintain the long-term prosperity and stability of Hong Kong. To improve the electoral system of the HKSAR and develop a democratic system suited to the HKSAR's realities, the NPC has made the following decision pursuant to Articles 31 and 62(2), (14) and (16) of the Constitution of the PRC and the relevant provisions of the Basic Law of the HKSAR of the PRC and the Law of the PRC on Safeguarding National Security in the HKSAR:

Art 45, 68
Inst 23 (p 323)

1. Improving the electoral system of the HKSAR must fully and faithfully implement the policy of "one country, two systems" under which the people of Hong Kong administer Hong Kong with a high degree of autonomy, uphold the constitutional order in the HKSAR as established by the Constitution of the PRC and the Basic Law of the HKSAR of the PRC, ensure the administration of Hong Kong by Hong Kong people with patriots as the main body, effectively improve the governance efficacy of the HKSAR, and safeguard the right to vote and the right to stand for election of permanent residents of the HKSAR.

2. The HKSAR shall establish an Election Committee which is broadly representative, suited to the HKSAR's realities, and representative of the overall interests of its society. The Election Committee shall be responsible for electing the Chief Executive designate and part of the members of the LegCo. The Election Committee shall also be responsible for nominating candidates for the Chief Executive and LegCo members, as well as for other matters.

Anx I (p 125)

選舉委員會由工商、金融界，專業界，基層、勞工和宗教等界，立法會議員、地區組織代表等界，香港特別行政區全國人大代表、香港特別行政區全國政協委員和有關全國性團體香港成員的代表界等五個界別共1500名委員組成。

Art 45

三、香港特別行政區行政長官由選舉委員會選出，由中央人民政府任命。

行政長官候選人須獲得選舉委員會不少於188名委員聯合提名，且上述五個界別中每個界別參與提名的委員不少於15名。選舉委員會以一人一票無記名投票選出行政長官候任人，行政長官候任人須獲得選舉委員會全體委員過半數支持。

Anx II (p 142)

四、香港特別行政區立法會議員每屆90人。通過選舉委員會選舉、功能團體選舉、分區直接選舉三種方式分別選舉產生。

五、設立香港特別行政區候選人資格審查委員會，負責審查並確認選舉委員會委員候選人、行政長官候選人和立法會議員候選人的資格。香港特別行政區應當健全和完善有關資格審查制度

The Election Committee shall be composed of 1,500 members from the following five sectors: industrial, commercial and financial sectors; the professions; grassroots, labour, religious and other sectors; LegCo members and representatives of district organizations; Hong Kong deputies to the NPC, Hong Kong members of the National Committee of the Chinese People's Political Consultative Conference and representatives of Hong Kong members of related national organizations.

3. The Chief Executive shall be elected by the Election Committee and appointed by the Central People's Government.

   Art 45

   Candidates for the office of the Chief Executive shall be nominated jointly by not less than 188 members of the Election Committee, among whom the number of members of each sector should be not less than 15. The Election Committee shall elect the Chief Executive designate by secret ballot on a one-person-one-vote basis. The election of the Chief Executive designate shall require a simple majority vote of all the members of the Election Committee.

4. The LegCo of the HKSAR shall be composed of 90 members in each term. Members of the LegCo shall include members returned by the Election Committee, those returned by functional constituencies, and those by geographical constituencies through direct elections.

   Anx II (p 143)

5. A candidate qualification review committee of the HKSAR shall be established. The committee shall be responsible for reviewing and confirming the qualifications of candidates for the Election Committee members, the Chief Executive, and the LegCo members. The HKSAR shall improve the system and mechanisms

機制，確保候選人資格符合《中華人民共和國香港特別行政區基本法》、《中華人民共和國香港特別行政區維護國家安全法》、全國人民代表大會常務委員會關於《中華人民共和國香港特別行政區基本法》第一百零四條的解釋和關於香港特別行政區立法會議員資格問題的決定以及香港特別行政區本地有關法律的規定。

App 1 (p 378)

Inst 29 (p 368)

Inst 17 (p 296)

六、 授權全國人民代表大會常務委員會根據本決定修改《中華人民共和國香港特別行政區基本法》附件一《香港特別行政區行政長官的產生辦法》和附件二《香港特別行政區立法會的產生辦法和表決程序》。

Anx I (p 124)

Anx II (p 142)

七、 香港特別行政區應當依照本決定和全國人民代表大會常務委員會修改後的《中華人民共和國香港特別行政區基本法》附件一《香港特別行政區行政長官的產生辦法》和附件二《香港特別行政區立法會的產生辦法和表決程序》，修改香港特別行政區本地有關法律，依法組織、規管相關選舉活動。

Anx I (p 124)

Anx II (p 142)

八、 香港特別行政區行政長官應當就香港特別行政區選舉制度安排和選舉組織等有關重要情況，及時向中央人民政府提交報告。

Art 43

九、 本決定自公布之日起施行。

related to qualification review, to ensure that the qualifications of candidates are in conformity with the Basic Law, the Law on Safeguarding National Security in the HKSAR, the NPC Standing Committee's interpretation of Article 104 of the Basic Law, the NPC Standing Committee's decision on the qualification of HKSAR LegCo members, and provisions of relevant local laws of the HKSAR.

App 1 (p 379)

Inst 29 (p 369)

Inst 17(p 297)

6. The NPC Standing Committee is authorized to, in accordance with the decision on improving the electoral system of the HKSAR, amend Annex I: Method for the Selection of the Chief Executive of the Hong Kong Special Administrative Region and Annex II: Method for the Formation of the Legislative Council of the Hong Kong Special Administrative Region and Its Voting Procedures, to the Basic Law.

Anx I (p 125)

Anx II (p 143)

7. In accordance with this decision and the Basic Law's Annex I and Annex II amended by the NPC Standing Committee, the HKSAR shall amend relevant local laws, and organize and regulate election activities accordingly.

Anx I (p 125)

Anx II (p 143)

8. The Chief Executive of the HKSAR shall submit in a timely manner reports to the Central People's Government on relevant important situations including the institutional arrangements for elections of the HKSAR and the organization of the elections.

Art 43

9. The decision shall go into effect as of the date of promulgation.

全國人民代表大會常務委員會關於
《中華人民共和國香港特別行政區基本法》
附件三的決定

Decisions of the Standing Committee
of the National People's Congress
on Annex III to the Basic Law
of the Hong Kong Special Administrative Region
of the People's Republic of China

文件十九

Art 18,
Anx III (p 156)

全國人民代表大會常務委員會關於
《中華人民共和國香港特別行政區基本法》
附件三所列全國性法律增減的決定

（1997年7月1日第八屆全國人民代表大會
常務委員會第二十六次會議通過）

一、 在《中華人民共和國香港特別行政區基本法》附
件三中增加下列全國性法律：

1. 《中華人民共和國國旗法》；

2. 《中華人民共和國領事特權與豁免條例》；

3. 《中華人民共和國國徽法》；

4. 《中華人民共和國領海及毗連區法》；

Instrument 19

Art 18,
Anx III (p 157)

Decision of the Standing Committee of the National People's Congress on Adding to and Deleting from the List of the National Laws in Annex III to the Basic Law of the Hong Kong Special Administrative Region of the People's Republic of China

(Adopted at the Twenty-sixth Meeting of the Standing Committee
of the Eighth National People's Congress on 1 July 1997)

1. The following national laws shall be added to Annex III
    to the Basic Law of the Hong Kong Special Administrative
    Region of the People's Republic of China:

    (1) Law of the People's Republic of China on the
         National Flag

    (2) Regulations of the People's Republic of China
         Concerning Consular Privileges and Immunities;

    (3) Law of the People's Republic of China on the
         National Emblem;

    (4) Law of the People's Republic of China on the
         Territorial Sea and the Contiguous Zone;

Note:

    This English translation is reproduced from "The Laws of the People's Republic of
China 1997" compiled by the Legislative Affairs Commission of the Standing
Committee of the National People's Congress of the People's Republic of China. It
is for reference only and has no legislative effect.

　　　　5.　《中華人民共和國香港特別行政區駐軍法》。

　　以上全國性法律，自1997年7月1日起由香港特別行政區公布或立法實施。

二、　在《中華人民共和國香港特別行政區基本法》附件三中刪去下列全國性法律：

　　《中央人民政府公布中華人民共和國國徽的命令》附：國徽圖案、說明、使用辦法。

(5) Law of the People's Republic of China on Garrisoning the Hong Kong Special Administrative Region

Art 14

The national laws mentioned above shall be promulgated or implemented through legislation by the Hong Kong Special Administrative Region as of 1 July 1997.

2. The following national law shall be deleted from Annex III to the Basic Law of the Hong Kong Special Administrative Region of the People's Republic of China:

    Order on the National Emblem of the People's Republic of China Proclaimed by the Central People's Government Attached: Design of the national emblem, notes of explanation and instructions for use.

文件二十

文件二十

Art 18,
Anx III (p 156)

全國人民代表大會常務委員會關於增加
《中華人民共和國香港特別行政區基本法》
附件三所列全國性法律的決定

(1998年11月4日通過)

第九屆全國人民代表大會常務委員會第五次會議決定：在
《中華人民共和國香港特別行政區基本法》附件三中增加
全國性法律《中華人民共和國專屬經濟區和大陸架法》。

Instrument 20

Decision of the Standing Committee of the National People's Congress on Adding a Law to the List of the National Laws in Annex III to the Basic Law of the Hong Kong Special Administrative Region of the People's Republic of China

Art 18,
Anx III (p 157)

(Adopted on 4 November 1998)

At its 5th Meeting, the Standing Committee of the Ninth National People's Congress decides to add the National Law on the Exclusive Economic Zone and Continental Shelf of the People's Republic of China to Annex III to the Basic Law of the Hong Kong Special Administrative Region of the People's Republic of China.

Note:

This English translation is reproduced from "The Laws of the People's Republic of China 1998" compiled by the Legislative Affairs Commission of the Standing Committee of the National People's Congress of the People's Republic of China. It is for reference only and has no legislative effect.

文件二十一

全國人民代表大會常務委員會關於增加
《中華人民共和國香港特別行政區基本法》
附件三所列全國性法律的決定

(2005年10月27日通過)

第十屆全國人民代表大會常務委員會第十八次會議決定：
在《中華人民共和國香港特別行政區基本法》附件三中增
加全國性法律《中華人民共和國外國中央銀行財產司法強
制措施豁免法》。

Instrument 21

Decision of the Standing Committee of the National People's Congress on Adding a Law to the List of the National Laws in Annex III to the Basic Law of the Hong Kong Special Administrative Region of the People's Republic of China

Art 18, Anx III (p 157)

(Adopted on 27 October 2005)

At its 18th Meeting, the Standing Committee of the Tenth National People's Congress decides to add a national law to the list of the national laws in Annex III to the Basic Law of the Hong Kong Special Administrative Region of the People's Republic of China, i.e., the Law of the People's Republic of China on Judicial Immunity from Compulsory Measures Concerning the Property of Foreign Central Banks.

Note:
   This English translation is reproduced from "The Laws of the People's Republic of China 2005" compiled by the Legislative Affairs Commission of the Standing Committee of the National People's Congress of the People's Republic of China. It is for reference only and has no legislative effect.

文件二十二

文件二十二

全國人民代表大會常務委員會關於增加
《中華人民共和國香港特別行政區基本法》
附件三所列全國性法律的決定*

(2017年11月4日第十二屆全國人民代表大會
常務委員會第三十次會議通過)

第十二屆全國人民代表大會常務委員會第三十次會議決定：在《中華人民共和國香港特別行政區基本法》附件三中增加全國性法律《中華人民共和國國歌法》。

註：

* 本文件的中文文本轉載自《中華人民共和國全國人民代表大會常務委員會公報（2017年第六號）》。

Instrument 22

Decision of the Standing Committee of the National People's Congress on Adding a Law to the List of the National Laws in Annex III to the Basic Law of the Hong Kong Special Administrative Region of the People's Republic of China

Art 18,
Anx III (p 157)

(Adopted at the Thirtieth meeting of the Standing Committee of the Twelfth National People's Congress on November 4, 2017)

The Thirtieth Meeting of the Standing Committee of the Twelfth National People's Congress decides: the national law being the "Law of the People's Republic of China on the National Anthem" is added to the list of laws in Annex III to the Basic Law of the Hong Kong Special Administrative Region of the People's Republic of China.

Note:

This English translation is prepared by the Department of Justice, Government of the Hong Kong Special Administrative Region. It is for reference only and has no legislative effect.

文件二十三

Art 18,
Anx III (p 156),
App 1 (p 378)

全國人民代表大會常務委員會關於增加
《中華人民共和國香港特別行政區基本法》
附件三所列全國性法律的決定*

（2020年6月30日第十三屆全國人民代表大會常務委員會
第二十次會議通過）

Inst 15 (p 286)

根據《全國人民代表大會關於建立健全香港特別行政區維
護國家安全的法律制度和執行機制的決定》，第十三屆全國
人民代表大會常務委員會第二十次會議決定：在《中華人民
共和國香港特別行政區基本法》附件三中增加全國性法律
《中華人民共和國香港特別行政區維護國家安全法》，並由
香港特別行政區在當地公布實施。

註：

* 本文件的中文文本轉載自《中華人民共和國全國人民代表大會常務委員會公
報（2020年第三號）》。

Instrument 23

Decision of the Standing Committee of the National People's Congress on Adding a Law to the List of the National Laws in Annex III to the Basic Law of the Hong Kong Special Administrative Region of the People's Republic of China

Art 18,
Anx III (p 157),
App 1 (p 379)

(Adopted at the Twentieth Session of the Standing Committee of the Thirteenth National People's Congress on June 30, 2020)

In accordance with the "Decision of the National People's Congress on Establishing and Improving the Legal System and Enforcement Mechanism for the Hong Kong Special Administrative Region to Safeguard National Security", the Twentieth Session of the Standing Committee of the Thirteenth National People's Congress decides: the national law being the "Law of the People's Republic of China on Safeguarding National Security in the Hong Kong Special Administrative Region" is added to the list of laws in Annex III to the Basic Law of the Hong Kong Special Administrative Region of the People's Republic of China, and shall be applied locally by way of promulgation by the Region.

Inst 15 (p 287)

Note:
   This English translation is prepared by the Government of the Hong Kong Special Administrative Region. It is for reference purpose and has no legislative effect.

全國人民代表大會常務委員會關於
《中華人民共和國國籍法》和
《中華人民共和國香港特別行政區基本法》的解釋

Interpretations by the Standing Committee
of the National People's Congress
on the Nationality Law of the People's Republic
of China and on the Basic Law
of the Hong Kong Special Administrative Region
of the People's Republic of China

文件二十四

Art 158,
Anx III (p 156)

全國人民代表大會常務委員會
關於《中華人民共和國國籍法》
在香港特別行政區實施的幾個問題的解釋

（1996年5月15日第八屆全國人民代表大會
常務委員會第十九次會議通過）

根據《中華人民共和國香港特別行政區基本法》第十八條和附件三的規定，《中華人民共和國國籍法》自1997年7月1日起在香港特別行政區實施。考慮到香港的歷史背景和現實情況，對《中華人民共和國國籍法》在香港特別行政區實施作如下解釋：

Art 24

一、 凡具有中國血統的香港居民，本人出生在中國領土（含香港）者，以及其他符合《中華人民共和國國籍法》規定的具有中國國籍的條件者，都是中國公民。

Instrument 24

Art 158
Anx III (p 157)

Interpretation by the Standing Committee of the National People's Congress on Some Questions Concerning Implementation of the Nationality Law of the People's Republic of China in the Hong Kong Special Administrative Region

(Adopted at the Nineteenth Meeting of the Standing Committee
of the Eighth National People's Congress on 15 May 1996)

According to the provisions of Article 18 of the Basic Law of the Hong Kong Special Administrative Region of the People's Republic of China and of its Annex III, the Nationality Law of the People's Republic of China shall become effective in the Hong Kong Special Administrative Region as of 1 July 1997. In view of the historical background and the reality of Hong Kong, an interpretation regarding implementation of the Nationality Law of the People's Republic of China in the Hong Kong Special Administrative Region is made as follows:

1. Any Hong Kong resident of Chinese descent who was born in the territory of China (including Hong Kong), or any other person who meets the requirements for Chinese nationality as prescribed by the Nationality Law of the People's Republic of China is a Chinese national.

Art 24

Note:

This English translation is reproduced from "The Laws of the People's Republic of China 1996" compiled by the Legislative Affairs Commission of the Standing Committee of the National People's Congress of the People's Republic of China. It is for reference only and has no legislative effect.

二、 所有香港中國同胞,不論其是否持有"英國屬土公民護照"或者"英國國民(海外)護照",都是中國公民。自1997年7月1日起,上述中國公民可繼續使用英國政府簽發的有效旅行證件去其他國家或地區旅行,但在香港特別行政區和中華人民共和國其他地區不得因持有上述英國旅行證件而享有英國的領事保護的權利。

三、 任何在香港的中國公民,因英國政府的"居英權計劃"而獲得的英國公民身份,根據《中華人民共和國國籍法》不予承認。這類人仍為中國公民,在香港特別行政區和中華人民共和國其他地區不得享有英國的領事保護的權利。

四、 在外國有居留權的香港特別行政區的中國公民,可使用外國政府簽發的有關證件去其他國家或地區旅行,但在香港特別行政區和中華人民共和國其他地區不得因持有上述證件而享有外國領事保護的權利。

2. All Chinese compatriots residing in Hong Kong, whether they are holders of the British Dependent Territories Citizens' Passport or the British National (Overseas) Passport, are Chinese nationals. These Chinese nationals may, as of 1 July 1997, continue to use their valid travel documents issued by the British government for the purpose of travelling to other countries or regions. However, they shall not be entitled to British consular protection in the Hong Kong Special Administrative Region or in any other part of the People's Republic of China on account of their holding the British travel documents mentioned above.

3. The British citizen status of any Chinese national residing in Hong Kong granted by the British government under the British Nationality Selection Scheme shall not be recognized according to the Nationality Law of the People's Republic of China. Such person being still Chinese national, he or she shall not be entitled to British consular protection in the Hong Kong Special Administrative Region or in any other part of the People's Republic of China.

4. Any Chinese national who resides in the Hong Kong Special Administrative Region and has the right of abode in a foreign country may use the relevant document issued by the foreign government for the purpose of travelling to other countries or regions, but he or she shall not be entitled to the consular protection of the foreign country in the Hong Kong Special Administrative Region or in any other part of the People's Republic of China on account of his or her holding the foreign documents mentioned above.

Art 154

五、 香港特別行政區的中國公民的國籍發生變更，可
憑有效證件向香港特別行政區受理國籍申請的
機關申報。

六、 授權香港特別行政區政府指定其入境事務處為
香港特別行政區受理國籍申請的機關，香港特別
行政區入境事務處根據《中華人民共和國國籍
法》和以上規定對所有國籍申請事宜作出處理。

5. Any Chinese national residing in the Hong Kong Special Administrative Region who wishes to change his or her nationality may, by producing valid documents, apply to the competent authorities of the Hong Kong Special Administrative Region that handle nationality applications.

6. The Government of the Hong Kong Special Administrative Region is authorized to designate its Immigration Department as the competent authorities for handling nationality applications. The Immigration Department of the Hong Kong Special Administrative Region shall deal with all matters relating to nationality applications in accordance with the Nationality Law of the People's Republic of China and the provisions mentioned above.

Art 154

文件二十五

Art 158

全國人民代表大會常務委員會關於
《中華人民共和國香港特別行政區基本法》
第二十二條第四款和第二十四條第二款
第（三）項的解釋

（1999年6月26日第九屆全國人民代表大會
常務委員會第十次會議通過）

Art 22 (4),
24(2)

第九屆全國人民代表大會常務委員會第十次會議審議了
國務院《關於提請解釋〈中華人民共和國香港特別行政區
基本法〉第二十二條第四款和第二十四條第二款第（三）
項的議案》。國務院的議案是應香港特別行政區行政長官

Art 43, 48

根據《中華人民共和國香港特別行政區基本法》第四十三
條和第四十八條第（二）項的有關規定提交的報告提出
的。鑒於議案中提出的問題涉及香港特別行政區終審法院

Instrument 25

Interpretation by the Standing Committee of the National People's Congress Regarding Paragraph 4 in Article 22 and Category (3) of Paragraph 2 in Article 24 of the Basic Law of the Hong Kong Special Administrative Region of the People's Republic of China

Art 158

(Adopted at the Tenth Meeting of the Standing Committee
of the Ninth National People's Congress on 26 June 1999)

At its 10th Meeting, the Standing Committee of the Ninth National People's Congress discussed the State Council's Proposal for Giving an Interpretation to Paragraph 4 in Article 22 and Category (3) of Paragraph 2 in Article 24 of the Basic Law of the Hong Kong Special Administrative Region of the People's Republic of China. It is in order to respond to the report submitted by the Chief Executive of the Hong Kong Special Administrative Region in accordance with the relevant provisions of Article 43 and those of Category (2) of Article 48 of the Basic Law of the Hong Kong Special Administrative Region of the People's Republic of China that the State Council has put forward the proposal. In view of the fact that the issue raised in the proposal concerns the interpretation of the relevant articles of the Basic Law of the Hong Kong Special Administrative

*Art 22 (4),
24(2)*

Art 43, 48

Note:

This English translation is reproduced from "The Laws of the People's Republic of China 1999" compiled by the Legislative Affairs Commission of the Standing Committee of the National People's Congress of the People's Republic of China. It is for reference only and has no legislative effect.

1999年1月29日的判決對《中華人民共和國香港特別行政區基本法》有關條款的解釋，該有關條款涉及中央管理的事務和中央與香港特別行政區的關係，終審法院在判決前沒有依照《中華人民共和國香港特別行政區基本法》第一百五十八條第三款的規定請全國人民代表大會常務委員會作出解釋，而終審法院的解釋又不符合立法原意，經徵詢全國人民代表大會常務委員會香港特別行政區基本法委員會的意見，全國人民代表大會常務委員會決定，根據《中華人民共和國憲法》第六十七條第（四）項和《中華人民共和國香港特別行政區基本法》第一百五十八條第一款的規定，對《中華人民共和國香港特別行政區基本法》第二十二條第四款和第二十四條第二款第（三）項的規定，作如下解釋：

一、《中華人民共和國香港特別行政區基本法》第二十二條第四款關於"中國其他地區的人進入香港特別行政區須辦理批准手續"的規定，是指各省、自治區、直轄市的人，包括香港永久性居民在內地所生的中國籍子女，不論以何種事由要求

Region of the People's Republic of China by the Court of Final
Appeal of the Hong Kong Special Administrative Region in its
judgment made on 29 January 1999, that these provisions
concern affairs which are the responsibility of the Central
Authorities and the relationship between the Central Authorities
and the Hong Kong Special Administrative Region, that the
Court of Final Appeal, before making its judgment, failed to seek
an interpretation of the provisions from the Standing Committee
of the National People's Congress in accordance with the
provisions of Paragraph 3 in Article 158 of the Basic Law of the
Hong Kong Special Administrative Region of the People's
Republic of China and that the interpretation of the Court of
Final Appeal is not in conformity with the original legislative
intent, the Standing Committee of the National People's
Congress, after consulting its Committee for the Basic Law of
the Hong Kong Special Administrative Region, decides to give
the following interpretations to the relevant provisions in the
Basic Law of the Hong Kong Special Administrative Region of
the People's Republic of China in accordance with the provisions
of Category (4) of Article 67 of the Constitution of the People's
Republic of China and Paragraph 1 in Article 158 of the Basic
Law of the Hong Kong Special Administrative Region of the
People's Republic of China:

Art 158 (3)

1. The provisions of Paragraph 4 in Article 22 of the Basic
   Law of the Hong Kong Special Administrative Region
   of the People's Republic of China "for entry into the
   Hong Kong Special Administrative Region, people from
   other parts of China must apply for approval", mean that
   persons from provinces, autonomous regions and
   municipalities directly under the Central Government,
   including the children of permanent residents of the
   Hong Kong Special Administrative Region born in the
   mainland with Chinese nationality, who request to enter

Art 22 (4)

進入香港特別行政區，均須依照國家有關法律、行政法規的規定，向其所在地區的有關機關申請辦理批准手續，並須持有有關機關製發的有效證件方能進入香港特別行政區。各省、自治區、直轄市的人，包括香港永久性居民在內地所生的中國籍子女，進入香港特別行政區，如未按國家有關法律、行政法規的規定辦理相應的批准手續，是不合法的。

Art 24 (2)

二、《中華人民共和國香港特別行政區基本法》第二十四條第二款前三項規定："香港特別行政區永久性居民為：(一) 在香港特別行政區成立以前或以後在香港出生的中國公民；(二) 在香港特別行政區成立以前或以後在香港通常居住連續七年以上的中國公民；(三) 第(一)、(二) 兩項所列居民在香港以外所生的中國籍子女"。其中第(三) 項關於「第(一)、(二) 兩項所列居民在香港以外所生的中國籍子女」的規定，是指無論本人是在香港特別行政區成立以前或以後出生，在

the Hong Kong Special Administrative Region with whatever reason shall, in accordance with the provisions of relevant laws and administrative regulations of the State, apply for approval from the relevant government department in the place of their residence and may only enter the Hong Kong Special Administrative Region with valid certificates issued by relevant authorities. It is illegal for any persons or children mentioned above to enter the Hong Kong Special Administrative Region without going through due approval procedures in accordance with the provisions of relevant laws and administrative regulations of the State.

2. The first three categories of Paragraph 2 in Article 24 of the Basic Law of the Hong Kong Special Administrative Region of the People's Republic of China provide: "The permanent residents of the Hong Kong Special Administrative Region shall be: (1) Chinese citizens born in Hong Kong before or after the establishment of the Hong Kong Special Administrative Region; (2) Chinese citizens who have ordinarily resided in Hong Kong for a continuous period of not less than seven years before or after the establishment of the Hong Kong Special Administrative Region; (3) Persons of Chinese nationality born outside Hong Kong of those residents listed in categories (1) and (2)". "Among these people, the persons provided for in Category (3) "Persons of Chinese nationality born outside Hong Kong of those residents listed in categories (1) and (2)" mean that those persons, at the time of their birth, no matter whether they were born before or after the establishment of the Hong Kong Special Administrative Region, whose parents or whose

Art 24 (2)

其出生時，其父母雙方或一方須是符合《中華人民共和國香港特別行政區基本法》第二十四條第二款第 (一) 項或第 (二) 項規定條件的人。本解釋所闡明的立法原意以及《中華人民共和國香港特別行政區基本法》第二十四條第二款其他各項的立法原意，已體現在1996年8月10日全國人民代表大會香港特別行政區籌備委員會第四次全體會議通過的《關於實施〈中華人民共和國香港特別行政區基本法〉第二十四條第二款的意見》中。

本解釋公布之後，香港特別行政區法院在引用《中華人民共和國香港特別行政區基本法》有關條款時，應以本解釋為準。本解釋不影響香港特別行政區終審法院1999年1月29日對有關案件判決的有關訴訟當事人所獲得的香港特別行政區居留權。此外，其他任何人是否符合《中華人民共和國香港特別行政區基本法》第二十四條第二款第 (三) 項規定的條件，均須以本解釋為準。

fathers or mothers are Chinese citizens as provided for in Category (1) or Category (2) of Paragraph 2 in Article 24 of the Basic Law of the Hong Kong Special Administrative Region. The original legislative intent elucidated by this Interpretation and the original legislative intent of the other categories of Paragraph 2 in Article 24 of the Basic Law of the Hong Kong Special Administrative Region have been embodied in the Opinions on the Implementation of the Second Paragraph of Article 24 of the Basic Law of the Hong Kong Special Administrative Region of the People's Republic of China, which were adopted at the Fourth Plenary Meeting of the Preparatory Committee for the Hong Kong Special Administrative Region of the National People's Congress on 10 August 1996. *Art 24 (2)*

After promulgation of this Interpretation, the courts of the Hong Kong Special Administrative Region shall, in applying the relevant articles of the Basic Law of the Hong Kong Special Administrative Region of the People's Republic of China, follow this Interpretation. This Interpretation does not affect the right of abode in the Hong Kong Special Administrative Region granted to the litigating party in the case through the judgment made by the Court of Final Appeal of the Hong Kong Special Administrative Region on 29 January 1999. As to whether any other person conforms to the provisions of Category (3) of Paragraph 2 in Article 24 of the Basic Law of the Hong Kong Special Administrative Region, the matter shall be decided according to this Interpretation. *Art 24 (2), 158*

文件二十六

Art 158,
Anx I (p 124),
Anx II (p 142)

全國人民代表大會常務委員會關於
《中華人民共和國香港特別行政區基本法》
附件一第七條和附件二第三條的解釋

(2004年4月6日第十屆全國人民代表大會
常務委員會第八次會議通過)

第十屆全國人民代表大會常務委員會第八次會議審議了
委員長會議關於提請審議《全國人民代表大會常務委員會
關於〈中華人民共和國香港特別行政區基本法〉附件一第
七條和附件二第三條的解釋(草案)》的議案。經徵詢全國
人民代表大會常務委員會香港特別行政區基本法委員會
的意見,全國人民代表大會常務委員會決定,根據《中華
人民共和國憲法》第六十七條第四項和《中華人民共和國

Art 158 (1)

香港特別行政區基本法》第一百五十八條第一款的規定,

Instrument 26

Interpretation by the Standing Committee of the National People's Congress Regarding Annex I (7) and Annex II (III) to the Basic Law of the Hong Kong Special Administrative Region of the People's Republic of China

Art 158,
Anx I (p 125),
Anx II (p 143)

(Adopted at the Eighth Meeting of the Standing Committee
of the Tenth National People's Congress on 6 April 2004)

At its 8th Meeting, the Standing Committee of the Tenth National People's Congress examined the motion proposed by the Council of Chairmen requesting examination of the Draft Interpretation by the Standing Committee of the National People's Congress Regarding Annex I (7) and Annex II (III) to the Basic Law of the Hong Kong Special Administrative Region of the People's Republic of China. Having consulted the Committee for the Basic Law of the Hong Kong Special Administrative Region under the Standing Committee of the National People's Congress, the Standing Committee of the National People's Congress has decided, in accordance with the provisions in Subparagraph (4) of Article 67 of the Constitution of the People's Republic of China and the provisions in the first paragraph of Article 158 of the Basic Law of the Hong Kong Special Administrative Region of the People's Republic of China,

Art 158 (1)

Note:

This English translation is reproduced from "The Laws of the People's Republic of China 2004" compiled by the Legislative Affairs Commission of the Standing Committee of the National People's Congress of the People's Republic of China. It is for reference only and has no legislative effect.

Anx I (p 124)
Anx II (p 142)

對《中華人民共和國香港特別行政區基本法》附件一《香港特別行政區行政長官的產生辦法》第七條"二〇〇七年以後各任行政長官的產生辦法如需修改,須經立法會全體議員三分之二多數通過,行政長官同意,並報全國人民代表大會常務委員會批准"的規定和附件二《香港特別行政區立法會的產生辦法和表決程序》第三條"二〇〇七年以後香港特別行政區立法會的產生辦法和法案、議案的表決程序,如需對本附件的規定進行修改,須經立法會全體議員三分之二多數通過,行政長官同意,並報全國人民代表大會常務委員會備案"的規定,作如下解釋:

一、 上述兩個附件中規定的"二〇〇七年以後",含二〇〇七年。

二、 上述兩個附件中規定的二〇〇七年以後各任行政長官的產生辦法、立法會的產生辦法和法案、議案的表決程序"如需"修改,是指可以進行修改,也可以不進行修改。

to make the following interpretation of the provisions of Annex I (7) to the Basic Law of the Hong Kong Special Administrative Region of the People's Republic of China, under the Method for the Selection of the Chief Executive of the Hong Kong Special Administrative Region, which reads, "If there is a need to amend the method for selecting the Chief Executives for the terms subsequent to the year 2007, such amendments must be made with the endorsement of a two-thirds majority of all the members of the Legislative Council and the consent of the Chief Executive, and they shall be reported to the Standing Committee of the National People's Congress for approval", and the provisions of Annex II (III), under the Method for the Formation of the Legislative Council of the Hong Kong Special Administrative Region and its Voting Procedures, which reads, "With regard to the method for forming the Legislative Council of the Hong Kong Special Administrative Region and its procedures for voting on bills and motions after 2007, if there is a need to amend the provisions of this Annex, such amendments must be made with the endorsement of a two-thirds majority of all the members of the Council and the consent of the Chief Executive, and they shall be reported to the Standing Committee of the National People's Congress for the record":

Anx I (p 124)

Anx II (p 135)

1. The phrases "subsequent to the year 2007" and "after 2007" stipulated in the two Annexes mentioned above include the year 2007.

2. The provisions in the two Annexes mentioned above that "if there is a need" to amend the method for selecting the Chief Executives for the terms subsequent to the year 2007 or the method for forming the Legislative Council and its procedures for voting on bills and motions after 2007 mean that they may be amended or remain unamended.

三、 上述兩個附件中規定的須經立法會全體議員三分之二多數通過，行政長官同意，並報全國人民代表大會常務委員會批准或者備案，是指行政長官的產生辦法和立法會的產生辦法及立法會法案、議案的表決程序修改時必經的法律程序。只有經過上述程序，包括最後全國人民代表大會常務委員會依法批准或者備案，該修改方可生效。是否需要進行修改，香港特別行政區行政長官應向全國人民代表大會常務委員會提出報告，由全國人民代表大會常務委員會依照《中華人民共和國香港特別行政區基本法》第四十五條和第六十八條規定，根據香港特別行政區的實際情況和循序漸進的原則確定。修改行政長官產生辦法和立法會產生辦法及立法會法案、議案表決程序的法案及其修正案，應由香港特別行政區政府向立法會提出。

Art 43, 45, 68

Art 62 (5)

3.   The provisions in the two Annexes mentioned above that any amendment must be made with the endorsement of a two-thirds majority of all the members of the Legislative Council and the consent of the Chief Executive and shall be reported to the Standing Committee of the National People's Congress for approval or for the record mean the legislative process that must be gone through before the method for selecting the Chief Executive and the method for forming the Legislative Council and its procedures for voting on bills and motions are to be amended. Such an amendment may become effective only if it has gone through the said process, including the approval finally given by the said Committee in accordance with law or the reporting to the Committee for the record. The Chief Executive of the Hong Kong Special Administrative Region shall present a report to the Standing Committee of the National People's Congress as regards whether there is a need to make an amendment, and the Committee shall, in accordance with the provisions in Articles 45 and 68 of the Basic Law of the Hong Kong Special Administrative Region of the People's Republic of China, make a determination in the light of the actual situation in the Hong Kong Special Administrative Region and in accordance with the principle of gradual and orderly progress. The bills on amendments to the method for selecting the Chief Executive and the method for forming the Legislative Council and its procedures for voting on bills and motions and the proposed amendments to such bills shall be introduced by the Government of the Hong Kong Special Administrative Region into the Legislative Council.

Art 43, 45, 68

Art 62 (5)

Anx I (p 124),
Anx II (p 142)

四、 上述兩個附件中規定的行政長官的產生辦法、立法會的產生辦法和法案、議案的表決程序如果不作修改,行政長官的產生辦法仍適用附件一關於行政長官產生辦法的規定;立法會的產生辦法和法案、議案的表決程序仍適用附件二關於第三屆立法會產生辦法的規定和附件二關於法案、議案的表決程序的規定。

現予公告。

4. If no amendment is made to the method for selecting the Chief Executive, the method for forming the Legislative Council and its procedures for voting on bills and motions as stipulated in the two Annexes mentioned above, the provisions relating to the method for selecting the Chief Executive in Annex I will remain applicable to the method for selecting the Chief Executive, and the provisions relating to the method for forming the third term of the Legislative Council in Annex II and the provisions relating to its procedures for voting on bills and motions in Annex II will remain applicable to the method for forming the Legislative Council and its procedures for voting on bills and motions.

Anx I (p 125), Anx II (p 143)

This Interpretation is hereby announced.

文件二十七

Art 158,
Art 53

全國人民代表大會常務委員會關於
《中華人民共和國香港特別行政區基本法》
第五十三條第二款的解釋

（2005年4月27日第十屆全國人民代表大會
常務委員會第十五次會議通過）

Art 158 (1),
Inst 4 (p 194)

第十屆全國人民代表大會常務委員會第十五次會議審議了國務院《關於提請解釋〈中華人民共和國香港特別行政區基本法〉第五十三條第二款的議案》。根據《中華人民共和國憲法》第六十七條第四項和《中華人民共和國香港特別行政區基本法》第一百五十八條第一款的規定，並徵詢全國人民代表大會常務委員會香港特別行政區基本法委員會的意見，全國人民代表大會常務委員會對《中華人民共和國香港特別行政區基本法》第五十三條第二款的規定，作如下解釋：

Instrument 27

Interpretation by the Standing Committee of the National People's Congress Regarding the Second Paragraph in Article 53 of the Basic Law of the Hong Kong Special Administrative Region of the People's Republic of China

Art 158,
Art 53

(Adopted at the Fifteenth Meeting of the Standing Committee
of the Tenth National People's Congress on 27 April 2005)

At its 15th Meeting, the Standing Committee of the Tenth National People's Congress discussed the State Council's Proposal for Giving an Interpretation to the Second Paragraph in Article 53 of the Basic Law of the Hong Kong Special Administrative Region of the People's Republic of China. After consulting its Committee for the Basic Law of the Hong Kong Special Administrative Region, the Standing Committee of the National People's Congress, in accordance with the provisions of the fourth paragraph in Article 67 of the Constitution of the People's Republic of China and the first paragraph in Article 158 of the Basic Law of the Hong Kong Special Administrative Region of the People's Republic of China, gives the following interpretation to the provisions of the second paragraph in Article 53 of the Basic Law of the Hong Kong Special Administrative Region of the People's Republic of China:

Art 158 (1),
Inst 4 (p 195)

Note:

This English translation is reproduced from "The Laws of the People's Republic of China 2005" compiled by the Legislative Affairs Commission of the Standing Committee of the National People's Congress of the People's Republic of China. It is for reference only and has no legislative effect.

Art 53

　　《中華人民共和國香港特別行政區基本法》第五十三條第二款中規定："行政長官缺位時，應在六個月內依本法第四十五條的規定產生新的行政長官。"其中"依本法第四十五條的規定產生新的行政長官"，既包括新的行政長官應依據《中華人民共和國香港特別行政區基本法》第四十五條規定的產生辦法產生，也包括新的行政長官的任期應依據《中華人民共和國香港特別行政區基本法》第四十五條規定的產生辦法確定。

Art 45

　　《中華人民共和國香港特別行政區基本法》第四十五條第三款規定："行政長官產生的具體辦法由附件一《香港特別行政區行政長官的產生辦法》規定。"附件一第一條規定："行政長官由一個具有廣泛代表性的選舉委員會根據本法選出，由中央人民政府任命。"第二條規定："選舉委員會每屆任期五年。"第七條規定："二〇〇七年以後各任行政長官的產生辦法如需修改，須經立法會全體議員三分之二多數通過，行政長官同意，並報全國人民代表大會常務委員會批准。"上述規定表明，二〇〇七年以前，在

Art 45
Anx I (p 124)

The second paragraph in Article 53 of the Basic Law of the Hong Kong Special Administrative Region of the People's Republic of China stipulates, "In the event that the office of Chief Executive becomes vacant, a new Chief Executive shall be selected within six months in accordance with the provisions of Article 45 of this Law." The provision that "a new Chief Executive shall be selected within six months in accordance with the provisions of Article 45 of this Law" means that a new Chief Executive shall be selected in accordance with the method of selection provided for under Article 45 of the Basic Law, and that the term of office of the new Chief Executive shall be determined in accordance with the method of selection provided for under Article 45 of the Basic Law.

The third paragraph in Article 45 of the Basic Law of the Hong Kong Special Administrative Region of the People's Republic of China stipulates, "The specific method for selecting the Chief Executive is prescribed in Annex I 'Method for the Selection of the Chief Executive of the Hong Kong Special Administrative Region'." Clause 1 of Annex I stipulates, "The Chief Executive shall be elected by a broadly representative Election Committee in accordance with this Law and appointed by the Central People's Government." Under Clause 2 it is stipulated that, "The term of office of the Election Committee shall be five years." Clause 7 stipulates, " If there is a need to amend the method for selecting the Chief Executives for the terms subsequent to the year 2007, such amendments must be made with the endorsement of a two-thirds majority of all the members of the Legislative Council and the consent of the Chief Executive, and they shall be reported to the Standing Committee of the National People's Congress for approval." The provisions mentioned above indicate that before the year of 2007, under the arrangement made

行政長官由任期五年的選舉委員會選出的制度安排下，如
出現行政長官未任滿《中華人民共和國香港特別行政區基
本法》第四十六條規定的五年任期導致行政長官缺位的
情況，新的行政長官的任期應為原行政長官的剩餘任期；
二〇〇七年以後，如對上述行政長官產生辦法作出修改，
屆時出現行政長官缺位的情況，新的行政長官的任期應
根據修改後的行政長官具體產生辦法確定。

現予公告。

according to the system whereby the Chief Executive is elected by the Election Committee, the term of office of which is five years, in the event that the office of Chief Executive becomes vacant before the expiration of the five years prescribed in Article 46 of the Basic Law of the Hong Kong Special Administrative Region of the People's Republic of China, the term of office of the new Chief Executive shall be the remainder of the term of office of the previous Chief Executive; after 2007, should amendment be made to the above-mentioned method for selecting the Chief Executive, the term of office of the new Chief Executive shall be determined according to the specific method amended for selecting the Chief Executive, in the event that the office of the then Chief Executive becomes vacant.

Art 46

This Interpretation is hereby announced.

文件二十八

Art 158,
Art 13, 19

全國人民代表大會常務委員會關於 《中華人民共和國香港特別行政區基本法》 第十三條第一款和第十九條的解釋

(2011年8月26日第十一屆全國人民代表大會
常務委員會第二十二次會議通過)

Art 13, 19,
158 (3)

第十一屆全國人民代表大會常務委員會第二十二次會議
審議了委員長會議關於提請審議《全國人民代表大會常
務委員會關於〈中華人民共和國香港特別行政區基本法〉
第十三條第一款和第十九條的解釋(草案)》的議案。委
員長會議的議案是應香港特別行政區終審法院依據《中
華人民共和國香港特別行政區基本法》第一百五十八條
第三款的規定提請全國人民代表大會常務委員會解釋
《中華人民共和國香港特別行政區基本法》有關規定的報
告提出的。

Instrument 28

Interpretation by the Standing Committee of the National People's Congress Regarding the First Paragraph of Article 13 and Article 19 of the Basic Law of the Hong Kong Special Administrative Region of the People's Republic of China

Art 158,
Art 13, 19

(Adopted at the Twenty-second Meeting of the Standing Committee
of the Eleventh National People's Congress on 26 August 2011)

The Standing Committee of the Eleventh National People's Congress deliberated at its 22nd Meeting the Draft Interpretation by the Standing Committee of the National People's Congress Regarding the first paragraph of Article 13 and Article 19 of the Basic Law of the Hong Kong Special Administrative Region of the People's Republic of China which was proposed for deliberation by the Chairmen's Council. The proposal of the Chairmen's Council was submitted upon the report by the Court of Final Appeal of Hong Kong Special Administrative Region requesting the Standing Committee of the National People's Congress to interpret the relevant provisions of the Basic Law of the Hong Kong Special Administrative Region of the People's Republic of China, in accordance with the third paragraph of Article 158 of the Basic Law of the Hong Kong Special Administrative Region of the People's Republic of China.

Art 13, 19,
158 (3)

Note:

　　香港特別行政區終審法院在審理一起與剛果民主共和國有關的案件時，涉及香港特別行政區是否應適用中央人民政府決定採取的國家豁免規則或政策的問題。為此，香港特別行政區終審法院依據《中華人民共和國香港特別行政區基本法》第一百五十八條第三款的規定，提請全國人民代表大會常務委員會解釋如下問題："（1）根據第十三條第一款的真正解釋，中央人民政府是否有權力決定中華人民共和國的國家豁免規則或政策；（2）如有此權力的話，根據第十三條第一款和第十九條的真正解釋，香港特別行政區（'香港特區'）（包括香港特區的法院）是否：①有責任援用或實施中央人民政府根據第十三條第一款所決定的國家豁免規則或政策；或②反之，可隨意偏離中央人民政府根據第十三條第一款所決定的國家豁免規則或政策，並採取一項不同的規則；（3）中央人民政府決定國家豁免規則或政策是否屬於《基本法》第十九條第三款第一句中所說的'國防、外交等國家行為'；以及（4）香港特區成立後，第十三條第一款、第十九條和香港作為中華人民共和國的特別行政區的地位，對香港原有（即1997年7月1日之前）的有關國家豁免的普通法（如果這些法律

Art 13, 19, 158 (3)

The Court of Final Appeal of the Hong Kong Special Administrative Region needs to ascertain, in adjudicating a case involving the Democratic Republic of Congo, whether the Hong Kong Special Administrative Region should apply the rules or policies on state immunity as determined by the Central People's Government. For this purpose, in accordance with the provisions of the third paragraph of Article 158 of the Basic Law of the Hong Kong Special Administrative Region of the People's Republic of China, the Court of Final Appeal of the Hong Kong Special Administrative Region seeks an interpretation from the Standing Committee of the National People's Congress on the following questions: "(1) whether on the true interpretation of the first paragraph of Article 13, the Central People's Government has the power to determine the rule or policy of the People's Republic of China on state immunity; (2) if so, whether on the true interpretation of the first paragraph of Article 13 and Article 19, the Hong Kong Special Administrative Region (HKSAR) , including the courts of the HKSAR: (i) is bound to apply or give effect to the rule or policy on state immunity determined by the Central People's Government under the first paragraph of Article 13; or (ii) on the other hand, is at liberty to depart from the rule or policy on state immunity determined by the Central People's Government under the first paragraph of Article 13 and to adopt a different rule; (3) whether the determination by the Central People's Government as to the rule or policy on state immunity falls within 'acts of the State such as national defense and foreign affairs' in the first sentence of the third paragraph of Article 19 of the Basic Law; and (4) whether, upon the establishment of the HKSAR, the effect of the first paragraph of Article 13, Article 19 and the status of Hong Kong as a special administrative region of the People's Republic of China upon the common law on state immunity previously in force in Hong Kong (this is, before 1 July 1997), to the extent that such common law was

Art 8, 160

與中央人民政府根據第十三條第一款所決定的國家豁免規則或政策有抵觸）所帶來的影響，是否令到這些普通法法律，須按照《基本法》第八條和第一百六十條及於1997

Inst 7 (p 202)

年2月23日根據第一百六十條作出的《全國人民代表大會常務委員會的決定》的規定，在適用時作出必要的變更、適應、限制或例外，以確保關於這方面的普通法符合中央人民政府所決定的國家豁免規則或政策。"香港特別行政區終審法院上述提請解釋的做法符合《中華人民共和國香港特別行政區基本法》第一百五十八條第三款的規定。

Art 13, 19, 158

根據《中華人民共和國憲法》第六十七條第（四）項和《中華人民共和國香港特別行政區基本法》第一百五十八條的規定，並徵詢全國人民代表大會常務委員會香港特別行政區基本法委員會的意見，全國人民代表大會常務委員會就香港特別行政區終審法院提請解釋的《中華人民共和國香港特別行政區基本法》第十三條第一款和第十九條的規定以及相關問題，作如下解釋：

inconsistent with the rule or policy on state immunity as *Art 8, 160*
determined by the Central People's Government pursuant to the
first paragraph of Article 13, was to require such common law to
be applied subject to such modifications, adaptations, limitations
or exceptions as were necessary to ensure that such common law
is consistent with the rule or policy on state immunity as
determined by the Central People's Government, in accordance *Inst 7 (p 203)*
with Article 8 and Article 160 of the Basic Law and the Decisions
of the Standing Committee of the National People's Congress
issued on 23 February 1997 made pursuant to Article 160." The
above request for interpretation by the Court of Final Appeal of
the Hong Kong Special Administrative Region complies with the
provisions of the third paragraph of Article 158 of the Basic Law
of the Hong Kong Special Administrative Region of the People's
Republic of China.

Pursuant to Subparagraph (4) of Article 67 of the Constitution *Art 13, 19, 158*
of the People's Republic of China and Article 158 of the Basic
Law of the Hong Kong Special Administrative Region of the
People's Republic of China, and after consulting the Committee
for the Basic Law of the Hong Kong Special Administrative
Region under the Standing Committee of the National People's
Congress, the Standing Committee of the National People's
Congress, in relation to the request for interpretation by the
Court of Final Appeal of the Hong Kong Special Administrative
Region, hereby makes the following interpretation of the
provisions of the first paragraph of Article 13 and Article 19 of
the Basic Law of the Hong Kong Special Administrative Region
of the People's Republic of China and related issues:

一、 關於香港特別行政區終審法院提請解釋的第 (1) 個問題。依照《中華人民共和國憲法》第八十九條第 (九) 項的規定,國務院即中央人民政府行使管理國家對外事務的職權,國家豁免規則或政策屬於國家對外事務中的外交事務範疇,中央人民政府有權決定中華人民共和國的國家豁免規則或政策,在中華人民共和國領域內統一實施。基於上述,根據《中華人民共和國香港特別行政區基本法》第十三條第一款關於“中央人民政府負責管理與香港特別行政區有關的外交事務”的規定,管理與香港特別行政區有關的外交事務屬於中央人民政府的權力,中央人民政府有權決定在香港特別行政區適用的國家豁免規則或政策。

二、 關於香港特別行政區終審法院提請解釋的第 (2) 個問題。依照《中華人民共和國香港特別行政區基本法》第十三條第一款和本解釋第一條的規定,中央人民政府有權決定在香港特別行政

1.   On question (1) on which an interpretation is sought by
      the Court of Final Appeal of the Hong Kong Special
      Administrative Region. According to Subparagraph (9),
      Article 89 of the Constitution of the People's Republic
      of China, the State Council as the Central People's
      Government exercises the function and power to conduct
      the foreign affairs of the State; as the rules or policies on
      state immunity fall within diplomatic affairs in the realm
      of the foreign affairs of the state, the Central People's
      Government has the power to determine the rules or
      policies of the People's Republic of China on state
      immunity to be given effect to uniformly in the territory
      of the People's Republic of China. Based on the above,
      in accordance with the provisions of the first paragraph
      of Article 13 of the Basic Law of the Hong Kong Special
      Administrative Region of the People's Republic of China
      that "the Central People's Government shall be
      responsible for the foreign affairs relating to the Hong
      Kong Special Administrative Region", the conduct of the
      foreign affairs relating to the Hong Kong Special
      Administrative Region falls within the power of the
      Central People's Government. The Central People's
      Government has the power to determine the rules or
      policies on state immunity to be applied in the Hong
      Kong Special Administrative Region.

Art 13

2.   On question (2) on which an interpretation is sought by
      the Court of Final Appeal of the Hong Kong Special
      Administrative Region. According to the provisions of
      the first paragraph of Article 13 of the Basic Law of the
      Hong Kong Special Administrative Region of the
      People's Republic of China and Article 1 of this
      Interpretation, the Central People's Government has the
      power to determine the rules or policies on state

Art 13, 19

區適用的國家豁免規則或政策；依照《中華人民共和國香港特別行政區基本法》第十九條和本解釋第三條的規定，香港特別行政區法院對中央人民政府決定國家豁免規則或政策的行為無管轄權。因此，香港特別行政區法院在審理案件時遇有外國國家及其財產管轄豁免和執行豁免問題，須適用和實施中央人民政府決定適用於香港特別行政區的國家豁免規則或政策。基於上述，根據《中華人民共和國香港特別行政區基本法》第十三條第一款和第十九條的規定，香港特別行政區，包括香港特別行政區法院，有責任適用或實施中央人民政府決定採取的國家豁免規則或政策，不得偏離上述規則或政策，也不得採取與上述規則或政策不同的規則。

Art 19

三、 關於香港特別行政區終審法院提請解釋的第(3)個問題。國家豁免涉及一國法院對外國國家及其財產是否擁有管轄權，外國國家及其財產在一國法院是否享有豁免，直接關係到該國的對

immunity to be applied in the Hong Kong Special Administrative Region. According to the provisions of Article 19 of the Basic Law of the Hong Kong Special Administrative Region of the People's Republic of China and Article 3 of this Interpretation, the courts of the Hong Kong Special Administrative Region have no jurisdiction over the act of the Central People's Government in determining the rules or policies on state immunity. Therefore, when questions of immunity from jurisdiction and immunity from execution of foreign states and their properties arise in the adjudication of cases, the courts of the Hong Kong Special Administrative Region must apply and give effect to the rules or policies on state immunity determined by the Central People's Government as being applicable to the Hong Kong Special Administrative Region. Based on the above, in accordance with the provisions of the first paragraph of Article 13 and Article 19 of the Basic Law of the Hong Kong Special Administrative Region of the People's Republic of China, the Hong Kong Special Administrative Region, including the courts of the Hong Kong Special Administrative Region, is under a duty to apply or give effect to the rules or policies on state immunity that the Central People's Government has determined, and must not depart from the abovementioned rules or policies nor adopt a rule that is inconsistent with the abovementioned rules or policies.

3. On question (3) on which an interpretation is sought by the Court of Final Appeal of the Hong Kong Special Administrative Region. State immunity concerns whether the courts of a state have jurisdiction over foreign states and their properties and whether foreign states and their properties enjoy immunity in the courts of a state. It

Art 19

363

外關係和國際權利與義務。因此，決定國家豁免規則或政策是一種涉及外交的國家行為。基於上述，《中華人民共和國香港特別行政區基本法》第十九條第三款規定的"國防、外交等國家行為"包括中央人民政府決定國家豁免規則或政策的行為。

Art 8, 160

四、 關於香港特別行政區終審法院提請解釋的第 (4) 個問題。依照《中華人民共和國香港特別行政區基本法》第八條和第一百六十條的規定，香港原有法律只有在不抵觸《中華人民共和國香港特別行政區基本法》的情況下才予以保留。根據

Inst 7 (p 202)

《全國人民代表大會常務委員會關於根據〈中華人民共和國香港特別行政區基本法〉第一百六十條處理香港原有法律的決定》第四條的規定，採用為香港特別行政區法律的香港原有法律，自1997年7月1日起，在適用時，應作出必要的變更、適應、限制或例外，以符合中華人民共和國

directly relates to the state's foreign relations and international rights and obligations. Therefore, the determination as to the rules or policies on state immunity is an act of state involving foreign affairs. Based on the above, "acts of the State such as national defense and foreign affairs" as stipulated in the third paragraph of Article 19 of the Basic Law of the Hong Kong Special Administrative Region of the People's Republic of China includes the act of determination by the Central People's Government as to the rules or policies on state immunity.

4.   On question (4) on which an interpretation is sought by the Court of Final Appeal of the Hong Kong Specials Administrative Region. According to the provisions of Articles 8 and 160 of the Basic Law of the Hong Kong Special Administrative Region of the People's Republic of China, the laws previously in force in Hong Kong shall be maintained only if there is no contravention of the Basic Law of the Hong Kong Special Administrative Region of the People's Republic of China. In accordance with the provisions of Article 4 of the Decision of the Standing Committee of the National People's Congress Concerning the Handling of the Laws Previously in Force in Hong Kong in Accordance with Article 160 of the Basic Law of the Hong Kong Special Administrative Region of the People's Republic of China, such of the laws previously in force in Hong Kong which have been adopted as the laws of the Hong Kong Special Administrative Region shall, as from 1 July 1997, be applied subject to such modification, adaptations, limitations or exceptions as are necessary so as to bring them into conformity with the status of Hong Kong after resumption by the People's Republic of China of the exercise of sovereignty over Hong Kong as well as to be

Art 8, 160

Inst 7 (p 203)

Art 12, 13,
19, 160

對香港恢復行使主權後香港的地位和《基本法》的有關規定。香港特別行政區作為中華人民共和國一個享有高度自治權的地方行政區域，直轄於中央人民政府，必須執行中央人民政府決定的國家豁免規則或政策。香港原有法律中有關國家豁免的規則必須符合上述規定才能在1997年7月1日後繼續適用。基於上述，根據《中華人民共和國香港特別行政區基本法》第十三條第一款和第十九條的規定，依照《全國人民代表大會常務委員會關於根據〈中華人民共和國香港特別行政區基本法〉第一百六十條處理香港原有法律的決定》採用為香港特別行政區法律的香港原有法律中有關國家豁免的規則，從1997年7月1日起，在適用時，須作出必要的變更、適應、限制或例外，以符合中央人民政府決定採取的國家豁免規則或政策。

現予公告。

in conformity with the relevant provisions of the Basic Law. The Hong Kong Special Administrative Region, as a local administrative region of the People's Republic of China that enjoys a high degree of autonomy and comes directly under the Central People's Government, must give effect to the rules or policies on state immunity as determined by the Central People's Government. The laws previously in force in Hong Kong relating to the rules on state immunity may continue to be applied after 1 July 1997 only if they comply with the above requirements. Based on the above, in accordance with the provisions of the first paragraph of Article 13 and Article 19 of the Basic Law of the Hong Kong Special Administrative Region of the People's Republic of China, such of the laws previously in force in Hong Kong concerning the rules on state immunity which have been adopted as the laws of the Hong Kong Special Administrative Region according to the Decision of the Standing Committee of the National People's Congress Concerning the Handling of the Laws Previously in Force in Accordance with Article 160 of the Basic Law of the Hong Kong Special Administrative Region of the People's Republic of China, which applied as from 1 July 1997, must be subject to such modifications, adaptations, limitations or exceptions as are necessary so as to be consistent with the rules or policies on state immunity that the Central People's Government has determined.

The interpretation is hereby announced.

Art 12, 13, 19, 160

文件二十九

Art 158,
Art 104

全國人民代表大會常務委員會關於
《中華人民共和國香港特別行政區基本法》
第一百零四條的解釋

(2016年11月7日第十二屆全國人民代表大會
常務委員會第二十四次會議通過)

Art 158 (1),
Inst 4 (p 194)

第十二屆全國人民代表大會常務委員會第二十四次會議審議了委員長會議提請審議《全國人民代表大會常務委員會關於〈中華人民共和國香港特別行政區基本法〉第一百零四條的解釋(草案)》的議案。經徵詢全國人民代表大會常務委員會香港特別行政區基本法委員會的意見,全國人民代表大會常務委員會決定,根據《中華人民共和國憲法》第六十七條第四項和《中華人民共和國香港特別行政區基本法》第一百五十八條第一款的規定,對《中華人民共和國香港特別行政區基本法》第一百零四條"香港特別行政區行政長官、主要官員、行政會議成員、立法會議

Instrument 29

Interpretation of Article 104 of the Basic Law of the Hong Kong Special Administrative Region of the People's Republic of China by the Standing Committee of the National People's Congress

Art 158,
Art 104

(Adopted by the Standing Committee of the Twelfth National People's Congress at its Twenty-fourth Session on 7 November 2016)

Art 158 (1),
Inst 4 (p 195)

The Standing Committee of the Twelfth National People's Congress examined at its Twenty-fourth Session the motion regarding the request for examination of the Draft Interpretation of Article 104 of the Basic Law of the Hong Kong Special Administrative Region of the People's Republic of China submitted by the Council of Chairmen. Having consulted the Committee for the Basic Law of the Hong Kong Special Administrative Region under the Standing Committee of the National People's Congress, the Standing Committee of the National People's Congress has decided to make, under the provisions of Article 67(4) of the Constitution of the People's Republic of China and Article 158(1) of the Basic Law of the Hong Kong Special Administrative Region of the People's Republic of China, an interpretation of the provisions of Article 104 of the Basic Law of the Hong Kong Special Administrative Region of the People's Republic of China regarding "When assuming office, the Chief Executive, principal officials, members

Note:
    This is an English translation of the original instrument in Chinese and is published for information.

員、各級法院法官和其他司法人員在就職時必須依法宣誓擁護中華人民共和國香港特別行政區基本法,效忠中華人民共和國香港特別行政區"的規定,作如下解釋:

Art 104

一、《中華人民共和國香港特別行政區基本法》第一百零四條規定的"擁護中華人民共和國香港特別行政區基本法,效忠中華人民共和國香港特別行政區",既是該條規定的宣誓必須包含的法定內容,也是參選或者出任該條所列公職的法定要求和條件。

Art 104

二、《中華人民共和國香港特別行政區基本法》第一百零四條規定相關公職人員"就職時必須依法宣誓",具有以下含義:

(一) 宣誓是該條所列公職人員就職的法定條件和必經程序。未進行合法有效宣誓或者拒絕宣誓,不得就任相應公職,不得行使相應職權和享受相應待遇。

of the Executive Council and of the Legislative Council, judges of the courts at all levels and other members of the judiciary in the Hong Kong Special Administrative Region must, in accordance with law, swear to uphold the Basic Law of the Hong Kong Special Administrative Region of the People's Republic of China and swear allegiance to the Hong Kong Special Administrative Region of the People's Republic of China" as follows:

1. "To uphold the Basic Law of the Hong Kong Special Administrative Region of the People's Republic of China" and to bear "allegiance to the Hong Kong Special Administrative Region of the People's Republic of China" as stipulated in Article 104 of the Basic Law of the Hong Kong Special Administrative Region of the People's Republic of China, are not only the legal content which must be included in the oath prescribed by the Article, but also the legal requirements and preconditions for standing for election in respect of or taking up the public office specified in the Article.

   Art 104

2. The provisions in Article 104 of the Basic Law of the Hong Kong Special Administrative Region of the People's Republic of China that "When assuming office", the relevant public officers "must, in accordance with law, swear" bear the following meaning:

   Art 104

   (1) Oath taking is the legal prerequisite and required procedure for public officers specified in the Article to assume office. No public office shall be assumed, no corresponding powers and functions shall be exercised, and no corresponding entitlements shall be enjoyed by anyone who fails to lawfully and validly take the oath or who declines to take the oath.

(二) 宣誓必須符合法定的形式和內容要求。宣誓人必須真誠、莊重地進行宣誓，必須準確、完整、莊重地宣讀包括"擁護中華人民共和國香港特別行政區基本法，效忠中華人民共和國香港特別行政區"內容的法定誓言。

(三) 宣誓人拒絕宣誓，即喪失就任該條所列相應公職的資格。宣誓人故意宣讀與法定誓言不一致的誓言或者以任何不真誠、不莊重的方式宣誓，也屬於拒絕宣誓，所作宣誓無效，宣誓人即喪失就任該條所列相應公職的資格。

(四) 宣誓必須在法律規定的監誓人面前進行。監誓人負有確保宣誓合法進行的責任，對符合本解釋和香港特別行政區法律規定的宣誓，應確定為有效宣誓；對不符合本解釋和香港特別行政區法律規定的宣誓，應確定為無效宣誓，並不得重新安排宣誓。

(2) Oath taking must comply with the legal requirements in respect of its form and content. An oath taker must take the oath sincerely and solemnly, and must accurately, completely and solemnly read out the oath prescribed by law, the content of which includes "will uphold the Basic Law of the Hong Kong Special Administrative Region of the People's Republic of China, bear allegiance to the Hong Kong Special Administrative Region of the People's Republic of China".

(3) An oath taker is disqualified forthwith from assuming the public office specified in the Article if he or she declines to take the oath. An oath taker who intentionally reads out words which do not accord with the wording of the oath prescribed by law, or takes the oath in a manner which is not sincere or not solemn, shall be treated as declining to take the oath. The oath so taken is invalid and the oath taker is disqualified forthwith from assuming the public office specified in the Article.

(4) The oath must be taken before the person authorized by law to administer the oath. The person administering the oath has the duty to ensure that the oath is taken in a lawful manner. He or she shall determine that an oath taken in compliance with this Interpretation and the requirements under the laws of the Hong Kong Special Administrative Region is valid, and that an oath which is not taken in compliance with this Interpretation and the requirements under the laws of the Hong Kong Special Administrative Region is invalid. If the oath taken is determined as invalid, no arrangement shall be made for retaking the oath.

三、《中華人民共和國香港特別行政區基本法》第
　　一百零四條所規定的宣誓，是該條所列公職人員
　　對中華人民共和國及其香港特別行政區作出的
　　法律承諾，具有法律約束力。宣誓人必須真誠信
　　奉並嚴格遵守法定誓言。宣誓人作虛假宣誓或
　　者在宣誓之後從事違反誓言行為的，依法承擔法
　　律責任。

現予公告。

3. The taking of the oath stipulated by Article 104 of the **Art 79, 104**
Basic Law of the Hong Kong Special Administrative
Region of the People's Republic of China is a legal pledge
made by the public officers specified in the Article to the
People's Republic of China and its Hong Kong Special
Administrative Region, and is legally binding. The oath
taker must sincerely believe in and strictly abide by the
relevant oath prescribed by law. An oath taker who makes
a false oath, or, who, after taking the oath, engages in
conduct in breach of the oath, shall bear legal
responsibility in accordance with law.

This Interpretation is hereby announced.

《中華人民共和國香港特別行政區維護國家安全法》

（2020年6月30日第十三屆全國人民代表大會常務委員會
第二十次會議通過）

The Law of the People's Republic of China on Safeguarding National Security in the Hong Kong Special Administrative Region

(Adopted by the Standing Committee of the Thirteenth National People's Congress at its Twenty Session on 30 June 2020)

第一章　總則

第一條

為堅定不移並全面準確貫徹"一國兩制"、"港人治港"、高度自治的方針，維護國家安全，防範、制止和懲治與香港特別行政區有關的分裂國家、顛覆國家政權、組織實施恐怖活動和勾結外國或者境外勢力危害國家安全等犯罪，保持香港特別行政區的繁榮和穩定，保障香港特別行政區居民的合法權益，根據中華人民共和國憲法、中華人民共和國香港特別行政區基本法和全國人民代表大會關於建立健全香港特別行政區維護國家安全的法律制度和執行機制的決定，制定本法。

第二條

關於香港特別行政區法律地位的香港特別行政區基本法第一條和第十二條規定是香港特別行政區基本法的根本性條款。香港特別行政區任何機構、組織和個人行使權利和自由，不得違背香港特別行政區基本法第一條和第十二條的規定。

Chapter I: General Principles

Article 1

This Law is enacted, in accordance with the Constitution of the People's Republic of China, the Basic Law of the Hong Kong Special Administrative Region of the People's Republic of China, and the Decision of the National People's Congress on Establishing and Improving the Legal System and Enforcement Mechanisms for Safeguarding National Security in the Hong Kong Special Administrative Region, for the purpose of: ensuring the resolute, full and faithful implementation of the policy of One Country, Two Systems under which the people of Hong Kong administer Hong Kong with a high degree of autonomy; safeguarding national security; preventing, suppressing and imposing punishment for the offences of secession, subversion, organisation and perpetration of terrorist activities, and collusion with a foreign country or with external elements to endanger national security in relation to the Hong Kong Special Administrative Region; maintaining prosperity and stability of the Hong Kong Special Administrative Region; and protecting the lawful rights and interests of the residents of the Hong Kong Special Administrative Region.

Article 2

The provisions in Articles 1 and 12 of the Basic Law of the Hong Kong Special Administrative Region on the legal status of the Hong Kong Special Administrative Region are the fundamental provisions in the Basic Law. No institution, organisation or individual in the Region shall contravene these provisions in exercising their rights and freedoms.

第三條

中央人民政府對香港特別行政區有關的國家安全事務負有根本責任。

香港特別行政區負有維護國家安全的憲制責任，應當履行維護國家安全的職責。

香港特別行政區行政機關、立法機關、司法機關應當依據本法和其他有關法律規定有效防範、制止和懲治危害國家安全的行為和活動。

第四條

香港特別行政區維護國家安全應當尊重和保障人權，依法保護香港特別行政區居民根據香港特別行政區基本法和《公民權利和政治權利國際公約》、《經濟、社會與文化權利的國際公約》適用於香港的有關規定享有的包括言論、新聞、出版的自由，結社、集會、遊行、示威的自由在內的權利和自由。

第五條

防範、制止和懲治危害國家安全犯罪，應當堅持法治原則。法律規定為犯罪行為的，依照法律定罪處刑；法律沒有規定為犯罪行為的，不得定罪處刑。

任何人未經司法機關判罪之前均假定無罪。保障犯罪嫌疑人、被告人和其他訴訟參與人依法享有的辯護權和

Article 3

The Central People's Government has an overarching responsibility for national security affairs relating to the Hong Kong Special Administrative Region.

It is the duty of the Hong Kong Special Administrative Region under the Constitution to safeguard national security and the Region shall perform the duty accordingly.

The executive authorities, legislature and judiciary of the Region shall effectively prevent, suppress and impose punishment for any act or activity endangering national security in accordance with this Law and other relevant laws.

Article 4

Human rights shall be respected and protected in safeguarding national security in the Hong Kong Special Administrative Region. The rights and freedoms, including the freedoms of speech, of the press, of publication, of association, of assembly, of procession and of demonstration, which the residents of the Region enjoy under the Basic Law of the Hong Kong Special Administrative Region and the provisions of the International Covenant on Civil and Political Rights and the International Covenant on Economic, Social and Cultural Rights as applied to Hong Kong, shall be protected in accordance with the law.

Article 5

The principle of the rule of law shall be adhered to in preventing, suppressing, and imposing punishment for offences endangering national security. A person who commits an act which constitutes an offence under the law shall be convicted and punished in accordance with the law. No one shall be convicted and punished for an act which does not constitute an offence under the law.

A person is presumed innocent until convicted by a judicial body. The right to defend himself or herself and other rights in

其他訴訟權利。任何人已經司法程序被最終確定有罪或者宣告無罪的，不得就同一行為再予審判或者懲罰。

第六條

維護國家主權、統一和領土完整是包括香港同胞在內的全中國人民的共同義務。

在香港特別行政區的任何機構、組織和個人都應當遵守本法和香港特別行政區有關維護國家安全的其他法律，不得從事危害國家安全的行為和活動。

香港特別行政區居民在參選或者就任公職時應當依法簽署文件確認或者宣誓擁護中華人民共和國香港特別行政區基本法，效忠中華人民共和國香港特別行政區。

judicial proceedings that a criminal suspect, defendant, and other parties in judicial proceedings are entitled to under the law shall be protected. No one shall be liable to be tried or punished again for an offence for which he or she has already been finally convicted or acquitted in judicial proceedings.

Article 6

It is the common responsibility of all the people of China, including the people of Hong Kong, to safeguard the sovereignty, unification and territorial integrity of the People's Republic of China.

Any institution, organisation or individual in the Hong Kong Special Administrative Region shall abide by this Law and the laws of the Region in relation to the safeguarding of national security, and shall not engage in any act or activity which endangers national security.

A resident of the Region who stands for election or assumes public office shall confirm in writing or take an oath to uphold the Basic Law of the Hong Kong Special Administrative Region of the People's Republic of China and swear allegiance to the Hong Kong Special Administrative Region of the People's Republic of China in accordance with the law.

第二章 香港特別行政區維護國家安全 的職責和機構

第一節 職責

第七條

香港特別行政區應當儘早完成香港特別行政區基本法規定的維護國家安全立法，完善相關法律。

第八條

香港特別行政區執法、司法機關應當切實執行本法和香港特別行政區現行法律有關防範、制止和懲治危害國家安全行為和活動的規定，有效維護國家安全。

第九條

香港特別行政區應當加強維護國家安全和防範恐怖活動的工作。對學校、社會團體、媒體、網絡等涉及國家安全的事宜，香港特別行政區政府應當採取必要措施，加強宣傳、指導、監督和管理。

Chapter II: The Duties and the Government Bodies of the Hong Kong Special Administrative Region for Safeguarding National Security

Part 1: Duties

Article 7
The Hong Kong Special Administrative Region shall complete, as early as possible, legislation for safeguarding national security as stipulated in the Basic Law of the Hong Kong Special Administrative Region and shall refine relevant laws.

Article 8
In order to safeguard national security effectively, the law enforcement and judicial authorities of the Hong Kong Special Administrative Region shall fully enforce this Law and the laws in force in the Region concerning the prevention of, suppression of, and imposition of punishment for acts and activities endangering national security.

Article 9
The Hong Kong Special Administrative Region shall strengthen its work on safeguarding national security and prevention of terrorist activities. The Government of the Hong Kong Special Administrative Region shall take necessary measures to strengthen public communication, guidance, supervision and regulation over matters concerning national security, including those relating to schools, universities, social organisations, the media, and the internet.

第十條

香港特別行政區應當通過學校、社會團體、媒體、網絡等開展國家安全教育，提高香港特別行政區居民的國家安全意識和守法意識。

第十一條

香港特別行政區行政長官應當就香港特別行政區維護國家安全事務向中央人民政府負責，並就香港特別行政區履行維護國家安全職責的情況提交年度報告。

　　如中央人民政府提出要求，行政長官應當就維護國家安全特定事項及時提交報告。

第二節　機構

第十二條

香港特別行政區設立維護國家安全委員會，負責香港特別行政區維護國家安全事務，承擔維護國家安全的主要責任，並接受中央人民政府的監督和問責。

第十三條

香港特別行政區維護國家安全委員會由行政長官擔任主席，成員包括政務司長、財政司長、律政司長、保安局局

Article 10

The Hong Kong Special Administrative Region shall promote national security education in schools and universities and through social organisations, the media, the internet and other means to raise the awareness of Hong Kong residents of national security and of the obligation to abide by the law.

Article 11

The Chief Executive of the Hong Kong Special Administrative Region shall be accountable to the Central People's Government for affairs relating to safeguarding national security in the Hong Kong Special Administrative Region and shall submit an annual report on the performance of duties of the Region in safeguarding national security.

The Chief Executive shall, at the request of the Central People's Government, submit in a timely manner a report on specific matters relating to safeguarding national security.

Part 2: Government Bodies

Article 12

The Hong Kong Special Administrative Region shall establish the Committee for Safeguarding National Security. The Committee shall be responsible for affairs relating to and assume primary responsibility for safeguarding national security in the Region. It shall be under the supervision of and accountable to the Central People's Government.

Article 13

The Chief Executive shall be the chairperson of the Committee for Safeguarding National Security of the Hong Kong Special

長、警務處處長、本法第十六條規定的警務處維護國家安全部門的負責人、入境事務處處長、海關關長和行政長官辦公室主任。

香港特別行政區維護國家安全委員會下設秘書處,由秘書長領導。秘書長由行政長官提名,報中央人民政府任命。

第十四條

香港特別行政區維護國家安全委員會的職責為:

(一)　分析研判香港特別行政區維護國家安全形勢,規劃有關工作,制定香港特別行政區維護國家安全政策;

(二)　推進香港特別行政區維護國家安全的法律制度和執行機制建設;

(三)　協調香港特別行政區維護國家安全的重點工作和重大行動。

香港特別行政區維護國家安全委員會的工作不受香港特別行政區任何其他機構、組織和個人的干涉,工作信息不予公開。香港特別行政區維護國家安全委員會作出的決定不受司法覆核。

Administrative Region. The other members of the Committee shall be the Chief Secretary for Administration, the Financial Secretary, the Secretary for Justice, the Secretary for Security, the Commissioner of Police, the head of the department for safeguarding national security of the Hong Kong Police Force established under Article 16 of this Law, the Director of Immigration, the Commissioner of Customs and Excise, and the Director of the Chief Executive's Office.

A secretariat headed by a Secretary-General shall be established under the Committee. The Secretary-General shall be appointed by the Central People's Government upon nomination by the Chief Executive.

Article 14

The duties and functions of the Committee for Safeguarding National Security of the Hong Kong Special Administrative Region shall be:

(1) Analysing and assessing developments in relation to safeguarding national security in the Hong Kong Special Administrative Region, making work plans, and formulating policies for safeguarding national security in the Region;

(2) Advancing the development of the legal system and enforcement mechanisms of the Region for safeguarding national security; and

(3) Coordinating major work and significant operations for safeguarding national security in the Region.

No institution, organisation or individual in the Region shall interfere with the work of the Committee. Information relating to the work of the Committee shall not be subject to disclosure. Decisions made by the Committee shall not be amenable to judicial review.

第十五條

香港特別行政區維護國家安全委員會設立國家安全事務顧問，由中央人民政府指派，就香港特別行政區維護國家安全委員會履行職責相關事務提供意見。國家安全事務顧問列席香港特別行政區維護國家安全委員會會議。

第十六條

香港特別行政區政府警務處設立維護國家安全的部門，配備執法力量。

　　警務處維護國家安全部門負責人由行政長官任命，行政長官任命前須書面徵求本法第四十八條規定的機構的意見。警務處維護國家安全部門負責人在就職時應當宣誓擁護中華人民共和國香港特別行政區基本法，效忠中華人民共和國香港特別行政區，遵守法律，保守秘密。

　　警務處維護國家安全部門可以從香港特別行政區以外聘請合格的專門人員和技術人員，協助執行維護國家安全相關任務。

Article 15

The Committee for Safeguarding National Security of the Hong Kong Special Administrative Region shall have a National Security Adviser, who shall be designated by the Central People's Government and provide advice on matters relating to the duties and functions of the Committee. The National Security Adviser shall sit in on meetings of the Committee.

Article 16

The Police Force of the Hong Kong Special Administrative Region shall establish a department for safeguarding national security with law enforcement capacity.

The head of the department for safeguarding national security of the Hong Kong Police Force shall be appointed by the Chief Executive. The Chief Executive shall seek in writing the opinion of the Office established under Article 48 of this Law before making the appointment. When assuming office, the head of the department for safeguarding national security of the Hong Kong Police Force shall swear to uphold the Basic Law of the Hong Kong Special Administrative Region of the People's Republic of China, swear allegiance to the Hong Kong Special Administrative Region of the People's Republic of China, and swear to abide by the law and to observe the obligation of secrecy.

The department for safeguarding national security of the Hong Kong Police Force may recruit qualified professionals and technical personnel from outside the Hong Kong Special Administrative Region to provide assistance in the performance of duties for safeguarding national security.

第十七條

警務處維護國家安全部門的職責為：

(一)　收集分析涉及國家安全的情報信息；

(二)　部署、協調、推進維護國家安全的措施和行動；

(三)　調查危害國家安全犯罪案件；

(四)　進行反干預調查和開展國家安全審查；

(五)　承辦香港特別行政區維護國家安全委員會交辦的維護國家安全工作；

(六)　執行本法所需的其他職責。

第十八條

香港特別行政區律政司設立專門的國家安全犯罪案件檢控部門，負責危害國家安全犯罪案件的檢控工作和其他相關法律事務。該部門檢控官由律政司長徵得香港特別行政區維護國家安全委員會同意後任命。

律政司國家安全犯罪案件檢控部門負責人由行政長官任命，行政長官任命前須書面徵求本法第四十八條規定的機構的意見。律政司國家安全犯罪案件檢控部門負責人在就職時應當宣誓擁護中華人民共和國香港特別行政

Article 17

The duties and functions of the department for safeguarding national security of the Hong Kong Police Force shall be:

(1) Collecting and analysing intelligence and information concerning national security;

(2) Planning, coordinating and enforcing measures and operations for safeguarding national security;

(3) Investigating offences endangering national security;

(4) Conducting counter-interference investigation and national security review;

(5) Carrying out tasks of safeguarding national security assigned by the Committee for Safeguarding National Security of the Hong Kong Special Administrative Region; and

(6) Performing other duties and functions necessary for the enforcement of this Law.

Article 18

The Department of Justice of the Hong Kong Special Administrative Region shall establish a specialised prosecution division responsible for the prosecution of offences endangering national security and other related legal work. The prosecutors of this division shall be appointed by the Secretary for Justice after obtaining the consent of the Committee for Safeguarding National Security of the Hong Kong Special Administrative Region.

The head of the specialised prosecution division of the Department of Justice shall be appointed by the Chief Executive, who shall seek in writing the opinion of the Office established under Article 48 of this Law before making the appointment. When assuming office, the head of the specialised prosecution division shall swear to uphold the Basic Law of the Hong Kong

區基本法，效忠中華人民共和國香港特別行政區，遵守法律，保守秘密。

第十九條

經行政長官批准，香港特別行政區政府財政司長應當從政府一般收入中撥出專門款項支付關於維護國家安全的開支並核准所涉及的人員編制，不受香港特別行政區現行有關法律規定的限制。財政司長須每年就該款項的控制和管理向立法會提交報告。

Special Administrative Region of the People's Republic of China,
swear allegiance to the Hong Kong Special Administrative Region
of the People's Republic of China, and swear to abide by the law
and to observe the obligation of secrecy.

Article 19

The Financial Secretary of the Hong Kong Special Administrative
Region shall, upon approval of the Chief Executive, appropriate
from the general revenue a special fund to meet the expenditure
for safeguarding national security and approve the establishment
of relevant posts, which are not subject to any restrictions in the
relevant provisions of the laws in force in the Region. The
Financial Secretary shall submit an annual report on the control
and management of the fund for this purpose to the Legislative
Council of the Hong Kong Special Administrative Region.

第三章　罪行和處罰

第一節　分裂國家罪

第二十條

任何人組織、策劃、實施或者參與實施以下旨在分裂國家、破壞國家統一行為之一的,不論是否使用武力或者以武力相威脅,即屬犯罪:

(一)　將香港特別行政區或者中華人民共和國其他任何部分從中華人民共和國分離出去;

(二)　非法改變香港特別行政區或者中華人民共和國其他任何部分的法律地位;

(三)　將香港特別行政區或者中華人民共和國其他任何部分轉歸外國統治。

犯前款罪,對首要分子或者罪行重大的,處無期徒刑或者十年以上有期徒刑;對積極參加的,處三年以上十年以下有期徒刑;對其他參加的,處三年以下有期徒刑、拘役或者管制。

第二十一條

任何人煽動、協助、教唆、以金錢或者其他財物資助他人實施本法第二十條規定的犯罪的,即屬犯罪。情節嚴重

Chapter III: Offences and Penalties

Part 1: Secession

Article 20

A person who organises, plans, commits or participates in any of the following acts, whether or not by force or threat of force, with a view to committing secession or undermining national unification shall be guilty of an offence:

(1) Separating the Hong Kong Special Administrative Region or any other part of the People's Republic of China from the People's Republic of China;

(2) Altering by unlawful means the legal status of the Hong Kong Special Administrative Region or of any other part of the People's Republic of China; or

(3) Surrendering the Hong Kong Special Administrative Region or any other part of the People's Republic of China to a foreign country.

A person who is a principal offender or a person who commits an offence of a grave nature shall be sentenced to life imprisonment or fixed-term imprisonment of not less than ten years; a person who actively participates in the offence shall be sentenced to fixed-term imprisonment of not less than three years but not more than ten years; and other participants shall be sentenced to fixed-term imprisonment of not more than three years, short-term detention or restriction.

Article 21

A person who incites, assists in, abets or provides pecuniary or other financial assistance or property for the commission by other persons of the offence under Article 20 of this Law shall be guilty of an offence. If the circumstances of the offence

的，處五年以上十年以下有期徒刑；情節較輕的，處五年
以下有期徒刑、拘役或者管制。

第二節　顛覆國家政權罪

第二十二條
任何人組織、策劃、實施或者參與實施以下以武力、威脅
使用武力或者其他非法手段旨在顛覆國家政權行為之一
的，即屬犯罪：

(一)　推翻、破壞中華人民共和國憲法所確立的中
華人民共和國根本制度；

(二)　推翻中華人民共和國中央政權機關或者香港
特別行政區政權機關；

(三)　嚴重干擾、阻撓、破壞中華人民共和國中央
政權機關或者香港特別行政區政權機關依法
履行職能；

(四)　攻擊、破壞香港特別行政區政權機關履職場
所及其設施，致使其無法正常履行職能。

committed by a person are of a serious nature, the person shall be sentenced to fixed-term imprisonment of not less than five years but not more than ten years; if the circumstances of the offence committed by a person are of a minor nature, the person shall be sentenced to fixed-term imprisonment of not more than five years, short-term detention or restriction.

Part 2: Subversion

Article 22

A person who organises, plans, commits or participates in any of the following acts by force or threat of force or other unlawful means with a view to subverting the State power shall be guilty of an offence:

(1) Overthrowing or undermining the basic system of the People's Republic of China established by the Constitution of the People's Republic of China;

(2) Overthrowing the body of central power of the People's Republic of China or the body of power of the Hong Kong Special Administrative Region;

(3) Seriously interfering in, disrupting, or undermining the performance of duties and functions in accordance with the law by the body of central power of the People's Republic of China or the body of power of the Hong Kong Special Administrative Region; or

(4) Attacking or damaging the premises and facilities used by the body of power of the Hong Kong Special Administrative Region to perform its duties and functions, rendering it incapable of performing its normal duties and functions.

犯前款罪，對首要分子或者罪行重大的，處無期徒刑或者十年以上有期徒刑；對積極參加的，處三年以上十年以下有期徒刑；對其他參加的，處三年以下有期徒刑、拘役或者管制。

第二十三條

任何人煽動、協助、教唆、以金錢或者其他財物資助他人實施本法第二十二條規定的犯罪的，即屬犯罪。情節嚴重的，處五年以上十年以下有期徒刑；情節較輕的，處五年以下有期徒刑、拘役或者管制。

第三節　恐怖活動罪

第二十四條

為脅迫中央人民政府、香港特別行政區政府或者國際組織或者威嚇公眾以圖實現政治主張，組織、策劃、實施、參與實施或者威脅實施以下造成或者意圖造成嚴重社會危害的恐怖活動之一的，即屬犯罪：

A person who is a principal offender or a person who commits an offence of a grave nature shall be sentenced to life imprisonment or fixed-term imprisonment of not less than ten years; a person who actively participates in the offence shall be sentenced to fixed-term imprisonment of not less than three years but not more than ten years; and other participants shall be sentenced to fixed-term imprisonment of not more than three years, short-term detention or restriction.

Article 23

A person who incites, assists in, abets or provides pecuniary or other financial assistance or property for the commission by other persons of the offence under Article 22 of this Law shall be guilty of an offence. If the circumstances of the offence committed by a person are of a serious nature, the person shall be sentenced to fixed-term imprisonment of not less than five years but not more than ten years; if the circumstances of the offence committed by a person are of a minor nature, the person shall be sentenced to fixed-term imprisonment of not more than five years, short-term detention or restriction.

Part 3: Terrorist Activities

Article 24

A person who organises, plans, commits, participates in or threatens to commit any of the following terrorist activities causing or intended to cause grave harm to the society with a view to coercing the Central People's Government, the Government of the Hong Kong Special Administrative Region or an international organisation or intimidating the public in order to pursue political agenda shall be guilty of an offence:

（一）　針對人的嚴重暴力；

（二）　爆炸、縱火或者投放毒害性、放射性、傳染病病原體等物質；

（三）　破壞交通工具、交通設施、電力設備、燃氣設備或者其他易燃易爆設備；

（四）　嚴重干擾、破壞水、電、燃氣、交通、通訊、網絡等公共服務和管理的電子控制系統；

（五）　以其他危險方法嚴重危害公眾健康或者安全。

犯前款罪，致人重傷、死亡或者使公私財產遭受重大損失的，處無期徒刑或者十年以上有期徒刑；其他情形，處三年以上十年以下有期徒刑。

第二十五條

組織、領導恐怖活動組織的，即屬犯罪，處無期徒刑或者十年以上有期徒刑，並處沒收財產；積極參加的，處三年以上十年以下有期徒刑，並處罰金；其他參加的，處三年以下有期徒刑、拘役或者管制，可以並處罰金。

(1) Serious violence against a person or persons;

(2) Explosion, arson, or dissemination of poisonous or radioactive substances, pathogens of infectious diseases or other substances;

(3) Sabotage of means of transport, transport facilities, electric power or gas facilities, or other combustible or explosible facilities;

(4) Serious interruption or sabotage of electronic control systems for providing and managing public services such as water, electric power, gas, transport, telecommunications and the internet; or

(5) Other dangerous activities which seriously jeopardise public health, safety or security.

A person who commits the offence causing serious bodily injury, death or significant loss of public or private property shall be sentenced to life imprisonment or fixed-term imprisonment of not less than ten years; in other circumstances, a person who commits the offence shall be sentenced to fixed-term imprisonment of not less than three years but not more than ten years.

Article 25

A person who organises or takes charge of a terrorist organisation shall be guilty of an offence and shall be sentenced to life imprisonment or fixed-term imprisonment of not less than ten years, and shall be subject to confiscation of property; a person who actively participates in a terrorist organisation shall be sentenced to fixed-term imprisonment of not less than three years but not more than ten years and shall be imposed with a criminal fine; and other participants shall be sentenced to fixed-term imprisonment of not more than three years, short-term detention or restriction, and shall be liable to a criminal fine.

　　本法所指的恐怖活動組織，是指實施或者意圖實施本法第二十四條規定的恐怖活動罪行或者參與或者協助實施本法第二十四條規定的恐怖活動罪行的組織。

第二十六條

為恐怖活動組織、恐怖活動人員、恐怖活動實施提供培訓、武器、信息、資金、物資、勞務、運輸、技術或者場所等支持、協助、便利，或者製造、非法管有爆炸性、毒害性、放射性、傳染病病原體等物質以及以其他形式準備實施恐怖活動的，即屬犯罪。情節嚴重的，處五年以上十年以下有期徒刑，並處罰金或者沒收財產；其他情形，處五年以下有期徒刑、拘役或者管制，並處罰金。

　　有前款行為，同時構成其他犯罪的，依照處罰較重的規定定罪處罰。

For the purpose of this Law, a terrorist organisation means an organisation which commits or intends to commit the offence under Article 24 of this Law or participates or assists in the commission of the offence.

Article 26

A person who provides support, assistance or facility such as training, weapons, information, funds, supplies, labour, transport, technologies or venues to a terrorist organisation or a terrorist, or for the commission of a terrorist activity; or manufactures or illegally possesses substances such as explosive, poisonous or radioactive substances and pathogens of infectious diseases or uses other means to prepare for the commission of a terrorist activity, shall be guilty of an offence. If the circumstances of the offence committed by a person are of a serious nature, the person shall be sentenced to fixed-term imprisonment of not less than five years but not more than ten years, and shall be imposed with a criminal fine or subject to confiscation of property; in other circumstances, a person shall be sentenced to fixed-term imprisonment of not more than five years, short-term detention or restriction, and shall be imposed with a criminal fine.

If the act referred to in the preceding paragraph also constitutes other offences, the person who commits the act shall be convicted and sentenced for the offence that carries a more severe penalty.

第二十七條

宣揚恐怖主義、煽動實施恐怖活動的，即屬犯罪。情節嚴重的，處五年以上十年以下有期徒刑，並處罰金或者沒收財產；其他情形，處五年以下有期徒刑、拘役或者管制，並處罰金。

第二十八條

本節規定不影響依據香港特別行政區法律對其他形式的恐怖活動犯罪追究刑事責任並採取凍結財產等措施。

第四節　勾結外國或者境外勢力危害國家安全罪

第二十九條

為外國或者境外機構、組織、人員竊取、刺探、收買、非法提供涉及國家安全的國家秘密或者情報的；請求外國或者境外機構、組織、人員實施，與外國或者境外機構、組織、

Article 27

A person who advocates terrorism or incites the commission of a terrorist activity shall be guilty of an offence. If the circumstances of the offence committed by a person are of a serious nature, the person shall be sentenced to fixed-term imprisonment of not less than five years but not more than ten years, and shall be imposed with a criminal fine or subject to confiscation of property; in other circumstances, a person shall be sentenced to fixed-term imprisonment of not more than five years, short-term detention or restriction, and shall be imposed with a criminal fine.

Article 28

The provisions of this Part shall not affect the prosecution of terrorist offences committed in other forms or the imposition of other measures such as freezing of property in accordance with the laws of the Hong Kong Special Administrative Region.

Part 4: Collusion with a Foreign Country or with External Elements to Endanger National Security

Article 29

A person who steals, spies, obtains with payment, or unlawfully provides State secrets or intelligence concerning national security for a foreign country or an institution, organisation or individual outside the mainland, Hong Kong, and Macao of the People's Republic of China shall be guilty of an offence; a person who requests a foreign country or an institution, organisation or individual outside the mainland, Hong Kong, and Macao of the People's Republic of China, or conspires with a foreign country

人員串謀實施，或者直接或者間接接受外國或者境外機構、組織、人員的指使、控制、資助或者其他形式的支援實施以下行為之一的，均屬犯罪：

(一) 對中華人民共和國發動戰爭，或者以武力或者武力相威脅，對中華人民共和國主權、統一和領土完整造成嚴重危害；

(二) 對香港特別行政區政府或者中央人民政府制定和執行法律、政策進行嚴重阻撓並可能造成嚴重後果；

(三) 對香港特別行政區選舉進行操控、破壞並可能造成嚴重後果；

(四) 對香港特別行政區或者中華人民共和國進行制裁、封鎖或者採取其他敵對行動；

(五) 通過各種非法方式引發香港特別行政區居民對中央人民政府或者香港特別行政區政府的憎恨並可能造成嚴重後果。

犯前款罪，處三年以上十年以下有期徒刑；罪行重大的，處無期徒刑或者十年以上有期徒刑。

or an institution, organisation or individual outside the mainland, Hong Kong, and Macao of the People's Republic of China, or directly or indirectly receives instructions, control, funding or other kinds of support from a foreign country or an institution, organisation or individual outside the mainland, Hong Kong, and Macao of the People's Republic of China, to commit any of the following acts shall be guilty of an offence:

(1) Waging a war against the People's Republic of China, or using or threatening to use force to seriously undermine the sovereignty, unification and territorial integrity of the People's Republic of China;

(2) Seriously disrupting the formulation and implementation of laws or policies by the Government of the Hong Kong Special Administrative Region or by the Central People's Government, which is likely to cause serious consequences;

(3) Rigging or undermining an election in the Hong Kong Special Administrative Region, which is likely to cause serious consequences;

(4) Imposing sanctions or blockade, or engaging in other hostile activities against the Hong Kong Special Administrative Region or the People's Republic of China; or

(5) Provoking by unlawful means hatred among Hong Kong residents towards the Central People's Government or the Government of the Region, which is likely to cause serious consequences.

A person who commits the offence shall be sentenced to fixed-term imprisonment of not less than three years but not more than ten years; a person who commits an offence of a grave nature shall be sentenced to life imprisonment or fixed-term imprisonment of not less than ten years.

　　本條第一款規定涉及的境外機構、組織、人員，按共同犯罪定罪處刑。

第三十條

為實施本法第二十條、第二十二條規定的犯罪，與外國或者境外機構、組織、人員串謀，或者直接或者間接接受外國或者境外機構、組織、人員的指使、控制、資助或者其他形式的支援的，依照本法第二十條、第二十二條的規定從重處罰。

第五節　　其他處罰規定

第三十一條

公司、團體等法人或者非法人組織實施本法規定的犯罪的，對該組織判處罰金。

　　公司、團體等法人或者非法人組織因犯本法規定的罪行受到刑事處罰的，應責令其暫停運作或者吊銷其執照或者營業許可證。

第三十二條

因實施本法規定的犯罪而獲得的資助、收益、報酬等違法所得以及用於或者意圖用於犯罪的資金和工具，應當予以追繳、沒收。

The institution, organisation and individual outside the mainland, Hong Kong, and Macao of the People's Republic of China referred to in the first paragraph of this Article shall be convicted and punished for the same offence.

Article 30

A person who conspires with or directly or indirectly receives instructions, control, funding or other kinds of support from a foreign country or an institution, organisation, or individual outside the mainland, Hong Kong, and Macao of the People's Republic of China to commit the offences under Article 20 or 22 of this Law shall be liable to a more severe penalty in accordance with the provisions therein respectively.

Part 5: Other Provisions on Penalty

Article 31

An incorporated or unincorporated body such as a company or an organisation which commits an offence under this Law shall be imposed with a criminal fine.

The operation of an incorporated or unincorporated body such as a company or an organisation shall be suspended or its licence or business permit shall be revoked if the body has been punished for committing an offence under this Law.

Article 32

Proceeds obtained from the commission of an offence under this Law including financial aid, gains and rewards, and funds and tools used or intended to be used in the commission of the offence shall be seized and confiscated.

第三十三條

有以下情形的，對有關犯罪行為人、犯罪嫌疑人、被告人可以從輕、減輕處罰；犯罪較輕的，可以免除處罰：

(一)　　在犯罪過程中，自動放棄犯罪或者自動有效地防止犯罪結果發生的；

(二)　　自動投案，如實供述自己的罪行的；

(三)　　揭發他人犯罪行為，查證屬實，或者提供重要線索得以偵破其他案件的。

被採取強制措施的犯罪嫌疑人、被告人如實供述執法、司法機關未掌握的本人犯有本法規定的其他罪行的，按前款第二項規定處理。

第三十四條

不具有香港特別行政區永久性居民身份的人實施本法規定的犯罪的，可以獨立適用或者附加適用驅逐出境。

不具有香港特別行政區永久性居民身份的人違反本法規定，因任何原因不對其追究刑事責任的，也可以驅逐出境。

第三十五條

任何人經法院判決犯危害國家安全罪行的，即喪失作為候選人參加香港特別行政區舉行的立法會、區議會選舉或者出任香港特別行政區任何公職或者行政長官選舉委員

Article 33

A lighter penalty may be imposed, or the penalty may be reduced or, in the case of a minor offence, exempted, if an offender, criminal suspect, or defendant:

(1) In the process of committing an offence, voluntarily discontinues the commission of the offence or voluntarily and effectively forestalls its consequences;

(2) Voluntarily surrenders himself or herself and gives a truthful account of the offence; or

(3) Reports on the offence committed by other person, which is verified to be true, or provides material information which assists in solving other criminal case.

Sub-paragraph (2) of the preceding paragraph shall apply to a criminal suspect or defendant who is subjected to mandatory measures and provides a truthful account of other offences committed by him or her under this Law which are unknown to the law enforcement or judicial authorities.

Article 34

A person who is not a permanent resident of the Hong Kong Special Administrative Region may be subject to deportation as the sole or an additional punishment if he or she commits an offence under this Law.

A person who is not a permanent resident of the Region may be subject to deportation if he or she contravenes the provisions of this Law but is not prosecuted for any reason.

Article 35

A person who is convicted of an offence endangering national security by a court shall be disqualified from standing as a candidate in the elections of the Legislative Council and district councils of the Hong Kong Special Administrative Region, holding any public office in the Region, or serving as a member

會委員的資格；曾經宣誓或者聲明擁護中華人民共和國香港特別行政區基本法、效忠中華人民共和國香港特別行政區的立法會議員、政府官員及公務人員、行政會議成員、法官及其他司法人員、區議員，即時喪失該等職務，並喪失參選或者出任上述職務的資格。

前款規定資格或者職務的喪失，由負責組織、管理有關選舉或者公職任免的機構宣佈。

第六節 效力範圍

第三十六條

任何人在香港特別行政區內實施本法規定的犯罪的，適用本法。犯罪的行為或者結果有一項發生在香港特別行政區內的，就認為是在香港特別行政區內犯罪。

在香港特別行政區註冊的船舶或者航空器內實施本法規定的犯罪的，也適用本法。

of the Election Committee for electing the Chief Executive. If a person so convicted is a member of the Legislative Council, a government official, a public servant, a member of the Executive Council, a judge or a judicial officer, or a member of the district councils, who has taken an oath or made a declaration to uphold the Basic Law of the Hong Kong Special Administrative Region of the People's Republic of China and swear allegiance to the Hong Kong Special Administrative Region of the People's Republic of China, he or she shall be removed from his or her office upon conviction, and shall be disqualified from standing for the aforementioned elections or from holding any of the aforementioned posts.

The disqualification and removal from offices referred to in the preceding paragraph shall be announced by the authorities responsible for organising and managing the relevant elections or for the appointment and removal of holders of public office.

Part 6: Scope of Application

Article 36

This Law shall apply to offences under this Law which are committed in the Hong Kong Special Administrative Region by any person. An offence shall be deemed to have been committed in the Region if an act constituting the offence or the consequence of the offence occurs in the Region.

This Law shall also apply to offences under this Law committed on board a vessel or aircraft registered in the Region.

第三十七條

香港特別行政區永久性居民或者在香港特別行政區成立
的公司、團體等法人或者非法人組織在香港特別行政區以
外實施本法規定的犯罪的，適用本法。

第三十八條

不具有香港特別行政區永久性居民身份的人在香港特別
行政區以外針對香港特別行政區實施本法規定的犯罪的，
適用本法。

第三十九條

本法施行以後的行為，適用本法定罪處刑。

Article 37
This Law shall apply to a person who is a permanent resident of the Hong Kong Special Administrative Region or an incorporated or unincorporated body such as a company or an organisation which is set up in the Region if the person or the body commits an offence under this Law outside the Region.

Article 38
This Law shall apply to offences under this Law committed against the Hong Kong Special Administrative Region from outside the Region by a person who is not a permanent resident of the Region.

Article 39
This Law shall apply to acts committed after its entry into force for the purpose of conviction and imposition of punishment.

第四章　案件管轄、法律適用和程序

第四十條

香港特別行政區對本法規定的犯罪案件行使管轄權，但本法第五十五條規定的情形除外。

第四十一條

香港特別行政區管轄危害國家安全犯罪案件的立案偵查、檢控、審判和刑罰的執行等訴訟程序事宜，適用本法和香港特別行政區本地法律。

未經律政司長書面同意，任何人不得就危害國家安全犯罪案件提出檢控。但該規定不影響就有關犯罪依法逮捕犯罪嫌疑人並將其羈押，也不影響該等犯罪嫌疑人申請保釋。

香港特別行政區管轄的危害國家安全犯罪案件的審判循公訴程序進行。

審判應當公開進行。因為涉及國家秘密、公共秩序等情形不宜公開審理的，禁止新聞界和公眾旁聽全部或者一部分審理程序，但判決結果應當一律公開宣佈。

第四十二條

香港特別行政區執法、司法機關在適用香港特別行政區現行法律有關羈押、審理期限等方面的規定時，應當確保危

Chapter IV: Jurisdiction, Applicable Law and Procedure

Article 40

The Hong Kong Special Administrative Region shall have jurisdiction over cases concerning offences under this Law, except under the circumstances specified in Article 55 of this Law.

Article 41

This Law and the laws of the Hong Kong Special Administrative Region shall apply to procedural matters, including those related to criminal investigation, prosecution, trial, and execution of penalty, in respect of cases concerning offence endangering national security over which the Region exercises jurisdiction.

No prosecution shall be instituted in respect of an offence endangering national security without the written consent of the Secretary for Justice. This provision shall not prejudice the arrest and detention of a person who is suspected of having committed the offence or the application for bail by the person in accordance with the law.

Cases concerning offence endangering national security within the jurisdiction of the Hong Kong Special Administrative Region shall be tried on indictment.

The trial shall be conducted in an open court. When circumstances arise such as the trial involving State secrets or public order, all or part of the trial shall be closed to the media and the public but the judgment shall be delivered in an open court.

Article 42

When applying the laws in force in the Hong Kong Special Administrative Region concerning matters such as the detention

害國家安全犯罪案件公正、及時辦理，有效防範、制止和懲治危害國家安全犯罪。

　　對犯罪嫌疑人、被告人，除非法官有充足理由相信其不會繼續實施危害國家安全行為的，不得准予保釋。

第四十三條

香港特別行政區政府警務處維護國家安全部門辦理危害國家安全犯罪案件時，可以採取香港特別行政區現行法律准予警方等執法部門在調查嚴重犯罪案件時採取的各種措施，並可以採取以下措施：

(一)　搜查可能存有犯罪證據的處所、車輛、船隻、航空器以及其他有關地方和電子設備；

(二)　要求涉嫌實施危害國家安全犯罪行為的人員交出旅行證件或者限制其離境；

(三)　對用於或者意圖用於犯罪的財產、因犯罪所得的收益等與犯罪相關的財產，予以凍結，申請限制令、押記令、沒收令以及充公；

and time limit for trial, the law enforcement and judicial
authorities of the Region shall ensure that cases concerning
offence endangering national security are handled in a fair and
timely manner so as to effectively prevent, suppress and impose
punishment for such offence.

No bail shall be granted to a criminal suspect or defendant
unless the judge has sufficient grounds for believing that the
criminal suspect or defendant will not continue to commit acts
endangering national security.

Article 43

When handling cases concerning offence endangering national
security, the department for safeguarding national security of the
Police Force of the Hong Kong Special Administrative Region
may take measures that law enforcement authorities, including
the Hong Kong Police Force, are allowed to apply under the laws
in force in the Hong Kong Special Administrative Region in
investigating serious crimes, and may also take the following
measures:

(1) Search of premises, vehicles, vessels, aircraft and other
relevant places and electronic devices that may contain
evidence of an offence;

(2) Ordering any person suspected of having committed an
offence endangering national security to surrender travel
documents, or prohibiting the person concerned from
leaving the Region;

(3) Freezing of, applying for restraint order, charging order
and confiscation order in respect of, and forfeiture of
property used or intended to be used for the commission
of the offence, proceeds of crime, or other property
relating to the commission of the offence;

(四)　要求信息發佈人或者有關服務商移除信息或者提供協助；

(五)　要求外國及境外政治性組織，外國及境外當局或者政治性組織的代理人提供資料；

(六)　經行政長官批准，對有合理理由懷疑涉及實施危害國家安全犯罪的人員進行截取通訊和秘密監察；

(七)　對有合理理由懷疑擁有與偵查有關的資料或者管有有關物料的人員，要求其回答問題和提交資料或者物料。

香港特別行政區維護國家安全委員會對警務處維護國家安全部門等執法機構採取本條第一款規定措施負有監督責任。

授權香港特別行政區行政長官會同香港特別行政區維護國家安全委員會為採取本條第一款規定措施制定相關實施細則。

(4) Requiring a person who published information or the relevant service provider to delete the information or provide assistance;

(5) Requiring a political organisation of a foreign country or outside the mainland, Hong Kong, and Macao of the People's Republic of China, or an agent of authorities or a political organisation of a foreign country or outside the mainland, Hong Kong, and Macao of the People's Republic of China, to provide information;

(6) Upon approval of the Chief Executive, carrying out interception of communications and conducting covert surveillance on a person who is suspected, on reasonable grounds, of having involved in the commission of an offence endangering national security; and

(7) Requiring a person, who is suspected, on reasonable grounds, of having in possession information or material relevant to investigation, to answer questions and furnish such information or produce such material.

The Committee for Safeguarding National Security of the Hong Kong Special Administrative Region shall be responsible for supervising the implementation of the measures stipulated in the first paragraph of this Article by law enforcement authorities including the department for safeguarding national security of the Hong Kong Police Force.

The Chief Executive shall be authorised, in conjunction with the Committee for Safeguarding National Security of the Hong Kong Special Administrative Region, to make relevant implementation rules for the purpose of applying the measures under the first paragraph of this Article.

第四十四條

香港特別行政區行政長官應當從裁判官、區域法院法官、高等法院原訟法庭法官、上訴法庭法官以及終審法院法官中指定若干名法官，也可從暫委或者特委法官中指定若干名法官，負責處理危害國家安全犯罪案件。行政長官在指定法官前可徵詢香港特別行政區維護國家安全委員會和終審法院首席法官的意見。上述指定法官任期一年。

凡有危害國家安全言行的，不得被指定為審理危害國家安全犯罪案件的法官。在獲任指定法官期間，如有危害國家安全言行的，終止其指定法官資格。

在裁判法院、區域法院、高等法院和終審法院就危害國家安全犯罪案件提起的刑事檢控程序應當分別由各該法院的指定法官處理。

第四十五條

除本法另有規定外，裁判法院、區域法院、高等法院和終審法院應當按照香港特別行政區的其他法律處理就危害國家安全犯罪案件提起的刑事檢控程序。

Article 44

The Chief Executive shall designate a number of judges from the magistrates, the judges of the District Court, the judges of the Court of First Instance and the Court of Appeal of the High Court, and the judges of the Court of Final Appeal, and may also designate a number of judges from deputy judges or recorders, to handle cases concerning offence endangering national security. Before making such designation, the Chief Executive may consult the Committee for Safeguarding National Security of the Hong Kong Special Administrative Region and the Chief Justice of the Court of Final Appeal. The term of office of the aforementioned designated judges shall be one year.

A person shall not be designated as a judge to adjudicate a case concerning offence endangering national security if he or she has made any statement or behaved in any manner endangering national security. A designated judge shall be removed from the designation list if he or she makes any statement or behaves in any manner endangering national security during the term of office.

The proceedings in relation to the prosecution for offences endangering national security in the magistrates' courts, the District Court, the High Court and the Court of Final Appeal shall be handled by the designated judges in the respective courts.

Article 45

Unless otherwise provided by this Law, magistrates' courts, the District Court, the High Court and the Court of Final Appeal shall handle proceedings in relation to the prosecution for offences endangering national security in accordance with the laws of the Hong Kong Special Administrative Region.

第四十六條

對高等法院原訟法庭進行的就危害國家安全犯罪案件提起的刑事檢控程序，律政司長可基於保護國家秘密、案件具有涉外因素或者保障陪審員及其家人的人身安全等理由，發出證書指示相關訴訟毋須在有陪審團的情況下進行審理。凡律政司長發出上述證書，高等法院原訟法庭應當在沒有陪審團的情況下進行審理，並由三名法官組成審判庭。

凡律政司長發出前款規定的證書，適用於相關訴訟的香港特別行政區任何法律條文關於"陪審團"或者"陪審團的裁決"，均應當理解為指法官或者法官作為事實裁斷者的職能。

第四十七條

香港特別行政區法院在審理案件中遇有涉及有關行為是否涉及國家安全或者有關證據材料是否涉及國家秘密的認定問題，應取得行政長官就該等問題發出的證明書，上述證明書對法院有約束力。

Article 46

In criminal proceedings in the Court of First Instance of the High Court concerning offences endangering national security, the Secretary for Justice may issue a certificate directing that the case shall be tried without a jury on the grounds of, among others, the protection of State secrets, involvement of foreign factors in the case, and the protection of personal safety of jurors and their family members. Where the Secretary for Justice has issued the certificate, the case shall be tried in the Court of First Instance without a jury by a panel of three judges.

Where the Secretary for Justice has issued the certificate, the reference to "a jury" or "a verdict of the jury" in any provision of the laws of the Hong Kong Special Administrative Region applicable to the related proceedings shall be construed as referring to the judges or the functions of the judge as a judge of fact.

Article 47

The courts of the Hong Kong Special Administrative Region shall obtain a certificate from the Chief Executive to certify whether an act involves national security or whether the relevant evidence involves State secrets when such questions arise in the adjudication of a case. The certificate shall be binding on the courts.

第五章　中央人民政府駐
香港特別行政區維護國家安全機構

第四十八條

中央人民政府在香港特別行政區設立維護國家安全公署。中央人民政府駐香港特別行政區維護國家安全公署依法履行維護國家安全職責,行使相關權力。

駐香港特別行政區維護國家安全公署人員由中央人民政府維護國家安全的有關機關聯合派出。

第四十九條

駐香港特別行政區維護國家安全公署的職責為:

(一)　分析研判香港特別行政區維護國家安全形勢,就維護國家安全重大戰略和重要政策提出意見和建議;

(二)　監督、指導、協調、支持香港特別行政區履行維護國家安全的職責;

Chapter V: Office for Safeguarding National Security of the Central People's Government in the Hong Kong Special Administrative Region

Article 48

The Central People's Government shall establish in the Hong Kong Special Administrative Region an office for safeguarding national security. The Office for Safeguarding National Security of the Central People's Government in the Hong Kong Special Administrative Region shall perform its mandate for safeguarding national security and exercise relevant powers in accordance with the law.

The staff of the Office shall be jointly dispatched by relevant national security authorities under the Central People's Government.

Article 49

The Office for Safeguarding National Security of the Central People's Government in the Hong Kong Special Administrative Region shall perform the following mandate:

(1) Analysing and assessing developments in relation to safeguarding national security in the Hong Kong Special Administrative Region, and providing opinions and making proposals on major strategies and important policies for safeguarding national security;

(2) Overseeing, guiding, coordinating with, and providing support to the Region in the performance of its duties for safeguarding national security;

    （三）   收集分析國家安全情報信息；

    （四）   依法辦理危害國家安全犯罪案件。

第五十條

駐香港特別行政區維護國家安全公署應當嚴格依法履行職責，依法接受監督，不得侵害任何個人和組織的合法權益。

    駐香港特別行政區維護國家安全公署人員除須遵守全國性法律外，還應當遵守香港特別行政區法律。

    駐香港特別行政區維護國家安全公署人員依法接受國家監察機關的監督。

第五十一條

駐香港特別行政區維護國家安全公署的經費由中央財政保障。

第五十二條

駐香港特別行政區維護國家安全公署應當加強與中央人民政府駐香港特別行政區聯絡辦公室、外交部駐香港特別行政區特派員公署、中國人民解放軍駐香港部隊的工作聯繫和工作協同。

(3) Collecting and analysing intelligence and information concerning national security; and

(4) Handling cases concerning offence endangering national security in accordance with the law.

Article 50

The Office for Safeguarding National Security of the Central People's Government in the Hong Kong Special Administrative Region shall perform its mandate in strict compliance with the law and be subject to supervision in accordance with the law. It shall not infringe upon the lawful rights and interests of any individual or organisation.

The staff of the Office shall abide by the laws of the Hong Kong Special Administrative Region as well as national laws.

The staff of the Office shall be subject to the supervision of the national supervisory authorities in accordance with the law.

Article 51

The Office for Safeguarding National Security of the Central People's Government in the Hong Kong Special Administrative Region shall be funded by the Central People's Government.

Article 52

The Office for Safeguarding National Security of the Central People's Government in the Hong Kong Special Administrative Region shall strengthen working relations and cooperation with the Liaison Office of the Central People's Government in the Hong Kong Special Administrative Region, the Office of the Commissioner of the Ministry of Foreign Affairs in the Hong Kong Special Administrative Region, and the Hong Kong Garrison of the Chinese People's Liberation Army.

第五十三條

駐香港特別行政區維護國家安全公署應當與香港特別行政區維護國家安全委員會建立協調機制，監督、指導香港特別行政區維護國家安全工作。

駐香港特別行政區維護國家安全公署的工作部門應當與香港特別行政區維護國家安全的有關機關建立協作機制，加強信息共享和行動配合。

第五十四條

駐香港特別行政區維護國家安全公署、外交部駐香港特別行政區特派員公署會同香港特別行政區政府採取必要措施，加強對外國和國際組織駐香港特別行政區機構、在香港特別行政區的外國和境外非政府組織和新聞機構的管理和服務。

第五十五條

有以下情形之一的，經香港特別行政區政府或者駐香港特別行政區維護國家安全公署提出，並報中央人民政府批准，由駐香港特別行政區維護國家安全公署對本法規定的危害國家安全犯罪案件行使管轄權：

Article 53

The Office for Safeguarding National Security of the Central People's Government in the Hong Kong Special Administrative Region shall establish a mechanism of coordination with the Committee for Safeguarding National Security of the Hong Kong Special Administrative Region to oversee and provide guidance on the work of the Hong Kong Special Administrative Region for safeguarding national security.

The working departments of the Office shall establish mechanisms for collaboration with the relevant authorities of the Region responsible for safeguarding national security to enhance information sharing and operations coordination.

Article 54

The Office for Safeguarding National Security of the Central People's Government in the Hong Kong Special Administrative Region and the Office of the Commissioner of the Ministry of Foreign Affairs in the Hong Kong Special Administrative Region shall, together with the Government of the Hong Kong Special Administrative Region, take necessary measures to strengthen the management of and services for organs of foreign countries and international organisations in the Region, as well as non-governmental organisations and news agencies of foreign countries and from outside the mainland, Hong Kong, and Macao of the People's Republic of China in the Region.

Article 55

The Office for Safeguarding National Security of the Central People's Government in the Hong Kong Special Administrative Region shall, upon approval by the Central People's Government of a request made by the Government of the Hong Kong Special Administrative Region or by the Office itself, exercise jurisdiction over a case concerning offence endangering national security under this Law, if:

（一） 案件涉及外國或者境外勢力介入的複雜情
況，香港特別行政區管轄確有困難的；

（二） 出現香港特別行政區政府無法有效執行本法
的嚴重情況的；

（三） 出現國家安全面臨重大現實威脅的情況的。

第五十六條

根據本法第五十五條規定管轄有關危害國家安全犯罪案
件時，由駐香港特別行政區維護國家安全公署負責立案偵
查，最高人民檢察院指定有關檢察機關行使檢察權，最高
人民法院指定有關法院行使審判權。

第五十七條

根據本法第五十五條規定管轄案件的立案偵查、審查起
訴、審判和刑罰的執行等訴訟程序事宜，適用《中華人民
共和國刑事訴訟法》等相關法律的規定。

根據本法第五十五條規定管轄案件時，本法第
五十六條規定的執法、司法機關依法行使相關權力，其為
決定採取強制措施、偵查措施和司法裁判而簽發的法律
文書在香港特別行政區具有法律效力。對於駐香港特別

(1)   The case is complex due to the involvement of a foreign country or external elements, thus making it difficult for the Region to exercise jurisdiction over the case;

(2)   A serious situation occurs where the Government of the Region is unable to effectively enforce this Law; or

(3)   A major and imminent threat to national security has occurred.

Article 56

In exercising jurisdiction over a case concerning offence endangering national security pursuant to Article 55 of this Law, the Office for Safeguarding National Security of the Central People's Government in the Hong Kong Special Administrative Region shall initiate investigation into the case, the Supreme People's Procuratorate shall designate a prosecuting body to prosecute it, and the Supreme People's Court shall designate a court to adjudicate it.

Article 57

The Criminal Procedure Law of the People's Republic of China and other related national laws shall apply to procedural matters, including those related to criminal investigation, examination and prosecution, trial, and execution of penalty, in respect of cases over which jurisdiction is exercised pursuant to Article 55 of this Law.

When exercising jurisdiction over cases pursuant to Article 55 of this Law, the law enforcement and judicial authorities referred to in Article 56 of this Law shall exercise powers in accordance with the law. The legal documents issued by these authorities on their decisions to take mandatory and investigation measures and on their judicial decisions shall have legal force in the Hong Kong

行政區維護國家安全公署依法採取的措施，有關機構、組織和個人必須遵從。

第五十八條

根據本法第五十五條規定管轄案件時，犯罪嫌疑人自被駐香港特別行政區維護國家安全公署第一次訊問或者採取強制措施之日起，有權委託律師作為辯護人。辯護律師可以依法為犯罪嫌疑人、被告人提供法律幫助。

犯罪嫌疑人、被告人被合法拘捕後，享有儘早接受司法機關公正審判的權利。

第五十九條

根據本法第五十五條規定管轄案件時，任何人如果知道本法規定的危害國家安全犯罪案件情況，都有如實作證的義務。

第六十條

駐香港特別行政區維護國家安全公署及其人員依據本法執行職務的行為，不受香港特別行政區管轄。

Special Administrative Region. The institutions, organisations and individuals concerned must comply with measures taken by the Office for Safeguarding National Security of the Central People's Government in the Hong Kong Special Administrative Region in accordance with the law.

Article 58

In a case over which jurisdiction is exercised pursuant to Article 55 of this Law, a criminal suspect shall have the right to retain a lawyer to represent him or her from the day he or she first receives inquiry made by the Office for Safeguarding National Security of the Central People's Government in the Hong Kong Special Administrative Region or from the day a mandatory measure is taken against him or her. A defence lawyer may provide legal assistance to a criminal suspect or defendant in accordance with the law.

A criminal suspect or defendant who is arrested in accordance with the law shall be entitled to a fair trial before a judicial body without undue delay.

Article 59

In a case over which jurisdiction is exercised pursuant to Article 55 of this Law, any person who has information pertaining to an offence endangering national security under this Law is obliged to testify truthfully.

Article 60

The acts performed in the course of duty by the Office for Safeguarding National Security of the Central People's Government in the Hong Kong Special Administrative Region and its staff in accordance with this Law shall not be subject to the jurisdiction of the Hong Kong Special Administrative Region.

持有駐香港特別行政區維護國家安全公署制發的證件或者證明文件的人員和車輛等在執行職務時不受香港特別行政區執法人員檢查、搜查和扣押。

駐香港特別行政區維護國家安全公署及其人員享有香港特別行政區法律規定的其他權利和豁免。

第六十一條

駐香港特別行政區維護國家安全公署依據本法規定履行職責時，香港特別行政區政府有關部門須提供必要的便利和配合，對妨礙有關執行職務的行為依法予以制止並追究責任。

In the course of performing duty, a holder of an identification document or a document of certification issued by the Office and the articles including vehicles used by the holder shall not be subject to inspection, search or detention by law enforcement officers of the Region.

The Office and its staff shall enjoy other rights and immunities provided by laws of the Region.

Article 61

The relevant departments of the Government of the Hong Kong Special Administrative Region shall provide necessary facilitation and support to the Office for Safeguarding National Security of the Central People's Government in the Hong Kong Special Administrative Region in performing its mandate in accordance with this Law, and shall stop any act obstructing the performance of such mandate and hold those who commit such act liable in accordance with the law.

第六章 附則

第六十二條

香港特別行政區本地法律規定與本法不一致的，適用本法規定。

第六十三條

辦理本法規定的危害國家安全犯罪案件的有關執法、司法機關及其人員或者辦理其他危害國家安全犯罪案件的香港特別行政區執法、司法機關及其人員，應當對辦案過程中知悉的國家秘密、商業秘密和個人隱私予以保密。

擔任辯護人或者訴訟代理人的律師應當保守在執業活動中知悉的國家秘密、商業秘密和個人隱私。

配合辦案的有關機構、組織和個人應當對案件有關情況予以保密。

第六十四條

香港特別行政區適用本法時，本法規定的"有期徒刑""無期徒刑""沒收財產"和"罰金"分別指"監禁""終身監禁""充公犯罪所得"和"罰款"，"拘役"參照適用香港特別行政區相關法律規定的"監禁""入勞役中心"

Chapter VI: Supplementary Provisions

Article 62
This Law shall prevail where provisions of the local laws of the Hong Kong Special Administrative Region are inconsistent with this Law.

Article 63
The law enforcement and judicial authorities and their staff who handle cases concerning offence endangering national security under this Law, or the law enforcement and judicial authorities of the Hong Kong Special Administrative Region and their staff who handle other cases concerning offence endangering national security, shall keep confidential State secrets, trade secrets or personal information which they come to know in the process of handling such cases.

A lawyer who serves as defence counsel or legal representative shall keep confidential State secrets, trade secrets or personal information which he or she comes to know in the practice of law.

The relevant institutions, organisations and individuals who assist with the handling of a case shall keep confidential any information pertaining to the case.

Article 64
In the application of this Law in the Hong Kong Special Administrative Region, the terms "fixed-term imprisonment", "life imprisonment", "confiscation of property" and "criminal fine" in this Law respectively mean "imprisonment", "imprisonment for life", "confiscation of proceeds of crime" and "fine"; "short-term detention" shall be construed, with reference to the relevant laws of the Region, as "imprisonment", "detention in a detention centre" or "detention in a training centre";

"入教導所","管制"參照適用香港特別行政區相關法律規定的"社會服務令""入感化院","吊銷執照或者營業許可證"指香港特別行政區相關法律規定的"取消註冊或者註冊豁免,或者取消牌照"。

第六十五條

本法的解釋權屬於全國人民代表大會常務委員會。

第六十六條

本法自公佈之日起施行。

"restriction" shall be construed, with reference to the relevant
laws of the Region, as "community service" or "detention in a
reformatory school"; and "revoke licence or business permit"
means "revoke registration or exemption from registration, or
revoke licence" as provided for in the relevant laws of the Region.

Article 65
The power of interpretation of this Law shall be vested in the
Standing Committee of the National People's Congress.

Article 66
This Law shall come into force on the date of its promulgation.

全國人民代表大會常務委員會關於
《中華人民共和國香港特別行政區維護國家安全法》
第十四條和第四十七條的解釋

Interpretation by the Standing Committee of the
National People's Congress of Article 14 and Article 47
of the Law of the People's Republic of China
on Safeguarding National Security
in the Hong Kong Special Administrative Region

附件二　全國人民代表大會常務委員會關於《中華人民共和國香港特別行政區維護國家安全法》第十四條和第四十七條的解釋

（2022年12月30日第十三屆全國人民代表大會
常務委員會第三十八次會議通過）

第十三屆全國人民代表大會常務委員會第三十八次會議審議了《國務院關於提請解釋〈中華人民共和國香港特別行政區維護國家安全法〉有關條款的議案》。國務院的議案是應香港特別行政區行政長官向中央人民政府提交的有關報告提出的。根據《中華人民共和國憲法》第六十七條第四項和《中華人民共和國香港特別行政區維護國家安全法》第六十五條的規定，全國人民代表大會常務委員會對《中華人民共和國香港特別行政區維護國家安全法》第十四條和第四十七條規定的含義和適用作如下解釋：

　　一、根據《中華人民共和國香港特別行政區維護國家安全法》第十四條的規定，香港特別行政區維護

Appendix II: Interpretation by the Standing Committee of the National People's Congress of Article 14 and Article 47 of the Law of the People's Republic of China on Safeguarding National Security in the Hong Kong Special Administrative Region

(Adopted at the 38th Session of the Standing Committee of the Thirteenth National People's Congress on 30 December 2022)

At its 38th Session, the Standing Committee of the Thirteenth National People's Congress deliberated the State Council's Proposal Regarding the Request for an Interpretation of Relevant Articles of the Law of the People's Republic of China on Safeguarding National Security in the Hong Kong Special Administrative Region. The State Council's proposal was put forward in response to the relevant report submitted by the Chief Executive of the Hong Kong Special Administrative Region (HKSAR) to the Central People's Government. In accordance with the provisions of Subparagraph (4) of Article 67 of the Constitution of the People's Republic of China and Article 65 of the Law of the People's Republic of China on Safeguarding National Security in the Hong Kong Special Administrative Region, the Standing Committee of the National People's Congress hereby gives the following interpretation on the meaning and application of the provisions of Article 14 and Article 47 of the Law of the People's Republic of China on Safeguarding National Security in the Hong Kong Special Administrative Region:

1.   In accordance with the provisions of Article 14 of the Law of the People's Republic of China on Safeguarding

國家安全委員會承擔香港特別行政區維護國家安全的法定職責,有權對是否涉及國家安全問題作出判斷和決定,工作信息不予公開。香港特別行政區維護國家安全委員會作出的決定不受司法覆核,具有可執行的法律效力。香港特別行政區任何行政、立法、司法等機構和任何組織、個人均不得干涉香港特別行政區維護國家安全委員會的工作,均應當尊重並執行香港特別行政區維護國家安全委員會的決定。

二、 根據《中華人民共和國香港特別行政區維護國家安全法》第四十七條的規定,香港特別行政區法院在審理危害國家安全犯罪案件中遇有涉及有關行為是否涉及國家安全或者有關證據材料是否涉及國家秘密的認定問題,應當向行政長官提出並取得行政長官就該等問題發出的證明書,上述證明書對法院有約束力。

三、 香港特別行政區行政長官依據《中華人民共和國香港特別行政區維護國家安全法》第十一條的規定於11月28日向中央人民政府提交的有關報告認為,不具有香港特別行政區全面執業

National Security in the Hong Kong Special Administrative Region, the Committee for Safeguarding National Security of the HKSAR assumes statutory duties and functions for safeguarding national security in the HKSAR and has the power to make judgements and decisions on the question whether national security is involved; and information relating to its work is not subject to disclosure. Decisions made by the Committee for Safeguarding National Security of the HKSAR are not amenable to judicial review and have enforceable legal effect. No institution, including the executive authorities, legislature and judiciary, organisation or individual in the HKSAR shall interfere with the work of the Committee for Safeguarding National Security of the HKSAR; they shall all respect and implement the decisions of the Committee for Safeguarding National Security of the HKSAR.

2.   In accordance with the provisions of Article 47 of the Law of the People's Republic of China on Safeguarding National Security in the Hong Kong Special Administrative Region, the courts of the HKSAR shall request and obtain a certificate from the Chief Executive to certify whether an act involves national security or whether the relevant evidence involves State secrets when such questions arise in the adjudication of a case concerning an offence endangering national security. The certificate shall be binding on the courts.

3.   The relevant report submitted by the Chief Executive of the HKSAR to the Central People's Government on 28 November in accordance with the provisions of Article 11 of the Law of the People's Republic of China on Safeguarding National Security in the Hong Kong

資格的海外律師擔任危害國家安全犯罪案件的辯護人或者訴訟代理人可能引發國家安全風險。不具有香港特別行政區全面執業資格的海外律師是否可以擔任危害國家安全犯罪案件的辯護人或者訴訟代理人的問題,屬於《中華人民共和國香港特別行政區維護國家安全法》第四十七條所規定的需要認定的問題,應當取得行政長官發出的證明書。如香港特別行政區法院沒有向行政長官提出並取得行政長官就該等問題發出的證明書,香港特別行政區維護國家安全委員會應當根據《中華人民共和國香港特別行政區維護國家安全法》第十四條的規定履行法定職責,對該等情況和問題作出相關判斷和決定。

現予公告。